ENGAGING ENGLISH LEARNERS

Exploring Literature, Developing Literacy, and Differentiating Instruction

Carole Cox
California State University-Long Beach

Paul S. Boyd-Batstone
California State University-Long Beach

Allyn & Bacon
is an imprint of

Boston | New York | San Francisco
Mexico City | Montreal | Toronto | London | Madrid | Munich | Paris
Hong Kong | Singapore | Tokyo | Cape Town | Sydney

Vice President and Editor in Chief: Paul A. Smith
Senior Editor: Linda Ashe Bishop
Senior Managing Editor: Pamela D. Bennett
Senior Project Manager: Mary M. Irvin
Production Coordination: Vishal Harshvardhan, Aptara®, Inc.
Editorial Assistant: Demetrius Hall
Senior Art Director: Diane C. Lorenzo
Cover Design: Jeff Vanik
Cover Image: Jupiter Images
Operations Specialist: Matt Ottenweller
Director of Marketing: Quinn Perkson
Marketing Manager: Krista Clark
Marketing Coordinator: Brian Mounts
Photo Credits: p. 149, David Buffington/Getty Images, Inc., Photodisc; p 163, Carole Cox; p. 173, Anne Vega/Merill.

To obtain permission(s) to use material from this work, please submit a written request to Allyn and Bacon, Permissions Department, 501 Boylston Street, Boston, MA 02116 or fax your request to 617-671-2290.

For related titles and support materials, visit our online catalog at www.pearsonhighered.com.

Library of Congress Cataloging-in-Publication Data

Cox, Carole
   Engaging English learners: exploring literature, developing literacy, and differentiating instruction / Carole Cox, Paul S. Boyd-Batstone.—1st ed.
      p. cm.
   ISBN-13: 978-0-13-513088-9
   ISBN-10:   0-13-513088-3
   1. Literature—Study and teaching (Elementary)   2. English language—Study and teaching (Elementary)—Foreign speakers.   3. Group reading.   4. Individualized instruction.   I. Boyd-Batstone, Paul.   II. Title.
   LB1575.C798 2008
   372.64'044—dc22

                                        2008017765

Allyn & Bacon
is an imprint of

Printed in the United States of America

10 9 8 7 6 5 4 3 2 1   [RRD-OH]   12 11 10 09

*With thanks to all the smart, funny, terrific,
wonderful, amazing children we've written about in this book.*

Preface

This book is about engaging English learners through exploring literature in order to develop literacy and differentiate instruction. As a foundation for practice, this text maps the crossroads of theories of reader response and learning English as a second language, and it discusses this intersection within the context of theories of social construction of knowledge and sociocultural perspectives on learning and teaching. It also provides a model for teaching with literature that supports the language and literacy development of English learners and shows how to differentiate instruction for students who are at differing stages of English proficiency.

We have provided here a balance between theoretical and practical dimensions and have tried to showcase reader-response methods of teaching with literature that any classroom teacher can use when teaching any English learner. To communicate this content to our readers, we have laid out important background information and issues and have integrated them with narrative, interpretive case studies from the points of view of both a researcher engaged in teaching and a teacher who carries out research. You will hear the two distinct voices of the researcher/teacher and the teacher/researcher, often speaking together, as well as these voices of numerous children and their families.

We believe that all children—children who come to school already speaking English and those learning it as a new language—deserve the best that literature and teaching have to offer. We advocate an inclusive, reader-centered approach to developing language and literacy while differentiating instruction for all children.

ORGANIZATION OF THE BOOK

In the first three chapters of the book, Carole establishes why it is important to engage English learners in exploring literature to develop literacy and differentiate instruction.

▲ Chapter 1, "Teaching with Literature in a Classroom of English Learners," begins with an account of a visit to Paul Boyd-Batstone's third-grade classroom of English learners, whose home language was Spanish, and a conversation between the text's two authors about what happened that day.

▲ Chapter 2, "Reader Response and Learning English as a Second Language," maps out the crossroads of theories of reader response and learning English as a second language. It presents social constructivist and sociocultural perspectives on learning and teaching, as well as current research.

▲ Chapter 3, "Bridging Theory and Research into Practice," describes how to engage all English learners through exploring literature in order to develop literacy and differentiate instruction to meet the needs of individual students.

The last two chapters of the book show how Paul engages English learners by exploring literature and developing literacy through the use of literature circles. Paul writes about his own classroom when he was a third-grade bilingual teacher of students whose home language was Spanish. However, you don't have to be a bilingual teacher to make his ideas work. We believe that the principles and practices he describes can be extended by all classroom teachers to all English learners whose home language is other than English.

▲ Chapter 4, "Components of Student-Centered Instruction," provides an instructional model for Literature Circles, which Paul used with his class of English learners, and includes ways to assess levels of English language as a starting point.

▲ Chapter 5, "Engaging English Learners with Literature Circles in the Classroom," invites the reader inside Paul's classroom to see a day in the life of a teacher of English learners involved in Literature Circles, with a special in-depth look at Jackie and her journey of literary exploration and literacy development by way of Paul's differentiated instruction for her.

After Chapter 5, there is a "Compendium of Case Studies," which describes the background and home influences, language development, student experiences, and responses to literature of three children from kindergarten through fifth grade:

Juan: *A beginning English learner*
Anne: *A native English speaker*
Eduardo: *An intermediate/advanced English learner*

SPECIAL FEATURES

▲ *A Thought from Carole/A Thought from Paul* Throughout the text the authors provide a commentary on each other's writing and make connections between practice and theory.

▲ *Case Study boxes* These appear throughout the text with questions and prompts related to chapter content and refer the reader to case studies of Juan, Anne, or Eduardo to read, reflect, and apply ideas to practice.

▲ *Exploring Ideas* Each chapter ends with a list of questions and activities to guide the reader's reflection on the chapter content, to use as a discussion prompt, or to put the ideas in the chapter into practice.

▲ *Children's work* Examples of children's written and art work illustrate English language thinking and learning throughout the book.

ACKNOWLEDGEMENTS

From Carole Cox

Thanks to Merrill Vice President and Executive Publisher Jeff Johnston for his immediate interest in this project and especially for referring me to Linda Bishop for continued development and completion of the book. Linda's enthusiasm, warmth, vision, and talent as an editor are remarkable. All the reviewers' ideas were excellent and most useful, and we thank them: Flora V. Rodriguez-Brown, University of Illinois at Chicago; Julie Coppola, Boston University; Deanna Gilmore, Washington State University; Marjorie R. Hancock, Kansas State University; Paula M. Selvester, California State University, Chico; Margaret H. Shepherd, Kutztown University; and Gail Tompkins, California State University, Fresno.

Louise Rosenblatt's transactional theory gave me the explanatory power I needed to articulate my own classroom experiences and those of others. Our conversations and her support for my research and writing are deeply appreciated. My conversations with Paul about the transactional theory gave us a place to stand in mapping the terrain of exploring literature with English learners, and we are ever grateful to her. We have found that there is nothing more practical than a good theory.

Although the children in the case studies must remain anonymous, I must acknowledge them. Their ideas and insights into literature and life are among the most important presented in the book. These case studies were the result of my longitudinal study of children's responses to literature, including those of English learners, which was partially funded by several California State University–Long Beach Scholarly and Creative Activities Awards.

However, this book would never have happened if Paul hadn't allowed me into his classroom and been such a good friend and collaborator, which he continues to be.

From Paul Boyd-Batstone

I would like to echo Carole's deep appreciation for the excellent publishing team at Merrill. It is a pleasure to work with such gracious and thoughtful people. Special thanks to Dr. Flora Rodriguez-Brown and her graduate students at the University of Illinois–Chicago, who rekindled the need for this book when they invited me to speak about differentiating instruction for English learners. Dr. Rodriguez-Brown is a wise educator who understands the essential value of sociocultural practice in schools.

My former students who appear in this book continue to inspire me. Some have graduated from high school with honors and have continued on with university scholarships. Others have struggled with the challenges of living in poverty in urban society. Many remain in touch, which is the highest compliment any teacher can receive.

I will never forget the day that Carole Cox asked to come to my classroom to observe my instruction. At that time I had no idea what a significant moment in my career and life that would be. Throughout the years since, I have been overwhelmed by the great worth of a quality mentor and friend in education. All teachers should be so fortunate as to have Carole Cox step into their classrooms. To her I owe so much.

Contents

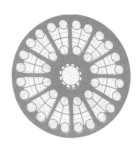

Prologue

Since this book is also a story about two teachers and their ongoing conversation about engaging English learners, exploring literature, developing literacy, and differentiating instruction, we think we should introduce ourselves to you and explain how this conversation started, how we have kept it going, how we came to collaborate on this book, and what the book is really about. Although we have written the book together, you will hear our separate voices in three ways. First, we wrote separate chapters: Carole wrote Chapters 1 through 3 and the Compendium of Case Studies. Paul wrote Chapters 4 and 5. Second, some of the book is written as conversation between us. Third, we make comments throughout that begin with a special heading: "A Thought from Carole" or "A Thought from Paul." In this way, the book reflects the conversational character of our ongoing collaboration on research and writing about teaching with literature and about language and literacy development.

THE AUTHORS MEET

One reviewer of this book said, "I would like to her the voices of Carole and Paul speaking together and speaking out together more often in the text. I believe that readers might like to know more about how they came to collaborate and to be able to do so for so long, as well as how they went about writing this text together."

A Thought from Carole

I was interested in talking to a teacher of English learners who also took a student-centered approach. Coincidentally, Paul, as an outstanding example of both, had been invited to address a meeting I attended at the university. At that time he taught a third-grade bilingual Spanish/English class in the Long Beach Unified School District. After I heard his remarks about teaching English learners, I asked if I might visit his classroom. He seemed very cautious, but I was determined. I wanted to see firsthand how a recognized effective teacher of English learners taught literacy and used literature in his classroom.

I knew when I finally walked into his classroom that it was the right place to be to observe a student-centered classroom of English learners. I just hoped he wouldn't mind my hanging out there awhile to be able to write about what he was doing in a meaningful way for other teachers. I tried to be quiet and not get in his way, but I was keenly interested to see how he would use literature in his third-grade class of English learners.

A Thought from Paul ────────────────────────────────

I first met Carole at a meeting I was invited to attend at California State University–Long Beach. A group of experienced teachers had been asked to speak to the teacher education faculty about what new teachers needed to know to be successful in the public schools. We spoke about teaching, much of it centering on the efforts to meet the needs of English learners. In my teaching, I had been setting aside the teacher's guide for language instruction, having become disenchanted with mechanistic approaches to developing literacy, and had begun to find answers to the challenge of teaching in the writings of Stephen Krashen and Jim Cummins. I remember one professor at the meeting asking about my approach to teaching English learners; I responded that a central tenet was that language instruction begins with the child.

At the end of the meeting, Carole introduced herself and asked whether she could observe my classroom. I had that sinking feeling of someone who has been shooting off at the mouth and then has to perform. When I inquired about what she was interested in, she invited me to her office and offered me a copy of her text *Teaching Language Arts: A Student-Centered Classroom*, some articles, and a book she had coedited on reader-response theory and research. At that point I had never even heard of reader-response theory. I told Carole I would look over her writing and get back to her about coming to my classroom.

During the following week, I looked over the materials Carole had given me. I was impressed to read such a comprehensive treatment of language development in theory and practice, and I was surprised at how far ahead of current thinking about literacy Carole's work was. That's when I became very nervous, wondering what this professor could actually gain by observing in my classroom. Even though I was an experienced classroom teacher and had worked as an English language development specialist and grant coordinator at the district level, all I was worried about at the time was that my students would embarrass me in front of this college professor. I wanted everything to go smoothly so that I would look like an effective teacher of English learners. Some of my students, however, had other ideas about what was going to happen in the classroom that day. Their responses to the story we were reading about a rabbit and a turnip initially set me on my ear but ultimately generated a major shift in my thinking about developing English learners' language and literacy with children's literature.

WHAT THE BOOK IS REALLY ABOUT

This book has emerged from our ongoing conversation about teaching all English learners and the ways all classroom teachers can engage them to develop literacy and differentiate instruction through explorations with literature. This book is not intended to be a comprehensive treatment of literacy instruction or methods of teaching English learners. The teaching approach we describe can be part of a balanced, comprehensive reading and writing program for English learners, one that includes rich, reader-oriented discussions of books in Literature Circles, student reading and writing on self-selected topics of interest as a result of these discussions, and integrated teaching of literacy and content areas.

In the recent review of research *Developing Literacy in Second-Language Learners: Report of the National Literacy Panel on Language-Minority Children and Youth* (August & Shanahan, 2006), a key recommendation is that all teachers develop more thorough discussions of reading material and literature with English learners. Our book offers a sound theoretical and research-based framework, along with a teaching model and practical strategies, to do just that.

We live and teach in Long Beach, California, the most diverse city in the country. The home language of the English learners we describe in the book is Spanish, as Paul was a bilingual Spanish/English teacher. You do not have to be a bilingual teacher yourself, however, or teach only English learners whose home language is Spanish, to make use of the ideas in this book or to make this approach work. The principles and practices of teaching the English learners we have written about are what every classroom teacher needs to know about teaching children whose home language—any language—is other than English. We hope you will try out these ideas in your own classrooms, and if you do, please contact us and tell us what happened: Carole Cox at cacox@csulb.edu and Paul Boyd-Batstone at pboydbat@csulb.edu. We look forward to hearing from you.

Meet the Authors

Carole Cox taught elementary school in Los Angeles, California and Madison, Wisconsin and received a Ph.D. from the University of Minnesota. As a professor at Louisiana State University, Baton Rouge and California State University, Long Beach she has taught courses in language arts, reading, and children's literature. Carole's research focuses on children's responses to literature from a reader-response perspective, specifically Louise Rosenblatt's transactional model of the reading process (1994, 1995). Carole and Joyce Many explored the relationship of children's responses to literature and literary understanding (Cox & Many, 1989a, 1989b, 1992a, 1992b, 1992c). With Jim Zarrillo, Carole looked at how teachers use literature in the classroom (Cox & Zarrillo, 1990, Zarrillo & Cox, 1992). She also conducted a 6-year longitudinal study of the development of the responses of a group of children from kindergarten through fifth grade (Cox, 1997, 1998, 2002). You will read about three of these children in the Compendium of Case Studies in this book.

Carole is the author of *Teaching language arts: A student-centered classroom,* (6th ed.) (2008), and many other books and articles in the field of language and literacy instruction. In 2001 she was named the Outstanding Professor at California State University, Long Beach. The greatest honor she has ever received, however, occurred when students she had taught in third through fifth grade in the 1960's and 1970's organized a reunion of her classes in Madison, Wisconsin and the mayor declared July 2, 2005 as Carole Cox Day. She and her former students are currently writing an historical ethnography of their classroom experiences together.

Paul Boyd-Batstone taught elementary school in Long Beach for 15 years. He began his teaching career as a first-grade teacher in a Spanish/English bilingual program. He also worked with immigrant students from Latin America and Southeast Asia as a language specialist in K-5, and coordinated a Title VII Federal Grant that developed the first Cambodian Khmer/English bilingual program in California. He was named Bilingual Educator of the Year by the Los Angeles County Office of Education, Bilingual Director's Association.

Paul met Carole Cox at a meeting at California State University, Long Beach and she asked to observe in his third-grade bilingual classroom. Little did he realize that a simple invitation to watch children responding to literature would lead to a professional collaboration that continues today. Paul received his Ph.D from Claremont Graduate University and is an Associate Professor at California State University, Long Beach. His writing addresses issues related to English learners, including reader-response centered instruction (Boyd-Batstone, 2002, 2003) and a book on *Differentiated early literacy for English learners: Practical strategies* (2006). Paul serves as Chair of the International Reading Association's Commission on Second Language Literacy and Learning and also works with the Guatemalan Reading Council to increase literacy development in Central America.

REFERENCES

August, E., & Shanahan, T. (Eds.). (2006). *Developing literacy in second-language learners: Report of the National Literacy Panel on Language-Minority Children and Youth.* Mahwah, NJ: Erlbaum.

Boyd-Batstone, P. (2002). Reading as co-authorship: A reader-response connection to culture. In M. Hunsberger & G. Labercane (Eds.), *Making meaning in the response-based classroom* (pp. 131–140). Boston: Allyn & Bacon.

Boyd-Batstone, P. (2003). Reading with a hero: A mediated and literate experience. In G. Garcia (Ed.). *English language learners: Reaching the highest level of English literacy* (pp. 333–356). Newark, DE: International Reading Association.

Boyd-Batstone, P. (2006). *Differentiated early literacy for English language learners: Practical strategies.* Boston: Allyn & Bacon.

Cox, C. (1997). Literature-based teaching: A student, response-centered classroom. In N. Karolides (Ed.). *Reader response in elementary classrooms* (pp. 29–49). Hillsdale, NJ: Erlbaum.

Cox, C. (1998, April). *Children's stance towards literature: A longitudinal study, K–5.* Paper presented at the annual meeting of the American Educational Research Association, San Diego, CA.

Cox, C. (2002). Resistance to reading in school. In M. Hunsberger & G. Labercane (Eds.). *Making meaning in the response-based classroom* (pp. 141–153). Boston: Allyn & Bacon.

Cox, C. (2008). *Teaching language arts: A student-centered classroom* (6th ed.). Boston: Pearson/Allyn & Bacon.

Cox, C., & Many, J. E. (1989a). Personal understanding from film and literature: Different paths reaching comparable heights. *Arts and Learning Research Journal, 7,* 29–39.

Cox, C., & Many, J. E. (1989b). Worlds of possibilities in response to literature, film, and life. *Language Arts, 66* (3), 287–294.

Cox, C., & Many, J. E. (1992a). Beyond choosing: Emergent categories of efferent and aesthetic stance. In J. Many & C. Cox (Eds.). *Reader stance and literary understanding: Exploring the theories, research, and practice* (pp. 103–126). Norwood, NJ: Ablex.

Cox, C., & Many, J. E. (1992b). Towards an understanding of the aesthetic response to literature. *Language Arts, 69,* 28–33.

Cox, C., & Many, J. E. (1992c). Stance towards a literary work: Applying the transactional theory to children's responses. *Reading Psychology, 13* (1), 37–72.

Cox, C., & Zarrillo, J. (1990). Teaching with literature in the elementary school: A descriptive study applying Rosenblatt's transactional theory. *Arts and Learning Research Journal, 7,* 29–37.

Rosenblatt, L. M. (1994). *The reader, the text, the poem: The transactional theory of the literary work.* Carbondale, IL: Southern Illinois University Press. (Original work published 1978).

Rosenblatt, L. M. (1995). *Literature as exploration* (5th ed.). New York: Modern Language Association. (Original work published 1938).

Zarrillo, J., & Cox, C. (1992). Efferent and aesthetic teaching. In J. Many & C. Cox (Eds.). *Reader stance and literary understanding: Exploring the theories, research, and practice* (pp. 235–249). Norwood, NJ: Ablex.

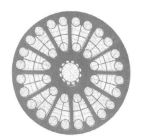

CHAPTER ONE

Teaching with Literature in a Classroom of English Learners

The first time I visited Paul's classroom, I checked in as a visitor at the office and said I was scheduled to see Mr. Boyd-Batstone. The office staff called a student from that room to escort me there, and when I told him I was going to be a visitor in Mr. Boyd-Batstone's class, he smiled graciously at my naiveté as he led me to the room, saying, "We call him Señor B.-B." (Paul asked his students to call him Señor or Mr. B.-B. after he became tired of the students innocently referring to him as Mr. Boys' Bathroom.)

A FIRST VISIT TO SEÑOR B.-B.'S THIRD-GRADE CLASS OF ENGLISH LEARNERS

Paul's third-grade classroom at Edison Elementary School in Long Beach was in the older part of the building, Art Deco circa 1930s. It was one of those bigger, high-ceilinged rooms with many coats of beige paint. It had survived many children as well as earthquakes.

The first thing I noticed was a sheet of chart paper titled "Literature Plan" (see photo Literature Plan for *The Rabbit and the Turnip*, p.6) hanging on a clothesline. The chart displayed a cluster with the book title "The Rabbit and the Turnip" in the middle, surrounded by two other clusters: "Projects" ("art work" and "a show to be done in the auditorium") and "Writing Analysis" ("setting," "characters," "events," and "problem").

A Thought from Carole

I liked the child-centered buzz in Paul's class right away. I was excited to see a plan for teaching with literature that could incorporate students' ideas and responses as "art projects" and "a show to be done in the auditorium" rather than simply following the teacher's guide for the commercial reading series used in the district. I'll admit to wondering about the label "Writing Analysis: setting, characters, events, and problem." Did it mean that the students would write about only these four things? Such analysis is a common practice in writing about literature. It does, however, reflect a more traditional and text-oriented view of teaching with literature. My acknowledged bias for a more reader-oriented approach is that students first be given the opportunity to reflect and talk or write about what they were thinking during reading before they attempted a more teacher-directed analysis of the text. In my own research, I had found that when children are first asked an open question after reading literature, such as "What did you think of the book?" they frequently also demonstrate an understanding of things like story structure and literary elements when talking and writing about their personal experience of the text, affording the teacher an immediate way to assess their comprehension of text and a way to plan further instruction. I was interested to see what would happen when Paul's students wrote about literature, what kind of approach he would take.

The walls of Paul's classroom were covered with student work, a Diego Rivera poster and pictures of Mexico, a calendar, the alphabet in cursive, and school memos. Songs that Paul's students had written were on large sheets of chart paper above two chalkboards where they could be easily seen and read by everyone for sing-alongs.

On one side of the room was a vintage computer, the Literature Plan display, and Paul's chair in front of a chalkboard next to a plastic rolling cart with supplies. Stacks of magazines (e.g., *National Geographic*) and catalogs were on the floor, and paperback books in Spanish and English lined the chalk tray: *Ramona la chinche/Ramona the Pest* by Beverly Cleary, *Sideways Stories from Wayside School* by Louis Sachar, and *Las telaranas de Carlota/Charlotte's Web* by E. B. White. A table in front of Paul's desk in the corner was home to In and Out boxes full of interactive journals. Under the table were plastic tubs with each child's literature folder.

A clothesline strung in front of the window wall held various Literature Plans in use. Papier-mâché models of the planets hung in front of a mural of the solar system on the same long wall. Models of volcanoes sat on the floor nearby in front of a volcano mural.

On the third wall were a sink, a coat room, another museum-quality PC, and student writing taped to a supply cupboard labeled "Escritura Excelente" (Excellent Writing). On the last long wall in front of the room were bookshelves, a copy of a Frida Kahlo self-portrait by the class artist Gustavo, a long chalkboard, and a wooden clothes drying rack with Big Books the class had made of interviews they had conducted with class visitors. The one prominently displayed was of Bubba, Paul's dog.

The Classroom Day

Paul scheduled content area instruction first thing in the morning, from 8:40 to 9:40, during which time he provided primary language support in Spanish for students still acquiring English. Next, he taught a language arts block in Spanish and English, from 9:40 to 10:50, followed by recess and back-to-back reading in Spanish and English before and after lunch, from 11:00 to 12:00 and 12:40 to 1:50, followed by another recess. The last hour of the day was content area instruction again, from 2:00 to 3:00.

Content Areas: Mathematics, Social Studies, and Science

A set of mathematics book rested on a shelf, with an In/Out box for mathematics homework and classwork on top of it. Above it on the chalkboard, Paul had written an assignment of page numbers and problems and a special Problem of the Week:

Conduct an opinion survey on "What is your favorite pet?" Directions for conducting this survey were in a folder on the shelf below the chalkboard.

The students were using textbooks that were in Spanish (maps in the social studies text were in English), but some of the same texts in English could be used depending on the level of English proficiency of the student. Although the home language of all Paul's students was Spanish, they varied in their level of English proficiency, ranging from very beginning to advanced fluency in speaking English as well as in reading and writing it. Paul also used an active, inquiry approach to science and social studies. Students were working on papier-mâché models of the planets, a mural of the solar system, and reports, written in Spanish, about a planet. They were also working in groups building models of types of volcanoes. One child reported to me that the volcanoes would "actually work." The students were also mapping locations of the volcano types in three parts of the world: Mexico, Hawaii, and the continental United States. Near the area where they were working on the models, mural, map, and reports was a rolling cart with books on space and volcanoes in both Spanish and English. The cart also had references: maps, an atlas, and encyclopedia volumes.

Paul was a bilingual Spanish/English teacher, so he taught in two languages. He used primary language support in Spanish, the home language of his students, during the teaching of mathematics and other content areas because of the higher cognitive demand of these subjects; consequently, his students learned these subjects while they were still acquiring English. He scheduled mathematics and the other content areas during the first and last hours of the day.

Language Arts/Reading

Paul organized the students for a 70-minute language arts/reading period from 9:40 to 10:50, centered around literature groups. After that was a school-adopted schedule of back-to-back reading—half the class at a time while the other half was on the playground—continuing the literature groups. Then students begin language arts/reading with a quick write about their stories.

After 5 minutes of writing, they read to a partner. A volunteer from each table read to the whole class.

Paul then discussed the various Literature Plans with each of several groups, moving from table to table as the groups got organized to work on projects. Some were making a mural; others, a 5-foot cobalt blue painted apron for *Katy No Pocket* by Emily Payne, masks for a play, and puppets; others, writing a puppet play. They were all talking animatedly. Each student had a literature folder with work in progress handy.

Paul next met with one of the groups: *Ratona Osa-Bear Mouse* by Berniece Freschet. They were writing a puppet play. Paul had made a cluster around the title "Los Animales"/"The Animals" on a sheet of chart paper. The students named all the characters in the story; each character got its own cluster. Following an extended, intense discussion of what each character would say, Paul wrote the words in each character's cluster. The play was then cast, and the names of the students were written in each character's cluster. Then a discussion of puppet making took place.

Paul moved from group to group, checking progress. Students were all over the room: reading stories; writing scripts; making paper bag puppets, masks, stick puppets; helping each other; referring back to the story text and pictures to extend through their projects; doing "writing analysis." They were always talking and interacting with each other in both Spanish and English about stories, the art-making process, the reading process, the writing process, and procedures. They were encouraging to each other. It was not a quiet room. It hummed, not roared, with the sounds of students actively engaged in listening, talking, reading, writing, creating projects, and sharing ideas. Many were missing recess.

Teaching with Literature

Paul's basic approach to teaching with literature was to use these literature groups, Literature Plans, and a combination of whole-class discussions, self-directed student learning, and conferences between himself and the groups. Paul scheduled conferences with the groups during the language arts block of time plus the two back-to-back reading periods.

Although the class discussion I describe next followed the format he had been using, it was significant because things didn't go the way he had planned. And because they didn't, Paul and I started our ongoing conversation about teaching with literature and English learners.

A Discussion of the Story: The Rabbit and the Turnip

Paul held this conference with *The Rabbit and the Turnip* by Richard Sadler group in English. The story is a Russian folktale about a rabbit who finds a turnip in the snow and gives it to another hungry animal, who passes it on to another, and so on until it comes back to the rabbit, who shares it with the other animals. Copies of the commercial readers were handed out.

On the back of the Literature Plan chart (see photo Discussion of the Rabbit and the Turnip, p.6) for this group, Paul had divided the paper into four sections with the titles "Setting," "Characters," "Events," and "Problem." He had already recorded the group's ideas about setting and characters in a cluster on the chart during other conferences. The setting cluster included "The rabbit lives in a house" and "There is snow in the mountains." The character cluster included each character's name with a remark: Little Rabbit—"Little Rabbit went out to look for food. He found a turnip." The event cluster included "The turnip was in the snow." Only the section on the problem remained.

Paul: *We need to talk about the problem. Take a minute and talk with each other. What would you call the problem in the story?*

(One child starts to speak very softly, and Paul leans forward to listen. Another child says, "Talk like at recess." Paul laughs out loud.)

Child: *Little rabbit . . .*
P: *Help her out. What's the problem with the turnip?*
C: *Threw in the snow.*

P: *Why is that a problem? Let's think. The turnip was in the snow. What's the big problem?*

C: *He gave to the donkey.*

P: *Why?*

C: *Because . . . because they don't have anything to eat.*

P: *Let's focus on eating.*

(One child lights up and starts talking excitedly.)

C: *Oh! The problem is they was cold.*

C: *They could put it in the microwave.*

P: *(Laughing) But do you think it was a problem because it was cold?*

C: *Yeah!*

P: *What time of year was it?*

C: *Navidad!*

(Paul writes on the chart "It was wintertime and Christmastime." Then he tells the group to go back and read page 248 in the story. He apparently wants them to understand that the problem was that it was winter and the animals were hungry. They read for a few minutes until one child speaks.)

C: *Oh. The rabbit ate the turnip.*

P: *How does he feel?*

C: *Happy.*

P: *Why?*

C: *The turnip was at his door again. It was a gift.*

P: *What happens at Christmastime?*

The Problem of the Story Versus the Problem Javier Was Having with the Story

(While Paul is trying to guide the students in the direction of identifying the problem found in the story itself, Javier takes a sudden detour by identifying the problem he's having with his personal experience of the story. The real problem for him is the lack of authenticity in the story.)

Javier: *The turnip was white and not red.*

P: *Is that a problem?*

J: *Yeah. No good. My grandpa has a farm in Mexico and grows turnips and carrots and vegetables. That turnip's [the one in the story] no good.*

P: *OK! You know more than I do. Then the illustrator didn't draw the turnip right. You might want to write about the turnip and how it should be.*

(Paul then summarizes what they've said, including Javier's response.)

P: *There are a few problems. The turnip's in the snow. The rabbit gave it to the donkey because there was nothing to eat. The turnip was at the door. The illustrator didn't draw it right.*

(Paul continues the discussion, apparently still hoping to reach a consensus among the group about the problem in the story.)

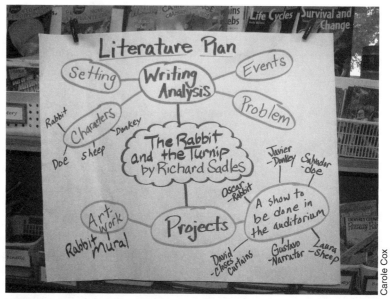

Literature Plan for *The Rabbit and the Turnip*

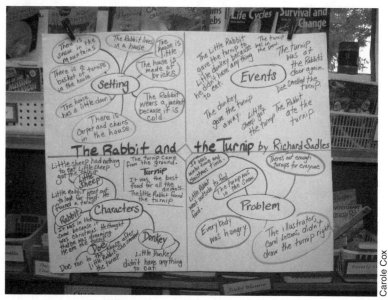

Discussion of *The Rabbit and the Turnip*

P: *Who was hungry in the story?*
C: *Little sheep.*
C: *Little donkey.*
C: *Little doe.*
P: *Everybody's hungry. Can we say that?*

C: *Yeah.*
P: *Everybody's hungry.*

(Paul writes this on the chart, too. They are close to a consensus, but Javier derails the discussion again by challenging the text.)

J: *Maybe the animals couldn't find anything because of the snow. But where did he find the turnip if there's snow all over?*
P: *This is a toughie. Talk it over and see if we can figure it out. Javier, you said something: "The rabbit ate and the others didn't. That's not fair."*
C: *They're poor and don't have enough to eat.*
P: *OK. You're saying, "Everybody's hungry."*
C: *Not enough turnips to go around, for the animals.*

(Javier jumps the rails again, and instead of just stating the problem, he offers a solution and rewrite of the story.)

J: *They could have cut the turnip in half so more people could have it!*
P: *What a good solution. Let's do a quick summary and start the play.*

(Paul reads and points to what he's written about the problem on the chart.)

P: *You need to write about the problem later on today and tomorrow. Let's talk about masks.*

(Now they plan a play of the story, and Paul shows them how they might make masks.)

A Thought from Carole

I honestly wondered why Paul, an obviously student-centered teacher, stayed focused on the idea of "the problem" in the story as long as he did. He seemed delighted when Javier brought his personal interpretation of the story to bear and triggered the richest part of the discussion up to that point. Paul made a final attempt, however, to focus the students' attention on the problem at the same time he celebrated the richness and honesty of Javier's response drawing on his personal experience with turnips.

I didn't know Paul well enough to come right out and ask him why he focused so much on the story problem rather than also using open questions and prompts—"What did you think of the story?" or "Tell about any similar experiences you've had," for example—and I liked what I saw so much in his classroom that I didn't want to seem to be critical and perhaps unwelcome later. I didn't have to wait long, however, for the issue of The Problem of the Story versus The Problem Javier Was Having with the Story to come up: only until the lunch bell, when we started talking, to be exact.

During lunch, we began to talk about what had happened in *The Rabbit and the Turnip* group and subsequently started a conversation we are still having about what's important in teaching with literature and language and literacy development.

A First Conversation Between Carole and Paul

This is not actually our first conversation, but rather our memories of it. We tried to re-create it, and it didn't work. We do remember it as important and as the beginning of our collaboration.

Carole: *I remember you seemed frustrated by the way the conference went, and I was hoping you weren't irritated because I was there, and we started talking about what happened. It seemed to me that the problem was that those students just weren't going to talk about what you wanted them to, and I wondered why you persisted.*

Paul: *I was frustrated with my students and embarrassed at first because they refused to comply with my inquiry about the problem of the story. Having sat in an in-service training about the use of commercial readers that stressed the importance of story structure, I thought that I was engaging the students in a significant exploration of the story. Teaching the problem of the story made sense to me. There was a nice logical progression in story structure. We would establish the setting first, then the characters, order the events of the story, identify the problem, and finish with the solution. I could have each literature group work through those elements and feel that I was covering the ground of the story. It all fit on paper and gave me a kind of handle on that elusive subject of language arts. Nevertheless, what fits on paper does not always match the reality of my students. What my students helped demonstrate was that the meaningful aspects of the story were far more personal than the abstractions of story structure or analysis.*

Carole: *Like Javier and the turnip?*

Paul: *With the turnip story, the problem was so obvious that it was almost stupid to have a conversation about it. In fact, I remember you and I concurred that it was a stupid story. But I was going to be the responsible teacher and plow through it.*

Carole: *Would you have stayed with it as long as you did if I hadn't been there? I sensed a tension, and it didn't fit with what I'd seen of your teaching style up to that point.*

Paul: *I was very aware of being observed by a professor. But I would probably have come back to it the next day. Javier has been a really difficult child to work with. And today he was really sabotaging the group. Every time I asked what the problem was, he'd start giggling or kicking another student or generally disrupting the discussion.*

Carole: *Until he got to express the problem he was having with the story.*

Paul: *I remember asking you what you would have done.*

Carole: *I said something about just asking an open question instead of focusing on "the problem." You got the best response from anybody—and it turned out to be Javier, the behavior problem—when he ignored what you were really asking for—the problem in the story—and started talking about the problem he was having with the story. An authentic response.*

Paul: *The discussion became engaging when I got fed up with the structure piece and threw it back on the students. When I finally let Javier tell me the problem* *with the whole story in general, he finally got to bring his grandfather into the story and tell his own story about the turnip farm in Mexico. What's most important here? Is it that he could identify that everybody was starving or that he began to see a relationship between himself and the story or that he had a valid critique of this story—the misrepresentation of turnips in it. Maybe he knew something that the author didn't.*

Carole: *Did you have similar struggles with other aspects of story structure?*

Paul: *Yes. The most difficult was the whole idea of the events in the story. Rarely did the students ever talk about the order. It was always a battle getting past what happened first, second, next. Sometimes just dealing with characters of a story is a struggle. They don't want to talk about all of them.*

Carole: *I remember feeling that we had a meaningful exchange going here and asking you whether you had ever read any reader-response theory. Like Louise Rosenblatt's transactional theory—the idea that meaning isn't found solely in the text or solely in the reader but is a transaction between the reader and the text.*

Paul: *When you first started talking about it, I didn't have a clue as to what you meant. The meaning isn't found solely in the text? Now it's so obvious having this thing hanging in front of your face—a student like Javier telling about his grandfather. At the time, the most important piece seemed to be to plow through this story so that I covered all my bases: the story elements. Seems so obvious now but not at the time. I do remember you waving your hand around and talking about a "to and fro" between the reader and the text.*

Carole: *I sensed you were intrigued. It certainly resonated with what had happened that day. I also thought, "OK, I know something he doesn't. I'll use this opportunity to ask about teaching English learners." I was feeling undereducated about teaching English learners at this time, and because we were revising our teacher education program to more fully address the needs of teachers of English learners, I thought I might as well get it from the horse's mouth. This is obviously a great teacher who also happens to be a teacher of English learners and is wrestling with what to do about literature, something I know about. Maybe we each had something to offer the other. I was eager to learn firsthand about teaching English learners, to spend more time in this room, and thinking that I didn't know nearly as much as I should about what went on in a classroom of English learners.*

Paul: *Yes, I remember being embarrassed because I hadn't heard of Rosenblatt, so I said, "Oh yes, Rosencrantz and Guildenstern." You get the joke?*

Carole: *I get it, Paul.*

A CHANGE IN THINKING ABOUT TEACHING WITH LITERATURE

After lunch, a child from *The Rabbit and the Turnip* group came up to Paul with his paper about the problem in the story and said he didn't "get it." Paul said, "Aha," and shared with the child that we'd been talking about it being a dumb story and said, "Why don't you write a better story?"

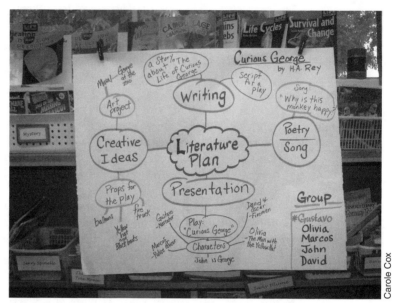

A new Literature Plan for *Curious George*

A New Literature Plan

The next time I visited Paul's class, he was trying something new for his Literature Plan chart (see photo A new Literature Plan for *Curious George*). He did not section off the side of the chart where he recorded the students' ideas about a story in separate parts for setting, character, events, and problem.

He said they had so much to say when he began by doing everything at once, so he encouraged them to talk about anything and everything. Evidently it was working better. It cut down conference time if they did it all at the same time. He also began by just asking them to "talk about the story," rather than about the conventions of literature. Paul's expression was "Talk to me." And then he waited for the ideas and language to emerge.

From the ideas that Paul recorded on the chart, the group members did four pieces of writing on self-selected topics generated during their open discussions of literature (e.g., Javier writing about life on a turnip farm) instead of three pieces of "writing analysis" based on story structure (e.g., the problem).

Curious George: A Discussion of the Story Using the New Literature Plan

Gustavo took over leading the *Curious George* group discussion while Paul was needed by another group (see photo Gustavo leading a Literature Circle discussion of *Curious George*, p.11). Because the approach was not a teacher-directed, text-centered one in which Paul (the teacher) would be necessary because he knew what the answers were (e.g., What is the problem in the story?), this was possible. Paul's new approach was to generate and record the students' ideas about the

Gustavo leading a Literature Circle discussion of *Curious George*

story, what they were thinking about while reading, and how it related to their own ideas and life experiences. Gustavo could now guide the group because his ideas were as important as the teacher's (or those in the teacher's guide).

Several ideas for writing and projects had emerged from the group discussion when Paul joined the group and began to write them on another piece of chart paper with three clusters for their ideas: "Curious George Play" with ideas for Act 1, Act II, and Act III in smaller clusters; "My Life with Curious George" with ideas for a story they could write, with smaller clusters with ideas like "I live with George," "We eat," "Everyday we go to . . .," and "We work"; and "Song: Why Is This Monkey

Paul leading a Literature Circle discussion of *Curious George*

Happy?" with ideas for verses. Paul also recorded what the students in the group would do on the new Literature Plan, in each of four areas:

> *Writing:* A story about the life of Curious George and a script for a play
> *Poetry/Song:* The song "Why Is This Monkey Happy?"
> *Creative Ideas:* An art project (a mural of George at the zoo) and props for the play
> *Presentation:* A play "Curious George" with students in the group cast as the
>   characters

The plan also identified the group with students' names in the bottom right corner: *Gustavo (the asterisk means he is the leader), Olivia, Marcos, John, and David.

Here is the finished song "Why Is This Monkey Happy?" (to the tune of "Twinkle, Twinkle, Little Star"):

Curious George in Africa

Caught by a man in a yellow hat

Taken far

So far, far away

Why, oh, why

Is George happy?

Learned to smoke

And stole balloons

Went to jail

And sat alone

Taken far

So far, far away

Why, oh, why

Is George happy?

More Conversation Between Carole and Paul

Before I left the first day, I told Paul I'd bring him a copy of Louise Rosenblatt's first book, *Literature as Exploration* (1995). I also took this opportunity to ask him what he'd recommend as reading in the field of teaching English learners. He gave me his copy of a book published by the California State Department of Education, *Schooling and Language-Minority Children: A Theoretical Framework* (1981).

After this, Paul and I really began to explore in our conversations the crossroads between reader-response theory and teaching with literature on the one hand, and theories of learning English as a second language on the other. I continued to observe, take notes, and participate in his classroom. And during lunch periods, we talked a lot about what it all meant.

Although we each came from a different experiential background and theoretical orientation, we found that reader-response theory provided a common ground and vocabulary for talking about children's responses to literature and life, engaging them and exploring literature, literacy development, and differentiating instruction. Paul showed me obvious connections among key ideas of reader response and learning English as a second language and ways he would apply them in his teaching with literature.

The common interest we shared was a drive to understand more about the importance of children's voices in the classroom. We never seem to tire of talking about how it plays out in children's language and literacy development. We listen for their voices through response to literature, through drama and dance and Shakespeare that I have done with children, and through songs and writing that Paul has done in his classroom. We hear it in informal conversations or chance remarks or the serendipitous metaphor spoken by a child that can become a central focus in learning to speak a second language or write in two or can become the raw material for a song or poem or drama or simply an image that sustains thought and talk beyond a teacher's expectations. It compels us both.

Through our conversations and writing, we have gained a deeper and richer understanding of processes that will always elude total understanding. But isn't that what makes them so intriguing in the first place? This book, then, is our effort to talk with each other, as well as with other teachers, about mapping the crossroads of literary understanding and teaching with literature with learning English as a second language.

Two caveats: First, this book is not intended to be a comprehensive treatment of all theories or methods of learning English as a second language, reader-response theory or methods of teaching with literature, or reading and language arts. Our discussion has always focused on the application of Rosenblatt's transactional theory to teaching with literature—in this case, Paul's third-grade classroom of English language learners. Furthermore, we see oral language development as a naturally occurring byproduct of student-centered teaching with literature across the curriculum, in combination with teaching reading and writing. It appears quite seamless to us, so we have not broken the discussion into separate parts for listening, speaking, reading, writing, and content area instruction. We see them as an integrally related whole.

Second, we live in Long Beach, California, the most diverse city in the country, where the largest number of English learners are native Spanish speakers. Paul was a teacher in a bilingual Spanish/English classroom, and classroom descriptions in this book reflect this. Of the three case studies of children that I write about from my research, one child was a native English speaker, and the other two were native Spanish speakers.

Keep in mind, however, that reader-response theories and theories of learning English as a second language have been broadly applied across cultural and linguistic groups and in the multilanguage classroom where the teacher speaks only English but uses approaches that foster English language and literacy development.

What Happened with the Problem Javier Was Having with the Story?

What Paul did with Javier's response to the story *The Rabbit and the Turnip* reflects his orientation as a student-centered teacher but clearly applied to teaching with literature. After his students just "didn't get" what they were supposed to say in response to the question "What's the problem in the story?" and after our conversation about what should be the focus of a literature discussion, Paul did what he did in every other aspect of his teaching: He recognized and validated Javier's challenge of the text concerning turnips: "The turnip was white and not red. No good. My grandpa has a farm in Mexico and grows turnips and carrots and vegetables. That turnip's no good" and "Maybe the animals couldn't find anything because of the snow. But where did he find the turnip if there's snow all over?"

Paul argues that the challenge for the educator of English learners for purposes of learning to speak English, maintaining their home language, becoming literate in both, and succeeding academically is to create the environment that invites students like Javier to share their lives and knowledge in the classroom. Paul points out the parallel between reader-response theory and theories of learning English as a second language. Learning becomes a two-way undertaking when transactional instruction happens in the classroom. Listening to students as they respond to a text becomes the first act of instruction.

Paul encouraged Javier to share more about turnips and his grandfather with the group. Javier brought a pile of photographs of his family's ranch in Mexico, showing him riding a mule with his brother, working the land, and harvesting turnips. Paul helped him make a display of the ranch pictures and write about life on their turnip ranch.

In this instance, Paul made a clear shift from a more text-oriented approach of asking the students to focus solely on the story to a more reader-oriented approach to teaching with literature by also focusing on the student's personal experience of the story. He encouraged Javier to draw on his own life experiences as a rich environment for literary understanding, spoken language, and literacy development. And a story became more than just a means to an end of gaining knowledge of story structure or even knowledge of the world, to the real purpose of literature as a means of self-knowledge.

A Thought from Paul

Javier and the turnip initiated a seminal moment in my understanding of exploring literature, developing literacy, and differentiating instruction. What was initially a frustrating teaching experience for me began a radical shift in my thinking. When Javier told me that his grandfather grew turnips at their ranch in Mexico, an opening to explore was presented. At that time I did not know the theoretical implications of this opening, nor did I imagine how a theory of literary response would organize a range of approaches to teaching English learners.

After the observation, my conversation with Carole posed critical questions about what substantive exploration of literature entailed. Story grammar analysis alone informs the reader about the structure, or bones, of a story; but the more interesting questions about the reader's "lived-through experience" (Rosenblatt, 1995) reveals the heart, the guts, and the meat of the story itself.

I followed Javier's lead intuitively, but at that point I was not yet aware of sociocultural theory or of exploring "funds of knowledge" (Moll & Greenberg, 1996). Javier, on the other hand, as a third grader, could not have been expected to articulate a clear-cut explanation of his knowledge funds. His reaction to my analysis-focused teaching about the story—acting out, balking at its inaccuracies—was understandable in retrospect, but not readily appreciated in the moment of instruction. Thank goodness, however, that he expressed his dissatisfaction. We had to work together. I like to think of it as exploring *mutual* funds of knowledge.

As the classroom teacher, I supplied pedagogical knowledge about language and literacy development; as the student, Javier supplied grounded knowledge drawn from his culture, family, and life experience. The dialogical nature of this kind of collaboration ran deeper than "response protocols" (Mohr & Mohr, 2007) or "instructional conversations" (Goldenberg, 1993). Sometimes I took the lead. At other times, Javier led the way, out of necessity, because the subject was his experience and knowledge in response to the story. The sociocultural implications of literary exploration were profound.

In addition, literacy development took place when I helped him recognize and craft his raw literary responses into differentiated and conventional formats, or response products. Those products were a combination of oral and written language activities and creative projects that matched his linguistic strengths and needs. Pedagogical knowledge and skills were manifold here. The situation required knowing the English learner's language level, as well as the curriculum, and district and state requirements. As teacher, I needed to know how to skillfully introduce a wide range of literacy development activities that could be differentiated according to the language level. Additionally, as teacher, I needed to learn about the cultural background of the English learner through dialogue with Javier and his family.

Further, differentiated instruction was naturally applied in this situation because it was tailored to Javier's literary response and his literacy needs. I suggested that he work on a presentation that involved listening, speaking, reading, writing, and visually representing turnip farming in Mexico. The differentiation was product driven. Javier brought pictures from home of the Mexican turnip farm and arranged them on tag board; then he wrote captions for each of the pictures that were consistent with his level of English proficiency. He presented his product to the class and responded to questions from fellow students. While the language requirements of the presentation were adjusted to his level, the content level remained constant.

For me, Rosenblatt's literary theory operated like a macrotheory that facilitated applying sociocultural practices, literacy development, and differentiated instruction. Inviting students to explore their own perceptions as they read opened up a wealth of experiences and ways of seeing. I began to see literature as part of a shared story; I began to see Javier as a knowledgeable explorer rather than a problem kid; and I began to see possibilities for engaging English learners with the raw stuff of story and their experiences.

EXPLORING IDEAS

1. If you have not had experience teaching English learners, think about the beliefs you had about what might go on in a class in which students were learning English as a second language. How do those beliefs compare with the description of Paul's class in this chapter?

2. If you have had experience teaching English learners, compare your knowledge of these students with the description of Paul's class in this chapter. How are they alike or different? What tentative conclusions can you draw from your comparison?

3. As you read the description of Paul's class and Carole's thoughts about it, what did you think about the way Paul taught and Carole's ideas?

4. What do you think is the most important thing to do when teaching with literature? How does your idea compare with Paul's or Carole's?

5. Sketch a cluster for the Literature Plan you might use in your own class. It could be different from the one Paul used. For example, if I did a Literature Plan, it would definitely have a heading for drama. What might yours look like? What ideas about language and teaching with literature would it reflect?

6. Read the books that Carole and Paul exchanged to inform each other about their respective interests in reader-response theory—specifically, Louise Rosenblatt's transactional theory and learning English as a second language:

On reader-response theory (transactional theory): Rosenblatt, L. M. (1995). *Literature as Exploration.* New York: Modern Language Association. (Original work published 1938)

On learning English as a second language: California State Department of Education. (1981). *Schooling and Language-Minority Children: A Theoretical Framework*. Los Angeles: California State University.

Jot down your own ideas about these books and their possible application in the classroom, and compare your ideas with those of Carole and Paul in this book.

CHILDREN'S BOOKS

Cleary, B. (1984). *Ramona la chinche* (edición en español). New York: William Morrow.

Freschet, B. (1973). *Bear mouse*. New York: Charles Scribner's & Sons.

Payne, E. (1973). *Katy no pocket*. New York: Houghton Mifflin.

Rey, H. A. (1973). *Curious George*. New York: Houghton Mifflin.

Sachar, L. (1978). *Sideways stories from Wayside School*. New York: Avon Books.

Sadler, R. (1968). *The rabbit and the turnip*. London: Richard Sadler Ltd.

White, E. B. (1988). *Las telarañas de Carlota*. Barcelona, Spain: Noguer.

REFERENCES

California State Department of Education. (1981). *Schooling and language-minority children: A theoretical framework*. Los Angles: California State University.

Goldenberg, C. (1993). Instructional conversations: Promoting comprehension through discussion. *The Reading Teacher, 46*, 221–238.

Mohr, K., & Mohr, E. (2007). Extending English language learner's classroom interactions using the Response Protocols. *The Reading Teacher, 60*(5), 440–450.

Moll, L. C., & Greenberg, J. (1996). Creating zones of possibilities: Combining social contexts for instruction. In L. C. Moll (Ed.), *Vygotsky in education: Instructional implications and applications of sociohistorical psychology*. Melbourne, Australia: Cambridge Press.

Rosenblatt, L. M. (1995). *Literature as exploration*. New York: Modern Language Association. (Original work published 1938)

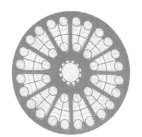

CHAPTER TWO

Reader Response and Learning English as a Second Language

All literary critics hope to explain how people make meaning when they read literature. Not all critics focus on the same aspects of the reading event, however. Although literary criticism may seem far removed from the classroom, it has, in fact, greatly influenced how literature has been taught and continues to do so. Knowledge of these theories may not be explicit in teachers' minds, but often the theories guide instruction implicitly if they were reflected in the way teachers were taught literature. With something as significant and also ephemeral as literature, it's important that teachers know not only what to do but also why they are doing it. In other words, there may be nothing more practical than a good theory.

READER-RESPONSE THEORY

Reader-response criticism emerged during the 20th century with a new emphasis on the reader, in contrast with the emphasis in the 19th and early 20th centuries on biographical and historical background and in the late 1930s and 1940s on the "New Criticism" of the text itself.

The Reader and the Text

The New Criticism changed literary scholarship when a new group of critics shifted the focus of attention to the works themselves, especially the use of figurative language and metaphor (Brooks & Warren, 1938; Wellek & Warren, 1949). This school of literary criticism reflected a positivistic epistemology, which sought to create "an objective, empirical and systematic foundation for knowledge . . . [where the] . . . ideal pursued is knowledge in the form of a mathematically formulated universal science" (Held, 1980, p. 164). Applied to literature, this meant that the New Critics sought to impose a universal system of structure upon a text. This shift in epistemological and literary theory influenced the way literature was taught in college and subsequently in K–12 reading and literature instruction.

The New Critics rejected the idea that the author's intention ("the intentional fallacy") or the reader's response ("the affective fallacy") had much bearing on the meaning of a text. Instead, they maintained that meaning could be found primarily within the text itself. The reader's subjective response was not stressed. Most important was a careful analysis of the text's language (e.g., figurative language)—not just what it "said," but the way it was said and what it symbolized. A proper reading of a text was like a careful dissection of a frog in biology class. Reading literature was more like science than art, although a literary work was viewed as a carefully constructed work of art that must be dissected and the parts carefully analyzed for the whole to be fully understood and appreciated. This view, incidentally, coincided with the heavy influence of behavioral psychology in education.

The first reader-response theorists, I. A. Richards (1935) and Louise Rosenblatt (1995), predated the New Critics, but their ideas did not influence instruction until a reaction to the strict formalism of the New Criticism in the late 1960s. Reader-response theorists argued the active role of the reader in the construction of meaning while reading. Because meaning is a creation of individual and unique readers, not everyone would necessarily agree on a single, "correct" meaning of a text.

The Transactional Theory

Reader-response theory is not essentially new. Louise Rosenblatt's landmark first book, *Literature as Exploration,* was initially published in 1938. It did not gain an influence in education until the 1960s, well after the new critical orientation of the 1940s had predominated literature instruction in the United States. The most widely referred to reader-response theory in education is Louise Rosenblatt's transactional theory of the literary work (Clifford, 1991; Cox, 2008; Cox & Zarrillo, 1993; Farrell & Squire, 1990; Hunsberger & Labercane, 2002; Karolides, 1992, 1997; Many & Cox, 1992).

In an explanation of her ideas in *Theoretical Models and Processes of Reading,* Rosenblatt (2004) begins by defining "the reader" for a new generation of educators. The definition is the same one she first wrote in *Literature as Explanation* in 1938:

> Terms such as "the reader" are somewhat misleading, though convenient, fictions. There is no such thing as a generic reader or a generic literary work; there are in reality only the potential millions of individual readers of individual literary works . . . the reading of any work of literature is, of necessity, an individual and unique occurrence involving the mind and emotions of some particular reader. (Rosenblatt, 2004, p. 1363)

The transactional theory focuses on the active role of the reader in creating meaning from a text, or literary work. She describes this creation of meaning as

> a complex, to-and-fro, self-correcting transaction between reader and verbal signs which continues until some final organization, more or less complete and coherent, is arrived at and thought of as corresponding to the text. The "meaning"—whether, e.g., poem, novel, play, scientific report, or legal brief—comes into being during the transaction. (1986, p. 123)

Rosenblatt describes this process as a "two-way transaction," a "live-circuit" between the reader and the text. She borrowed the term *transaction* from John Dewey (1938), who defined it as a reciprocal relationship among the parts in a single situation (see figure Two-way Transaction between Reader and Text, p.21). This is in contrast with the term *interaction,* which involves two separate entities acting on one another.

Each reading event is unique, involving a particular reader, text, and context and occurring at a particular moment in time. Both the reader and the text are two

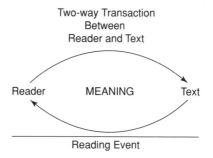

aspects of a totally dynamic situation. A reader may read the same text at different times and under different circumstances or in a different mood, and the result would be a new and different meaning. Reader and text are not two separate entities, but rather are factors in a total situation. The reader activates and draws from a linguistic-experiential reservoir, paying selective attention to those physical, personal, social, and cultural factors that enter into the reading situation and that will eventually be organized and synthesized into "meaning." Rosenblatt uses William James's (1890) phrase for reading as a "choosing activity."

Reader Stance

According to Rosenblatt (1994), although all reading occurs as experienced meaning, readers assume a stance, or focus their selective attention in different ways. *Stance* represents a reader's readiness to organize thinking about what is read according to a more efferent or more aesthetic framework (see figure Stance, p.22). The reader's adoption of a stance, either conscious or unconscious, guides the "choosing activity" in the stream of consciousness. Any text can be read efferently or aesthetically, and readers move back and forth on a continuum from more efferent to more aesthetic, eventually settling on one predominant stance.

During a more efferent reading, the reader's focus is on the information he or she will take away from the text, or the more public, lexical, analytical, abstracting aspects (e.g., reading the label on a bottle of prescription medicine to find the correct dosage). During a more aesthetic reading, the reader's focus is on the lived-through experience of the reading event, or the more private, experiential, affective, associational aspects (e.g., reading a novel and picturing yourself as one of the characters).

A more efferent reading focuses on what is in the text; a more aesthetic reading focuses on the associations, feelings, attitudes, and ideas that the text arouses in the reader. The lived-through experience of the work during the aesthetic transaction constitutes the "literary work." Rosenblatt calls this the "evocation" and "the poem" (not to be confused with a poetic text). And evocation, she argues, should be the center of literature response and interpretation, discussions and instruction, both during and after the reading event.

Most readings are a mix of both stances, and any text can be read more efferently or more aesthetically (e.g., reading the sports page to find out who won a baseball game and what the score was, or reading the same page and imagining yourself

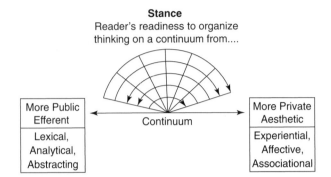

as a player in the game). Readers may adopt a different stance toward the same text at different times and in different situations: reading *Romeo and Juliet* in high school or college to study for a test on it in English; or reading it for pleasure and savoring the beauty of the language; or perhaps reading it while in love, thinking about whom they love. Rosenblatt maintains that, for most experiences with literature, "our primary responsibility is to encourage the aesthetic stance" (1982, p. 275).

A Higher Level of Understanding

Studies of children's and adolescents' stance towards literature from Rosenblatt's transactional perspective have shown that students who take a primarily aesthetic stance reach higher levels of understanding of a story (Cox & Many, 1989, 1992a, 1992b; Many, 2004). In a study of the effects of aesthetic and efferent stances on students in fourth, sixth, and eighth grades and level of understanding of stories, Many (1991) concluded that

> stance did significantly affect level of understanding, with higher levels of understanding associated with the aesthetic stance. . . . The subjects who focused in their responses on the lived-through experience of the story were significantly more likely to interpret story events, to apply the story to life, and to make abstract generalizations than were students who responded efferently. . . . The majority of efferent responses focusing on the literary elements tended to be trite and superficial. (p. 77)

However, in a study of teachers considered expert at teaching with literature, Jim Zarrillo and I found that they used a more efferent, less aesthetic, teacher- and text-centered approach (Zarrillo & Cox, 1992). Moreover, the teachers were basically atheoretical. Their instruction went unfettered by any guiding principles. Teacher's guides for commercial reading series, professional development books, and in-service sessions were the source of ideas for teaching with literature. Response was seen primarily as an artifact such as a piece of writing or a puppet, rather than what a child was experiencing or thinking while reading and the verbal expression or discussion of those thoughts.

   In comparing more efferent to more aesthetic teaching approaches, Many and Wiseman (1992) found that a literary-analysis, or more efferent approach, which emphasized identifying literary elements, resulted in children writing with a focus on the story. In contrast, a literary-experience, or more aesthetic, approach, which encouraged children to live through the reading experience, resulted in children's writing that was more involved and made connections between the story and their own lives.

These studies support Rosenblatt's conception of literary transactions and understanding and argue for teaching approaches that respect the reader's lived-through, personal experience of the text. With regard to research on teaching English learners, a key conclusion and recommendation on instructional approaches in *Developing Literacy in Second-Language Learners: Report of the National Literacy Panel on Language-Minority Children and Youth* (August & Shanahan, 2006) is that teachers should develop deeper, more thorough discussions of literature. Clearly, a means to do this is with a more reader-centered approach as described in Rosenblatt's transactional theory. To attach a child's face, experiences, and literary responses to this theory, see Box 2.1.

BOX 2.1   *Case Study of Juan: The Beginning English Learner*

Go to the Compendium of Case Studies, and read the "Case Study of Juan: The Beginning English Learner"—sections "Meet Juan" and "Juan's Response Style: Makes Personal Connections," pp. 149–61. Think about the following when you read, and jot down your ideas as you read and think:

▲ Pick one of Juan's responses. Look at each idea in a phrase or sentence, and classify it as efferent (focused on what is found in the text) or aesthetic (what is evoked in his mind as he heard the text). Tally up the two types of responses. Would you describe it as predominantly efferent or aesthetic? Why?

▲ In class, find a partner and compare your findings, and discuss the similarities and differences.

▲ Jot down some ideas about how you would teach Juan and why you would do it that way, keeping in mind Rosenblatt's suggestion that "our primary responsibility is to encourage the aesthetic stance" (1982, p. 275) when teaching with literature.

▲ Read one of the books that I read to Juan, and write a dialogue journal page. Draw a line down the middle of the page. On the left side, write the page number and a note about something that attracted your attention in that part of the book. On the right side, write your own response to it. Identify your responses as predominantly efferent or aesthetic as you did for Juan. What predominant stance did you take? What do you think occurred during the reading process? Use ideas from Rosenblatt's transactional theory to explain what happened and your comments.

THEORIES OF LEARNING ENGLISH AS A SECOND LANGUAGE

Like literary theory, theories of learning English as a second language often present contrasting views of how both a first and a second language are learned and have had varying effects on practice. Historically, the development of theory and of approaches to second language instruction has included an emphasis on grammar-translation approaches in the 19th century; behaviorist approaches, such as the audiolingual method in the mid-20th century; Noam Chomsky's notion of innate language ability and a universal grammar; and communicative approaches that influence teachers of English learners today, such as James Cummins's ideas on context-embedded communication and primary language support and Stephen Krashen's idea of comprehensible input and the natural approach. This is not intended to be a comprehensive overview, but rather a description of the major ideas that have most influenced practice. Viewed very broadly, approaches to learning a second language have ranged on a continuum from those that are predominantly grammar-based to those that are predominantly communicative-based.

Grammar

Grammar-based instruction has focused on accuracy in grammar usage. The goal of this type of instruction is to learn grammar or to produce grammatically correct sentences in a limited communicative context. This approach may seem familiar if you took a foreign language class in high school or college in which you used a textbook with sequential chapters on a language grammar system (e.g., present tense verbs, then past tense verbs; regular verb endings, then irregular verbs), did exercises at the end of the chapter in which you practiced these language forms, and were largely graded on written tests. You may have practiced set dialogues with other students or the teacher using the grammatical form. Your teacher taught lessons on the grammatical forms, corrected the exercises, and graded the tests. You probably spent less time actually communicating with the teacher or other students in the language, and little of that time would have been spent on communicating things of interest to you. The focus of instruction was on the grammar of the language as content.

Different grammar-based methods of language instruction have emphasized different strategies. From the 19th century through the 1950s, the grammar-translation approach dominated. Rules of grammar were taught by translating a text—which aptly illustrated that rule—from the foreign language into the student's first language. Lists of words, and sentences unrelated by meaning but illustrating the rule, were also used. Instruction was in the first language, and communication in the language was not important.

With the advent of World War II and a need to learn languages quickly, the audiolingual method was used by the military and began to replace grammar-translation. It was related to the work of structural linguists, such as Bloomfield (1933) and Fries (1945) in the 1930s and 1940s, who carefully listed and described the structure of languages. It also meshed well with behaviorism, the ruling learning theory of the period. This method used a sequence of oral patterned dialogues that were practiced and memorized through many repetitions to teach grammatical structures. Listening and speaking were emphasized over reading and writing, but still scant attention was paid to students' creative language production. A student's job was to repeat and memorize. Pronunciation was important and was often practiced with tapes and earphones in language laboratories. The direct, or Berlitz, method used more dialogue but still with a focus on a grammatical aspect of the language taught inductively in formal exchanges between the teacher and the student.

In the 1960s, cognitive methods focused on learning all the parts of a language, in order, from part to whole (e.g., letter sounds, then words, then phrases, then sentences) through structured lessons and drill of these subskills. By this time, the Chomskyan revolution in linguistics had occurred, replacing the predominance of structural linguistics. Noam Chomsky's (1957, 1965) theory of a transformational-generative grammar, which maintained that language had two levels—a deep and a surface structure—led to teachers leading students through sentence-recombining drills to understand grammar. These drills were used extensively by English teachers as well. Chomsky, however, did not suggest this use of his theory and, in fact, questioned it. His idea that humans had an innate cognitive ability to learn language was probably more influential in that it offered a direct challenge to behavioral psychology, the learning theory that predominated in schools when grammar-based methods were prevalent. Chomsky critiqued B. F. Skinner and behaviorism, maintaining that language was not learned through imitation and repetition because the ability of humans to produce sentences they had never heard before proved the creative nature of language production (Chomsky, 1964).

Support for Chomsky's ideas came from psycholinguistic research that described the commonalities of children's natural speech development over time and across languages. Chomsky's theory of innateness prompted interest in psycholinguistic research in children's language development in the 1960s and 1970s, particularly regarding the stages and rate of acquiring language structures (Cazden, 1972; C. Chomsky, 1969; Menyuk, 1963; Strickland, 1962), and opened the field of teaching English learners to methods that used students' own ideas and language production, or communicative-based methods, rather than behavioristic grammar-based methods that relied on imitation, repetition, memorization, and drills of skills.

Communication

Communicative-based approaches currently used in many classrooms with English learners apply methods relevant to the functional language needs of students who are learning to live in language environments different from those of their homes. The goal of this type of instruction is for students to be able to communicate messages in the language they are learning and to use it for meaningful purposes. Swain (1986) argues that the opportunity to engage in meaningful oral exchanges of "comprehensible output" in the classroom or community is an essential component of learning English as a second language. In conveying meaning when speaking, the speaker also learns the structure and form of the language.

Language forms will be learned, then, but the emphasis of instruction is on language as a medium of communication and on using language to learn, rather than as a subject to study. Teachers using this approach encourage English learners to initiate language events and to use language for functional and creative experiences and products. The teacher creates contexts in which this can occur. Much time is spent on students' ideas and interests as a focus of language and literacy experiences.

TABLE 2.1 Two Approaches to Teaching English Learners

Grammar	Communication
1. Focus is on language forms.	1. Focus is on meaningful instruction.
2. Success is based on mastery of language forms.	2. Success is based on using language to get things done.
3. Lessons are organized around types of language forms and structures: teacher-directed activities.	3. Lessons are organized around ideas and interests of students: student-centered activities.
4. Error correction is essential for mastery.	4. Errors in form are acceptable.
5. Learning is a conscious process of memorizing rules, forms, and structures.	5. Acquisition is unconscious and occurs through exposure to comprehensible input.
6. Emphasis on production skills may result in anxiety in early stages.	6. Emphasis on letting language production emerge naturally results in low anxiety.

A focus on communication rather than on grammar in language teaching was supported by sociolinguistic theoretical positions and research in the 1970s and 1980s (Cook-Gumperz, 1979; Halliday, 1975; Lindfors, 1987; Tough, 1977; Wells, 1981), which argued for the importance of the social aspects of language learning, and in several cases criticized Chomsky for his lack of attention to it. Dell Hymes (1974) argued that being proficient means demonstrating communicative competence, knowing how to use a language for specific purposes in real-life situations; and Michael Halliday (1975) defined language as "meaning potential, that is, as sets of opinions, or alternatives, in meaning, that are available to the speaker-hearer" (p. 63).

Several communicative models of learning English as a second language have evolved from these theories and this body of research and have had an impact on methods of teaching English learners. See Table 2.1 for a comparison of the major emphases of the two instructional approaches; it shows the contrast between traditional and predominantly grammar-based language learning and more current, predominantly communicative-based methods of teaching.

Context-Embedded Communication and Primary Language Support

The ideas of James Cummins (1981, 1989, 1992, 2000, 2005) have greatly influenced ideas about teaching English learners. Cummins argues that with context-embedded communication, which is the amount of contextual support present when someone is learning a second language, language meaning is actively negotiated between two speakers and is supported by many contextual clues. For example, contextual clues could include determining who is the ball monitor and takes the ball out to the yard at recess, or deciding whose turn it is in playing a game. In contrast, in context-reduced communication, there are very few clues to meaning—for example, answering a teacher's questions after a lecture. Each type of communication task also has a level of cognitive demand. Little thought is required in cognitively undemanding tasks, such as taking your turn in a game. Cognitively demanding tasks, such as writing a five-paragraph essay, however, are more difficult. According to Cummins (1984),

> A major aim of schooling is to develop students' ability to manipulate and interpret cognitively-demanding context-reduced text. The more initial reading and writing instruction can be embedded in a meaningful communicative context (i.e., related to a child's experience), the more successful it is likely to be. The same principle holds for second-language instruction. (p. 136)

The amount of context-embedded communication, or contextual support for learning English as a second language, determines a student's proficiency in English in two important dimensions of language:

1. Basic interpersonal communication skills (BICS) are used daily in social speaking situations, such as children talking together on the playground. These skills require up to 3 years of practice for proficiency.
2. Cognitive academic language proficiency (CALP) involves those language skills used in school tasks, such as taking notes on a lecture and writing a report using the information. CALP skills require 5 to 7 years of use for proficiency.

The relationship between these two dimensions of language proficiency is often illustrated with an iceberg and the adage about being deceived in seeing only its tip. The tip of the iceberg represents basic communicative language skills. In other words, teachers can hear basic communicative competence but can be misled in thinking that a student has also developed the academic language skills necessary for success in complex school tasks.

A teacher must ensure that English learners are able to develop both communicative and academic language skills in English. This doesn't mean, however, that the process will take twice as much time and effort. Students are able to manage the linguistic demand of more cognitively difficult, context-reduced school tasks because of a common underlying proficiency for both languages; that is, developing the ability to perform cognitively demanding tasks in context-reduced situations in one language is a basis for performing similar tasks in another language.

Cummins (2005) emphasizes the importance of primary language support, or using a child's home language, while learning English. This can be done in most classrooms in several ways. Cross-age tutoring allows older, more advanced English learners to work with younger, more beginning English learners. For example, in

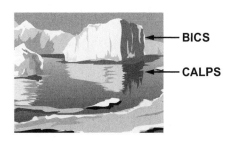

BICS

CALPS

many schools English learners in kindergarten have a fifth-grade "buddy" who is an advanced English speaker but who also speaks the same primary language as the younger children and meets with them on a regular schedule. Heterogeneous grouping of students in the same class who speak the same primary language, ranging from beginning to advanced levels of English proficiency, is another way to provide support in the primary language. Flexible scheduling and team teaching among teachers who speak only English and those who speak the primary language of students are another way to maintain primary language support, as well as using school staff, paraprofessionals, volunteers, and aides who speak the home languages of the students in the school.

Research-based recommendations regarding cross-linguistic relationships in second language learners and the issue of primary language support in teaching English learners are addressed in *Developing Literacy in Second-Language Learners: Report of the National Literacy Panel on Language-Minority Children and Youth* (August & Shanahan, 2006). This report concludes that proficiency in a child's first language positively influences acquisition of the second language with higher order academic skills development. In other words, the transfer of academically mediated skills is bidirectional between the first and second language. This means that academic skills such as reading comprehension, writing, and use of literacy strategies are interdependent among languages that a student knows and is learning. For example, with cognate vocabulary—that is, words that are the same or have a similar root in both languages, such as *color* and *calendario* in Spanish and *color* and *calendar* in English—transfer from the first to second language can enhance word reading and the comprehension of text (Nagy, Garcia, Durgunoglu, & Hancin-Bhatt, 1993). Furthermore, proficiency in word reading in the first language is highly correlated with proficient word reading in the second language. There is a solid base of research evidence for primary language support, then, in teaching English learners to speak, read, and write English (August & Shanahan, 2006; Proctor, August, Carlo, & Snow, 2006; Snow, Burns, & Griffin, 1998).

Comprehensible Input and the Natural Approach

The ideas of American linguist Stephen Krashen (1981, 1982, 1985a, 1985b, 2003, 2004; Crawford & Krashen, 2007) have also been influential in methods of teaching English learners, although not without controversy (Larsen-Freeman & Long, 1991; McLaughlin, 1987). Krashen argues that a key to learning English as a second language is comprehensible input. This means that students learn English by listening to and understanding input that's just a bit beyond their current level of proficiency. He describes this in a formula in which *i* stands for what we already know and *1* represents what we learn.

i + 1 = comprehensible input

For students to move to the next stage of learning English, they must increasingly understand language that's just a bit more difficult than what they already know, building on what they have already learned. (Compare this idea with Vygotsky's "zone of proximal development," which is described later in the chapter.) Characteristics of comprehensible input include the following:

▲ Language that's already known to the student, together with some new language

▲ Contextual clues, such as objects in familiar situations

▲ Paralinguistic clues, such as gestures and facial expressions

▲ Linguistic modifications, such as intonation, repetition, paraphrasing, simplification, clear pronunciation, and reduced speed

▲ Meaningful topics about which students have prior knowledge from their own experience

Krashen has described what he calls the monitor model, which has five hypotheses:

1. *Acquisition versus learning:* Second language learning involves two distinct processes: (a) language acquisition, or the subconscious, natural way people learn language by using it for real communication, and (b) language learning, or conscious knowing about a language, as when people are able to describe the rules. Children acquire their first language, picking it up naturally in informal settings, in a similar way to people who travel in other countries where a language they don't know is spoken. People acquire a second language in the same way they acquire their first, through the successful communication of meaningful messages.

2. *Natural order:* Grammatical structures are acquired in a somewhat predictable order, some early and some late. Not everyone acquires them in exactly the same order, nor do people acquire them in their second language in the same order they acquired them in their first language.

3. *The monitor:* This is the conscious knowledge about a second language, such as the ability to describe a grammar rule. Knowledge about a language won't make us more fluent speakers but may serve as self-correction for language we have acquired as long as we have the time to think—which may not happen in a rapid conversation. We must be thinking about the rule, and we must know the rule. Many people acquire a language without conscious knowledge of the rules behind it.

4. *Comprehensible input:* As just described, this key hypothesis in Krashen's model has important implications for teachers. Students acquire a second language when they obtain comprehensible input in a low-anxiety situation, when they are presented with interesting messages, and when they understand those messages.

5. *The affective filter:* Comprehensible input is necessary but not sufficient to acquire a second language. What Krashen calls the affective filter determines how much of the raw material of language (the comprehensible input) will be processed. If students are nervous, unmotivated to speak the new language, and lacking self-esteem, the affective filter will be high, and their learning will be limited. They will learn more if the affective filter is low because they are in a comfortable classroom environment and have high levels of motivation and self-confidence.

The natural approach to teaching English learners (Krashen & Terrell, 1983) is based on Krashen's hypotheses in the monitor model. The basic premise is that children acquire a second language in the same way they acquired their first: in natural situations focused on the communication of meaningful messages.

The goal for teaching English learners should be to focus on the communication of messages in English, rather than on grammatical accuracy. Speaking should be allowed to emerge in stages, from nonverbal communication to speaking single words, then short phrases, and so on. Students should be given time to begin speaking when they are ready, and correcting errors is not important or advisable in these early stages.

Teaching should also be based on students' own ideas, interests, and experiences. They should be learning to communicate for real purposes and in real situations. The classroom atmosphere should be warm and friendly, and teachers should create activities that fully engage English learners. Appropriate topics for students learning to speak English would therefore be things like their names and naming things, descriptions of the students and their families, numbers, clothing, colors, objects in the classroom, and pets. Appropriate situations for learning to speak English would be familiar greetings, classroom directions, playing games and sports, and sharing home experiences. Support for this approach is noted by Duran (1996):

> Research suggests that learners of a second language acquire the second language most effectively when it arises as comprehensible input (i.e., when the use of the second language arises in authentic social contexts with extended meaning and uses for practical problem solving). (p. 26)

To further explore these ideas, see Box 2.2.

BOX 2.2   *Case Study of Juan: The Beginning English Learner*

Go to the Compendium of Case Studies, and read more about Juan in the sections "Language Development: English as a Second Language" and "Juan as a Student," pp. 151–55. Think about the following as you read, and jot down your ideas:

▲ Think about Cummins's theory of context-embedded communication and primary language support with regard to Juan's experiences learning English as a second language and as a student. Identify instances where the theory and research were reflected or were not reflected in Juan's case. Explain your ideas with reference to the theory and research on context-embedded communication and primary language support.

▲ Do the same thing but think about Krashen's theory of comprehensible input and the natural approach.

▲ Based on the theories and research you have just read, jot down several ideas for how the school and Juan's teachers might have supported his English language development.

MAPPING THE CROSSROADS OF READER RESPONSE AND LEARNING ENGLISH AS A SECOND LANGUAGE

Transmission and Social Construction of Knowledge _____

Let's consider the crossroads of theories of reader response and learning English as a second language from a social constructivist view of learning. Reader-response and social constructivist theories are often linked in discussions of student-centered teaching. This perspective contrasts with the more traditional teacher- and text-centered teaching, with its origins in the New Critical literary theory that came about when a transmission model of learning was developed and applied in American classrooms.

Transmission Model

A traditional teacher- and text-centered classroom reflects the psychological theory of behaviorism and a transmission model of teaching. Educational applications of B. F. Skinner's behaviorist learning theory were popular in the 1950s. Early behaviorists, particularly Ivan Pavlov, conducted experiments with animals in laboratories. You may have heard of Pavlov's dogs, who salivated in response to the ringing of a bell that signaled mealtime. Behaviorists believe that learning follows a formula of stimulus-response conditioning, according to which acceptable responses are reinforced.

In a classroom based on a behaviorist view of learning, teaching language is based on the belief that children learn through a process of environmental conditioning and by imitating adult models. Teachers condition students' learning by modeling behaviors that the students are to imitate. If the students imitate those behaviors correctly, they receive positive reinforcement, such as praise or rewards. If they don't, they receive negative reinforcement, such as criticism or even punishment.

According to this traditional behaviorist approach, language learning is not believed to be instinctive. Moreover, language is supposedly learned in small increments, or skills. Mastering those skills means that a person learns them, one by one, and builds a repertoire until he or she can read and write. For example, children learn to read by first mastering the letters of the alphabet, then combine letters to master words, and then combine words to master sentences. Learning to read is thought to be a step-by-step, cumulative process, each step building on the previous one. The basal readers used to teach reading in this way have "scope and sequences" of these skills, prepared for each grade and building on the grade before.

Text-centered views of how students read and understand literature mesh well with the behaviorist, transmission model of learning and developing language. Assuming that literary meaning is found in the text means there is a set of knowledge about the literary conventions such as genre and style and literary elements. It is separate from a student's individual experience of a literary work. To facilitate a true understanding of the work—the meaning within the work itself—the teacher's job is to transmit the knowledge of literary conventions bit by bit until the student builds up enough of a repertoire of these to fully understand what he or she has read. For example, an elementary teacher explains that stories have main characters that carry the action of the stories. Then students are asked to identify the main characters and what they do in a particular story. The teacher can verify the students' knowledge of this literary convention by testing: asking students to define a main character and to identify the character in a story. Teachers who reflect this model of learning, language development, and understanding literature explain many literary conventions and genres, assign specific books or stories for reading that exemplify these conventions and genres, use worksheets or guides for students to practice learning them, and can verify "literary knowledge" through testing or grading book reports.

Social Constructivism

The *constructivist theory of learning* or cognitive development put forth by Jean Piaget (1973, 1977) maintains that learning is an active process in which the learner constructs meaning. This idea is also behind John Dewey's (1938) famous expression "learning by doing," which means that we discover or construct concepts by actively participating in our environments.

Piaget believed that children can construct a view of reality that's based on what they learn as they mature and also what they experience in their lives. In other words, they learn throughout their lives by exploring and discovering new things. Learning is a process of adding new bits of information to what one already knows. Given this, it is important that the teacher be aware of how children learn and develop and that he or she provide an environment and initiate experiences that help children engage in the active construction of meaning and knowledge about themselves and the world.

According to Piaget, language acquisition is an aspect of general cognitive development. Although he believed that thought (or cognition) and language were interdependent, he maintained that language development is rooted in the more fundamental development of cognition. In other words, conceptualization precedes language. These ideas were based on his observation of children at play. Through manipulating objects, children demonstrate that they understand concepts and can solve problems without verbalizing them. Children learn to understand language as they first assimilate and then accommodate language symbols to their symbolic structures, or schema. In the search for meaning, children symbolize before they verbalize.

Piaget viewed the adult's role in teaching language as creating situations in which children discover meaning themselves. According to the constructivist view, language will follow experience. To support language development, teachers provide students opportunities for self-discovery in the classroom, such as group work with materials for writing and art.

The *sociohistorical theory* of Lev Vygotsky (1962) proposes that children learn through meaningful interactions with their environments and other people and that these are essential factors in the development of new knowledge. Whereas Piaget suggested that children's learning is an individual, internalized cognitive process that does not depend on adult support, Vygotsky emphasizes the social, contextual nature of learning and language. For example, children learn to talk by listening to their parents, siblings, and others and eventually talking back. Similarly, children learn to read and write by having others read to them, by participating in shared storybook readings and writing events, and by eventually reading and writing on their own.

A key idea in Vygotsky's (1978) theory is the *zone of proximal development:* "the distance between the actual developmental level as determined by independent problem solving and the level of potential development as determined through problem solving under adult guidance or in collaboration with more capable peers" (p. 76). This means that children learn when they are supported by others who know more than they do—for instance, teachers, parents, and peers. A parallel idea is Krashen's i + 1.

Environment plays a more prominent role in sociohistorical theories than in cognitive constructivist theories. Sociohistorical theory assumes that language acquisition is determined by the interaction of physical, linguistic, and social factors, any and all of which may vary greatly for each child. Vygotsky (1978, 1986) believes that interaction with the environment, especially with adults and older children, plays a critical role in children's language development. As summarized by Vygotsky, "Language is a major stimulant for conceptual growth, and conceptual growth is also dependent on interaction with objects in the environment. Moreover, adults (and older children) have a role in stimulating language growth through a variety of means" (p. 11, quoted in Pflaum, 1986).

This stimulation should take place within the zone of proximal development, the center around which the child forms thought complexes (similar to schema) or symbolic structures. Piaget (1973, 1977) also identified the importance of connecting new experiences to prior knowledge and organizing that new information. His ideas differ from those of Vygotsky, however, in that Piaget believed that children verbalize structures that have already developed through firsthand experiences with objects in the environment. Vygotsky sees the verbal interaction between adult and child as the primary means by which a child achieves potential meaning through language. He clearly puts great emphasis on the role of the teacher in the cognitive and linguistic development of the child.

The key ideas in Piaget's cognitive constructivist theory and Vygotsky's sociohistorical theory have been loosely grouped together as a social constructivist perspective on language and literacy learning. The social constructivist framework also often takes into account the unique cultural aspects of each classroom, as well as the role of the family and the cultural and linguistic background of each child (Heath, 1983). On the basis of this framework, learning occurs in a particular context, which will vary from class to class and year to year. For instance, ideas and expectations will never be exactly the same. The teacher will initiate experiences, observe students, and set expectations based on the uniqueness of each child, group, and class. Reader-response theory in many ways mirrors the social constructivist perspective on language learning in that it describes reading as an active, social, and individual process unique to each reader.

Sociocultural Contexts for Learning English

Sociocultural contexts for learning English as described by Moll (1994) result in a teaching approach that views "literacy in connection to the complex social relationships and cultural practices of human beings, be it in classrooms or in community settings" (p. 211), a perspective that reflects Vygotsky's (1978) theory of learning (Moll, 1990; Moll & Greenberg, 1991). A key idea of this approach is the notion of teachers tapping into "funds of knowledge" from a child's home and community that Moll, Amanti, Neff, and Gonzalez (1992) define as "historically accumulated and culturally developed bodies of knowledge and skills essential for household or individual functioning and well-being" (p. 133).

This home–school connection supports students learning English as a second language when teachers and schools learn about the community and the families they serve and view them as resources in the classroom. This connection has the potential to make the curriculum relevant (Rodriguez-Brown, 2003, 2004). This clearly illustrates the importance of student-centered teaching of English learners and focusing on the unique cultural and linguistic backgrounds that children bring to the classroom. When teachers value and draw on the rich and unique experiences of each child and his or her family, everyone benefits. In examining the discourse in various contexts in schools, however, Gee (1996) found that children from mainstream middle-class backgrounds acquire literacy through experiences at home that relate to literacy required in schools, whereas children from nonmainstream homes, on the other hand, often acquire different forms. Teachers should be aware of these differences in differentiating instruction for all students, including English learners.

Gutierrez and Rogoff (2003) argue that it is also important to consider each child as a member of a dynamic cultural community with a unique experience within the cultural community as an individual. By cultural community, they mean "a coordinated group of people with some traditions and understandings in common, extending across several generations, with varied roles and practices and continual change among participants as well as transformation in the community's practices" (p. 21). These authors maintain that rather than view cultural ways of learning as individual traits and make deterministic generalizations about a child based on static characteristics such as Spanish surname or country of birth, teachers should focus on the child's dynamic history of varied experiences in activities within the cultural community. With regard to literacy development, for example, we can use the term *English learner* as a descriptor but not a complete and categorical classification of a child as an individual student. Teachers will, therefore, learn as much as they can about each child in order to differentiate instruction with regard to a whole range of characteristics, not just the fact that he or she is an English learner.

Sociocultural contexts and literacy development for English learners are addressed in *Developing Literacy in Second-Language Learners: Report of the National Literacy Panel on Language-Minority Children and Youth* (August & Shanahan, 2006) with the following key conclusions and recommendations: When teachers value students' first language, it tends to be accepted by their peers, and language status can positively influence academic achievement; when teachers fail to value the first language, students are less likely to value it. However, promoting language and literacy development takes more than just valuing students' first language. Language status is influenced by a variety of factors, and teachers need both school and community support to maintain first language status to support English learners' success in school. To further explore these ideas, see Box 2.3.

BOX 2.3:

Case Study of Juan: A Beginning English Learner

The first day I met Juan in kindergarten and took him out in the hall to read to him, he told me, "I don't know too much because I speak Spanish." Read the section in his case study titled "Background and Home Influences," pp. 150–51, and jot down your ideas about the following:

▲ What level of status do you think Juan felt his first language of Spanish had at school? What do you base your comment on?

▲ Reread the section "Juan as a Student," and comment on what level of status each of his different teachers from kindergarten through fifth grade gave to Spanish. Explain your comments.

▲ How would you describe some of Juan's "funds of knowledge," which a teacher might have tapped into to support his language and literacy development?

▲ In the section "Juan as a Student," identify an instance where a teacher might have tapped into these funds of knowledge to support his language and literacy learning, and describe what you would have done if you had been his teacher.

In the Classroom

Both reader-response and second language theory cover a lot of ground. Let's look at how these learning theories intersect in teaching practice with regard to the student, the language, the teacher, and the classroom (see Table 2.2).

The Student

Transactional theory describes reading as experienced meaning, a two-way transaction between the reader and the text. The focus of the reader's attention is on a personal evocation of the text while reading, what Rosenblatt refers to as "the poem." This emphasis on the lived-through experiences of readers affirms the importance of the role of the reader/student in constructing meaning from a text and is similar to the great importance placed on students' prior knowledge and life experience by the second language theorists Cummins and Krashen.

A pertinent idea here is Krashen's notion of a low-anxiety environment for language learning, in which students are motivated to speak and are confident. In a more student-centered discussion, motivation and confidence are highly likely because students' ideas or images about a literary text are welcomed. They are, in fact, a necessary part of talking and writing about literature. In a text-centered approach, questions are often a test of knowledge of the text itself. A common fear among students is not knowing the "right answer." The result is that students may not speak because they are afraid that their answers aren't the right ones (e.g., the teacher's idea about the text). As you read in the "Case Study of Juan," the first thing he said to me was "I don't know too much because I speak Spanish." From a sociocultural perspective, Juan identified himself as a child whose funds of knowledge, such as knowing how to speak Spanish, were not valued.

TABLE 2.2 Crossroads of Reader-Response and Learning English as a Second Language

	Reader Response	Second Language
Student	Reading as experienced meaning Personal evocation of a text Affirms important role of reader Each response unique and individual	Student's prior knowledge and life experience valued Low-anxiety environment required Self-esteem and motivation to speak important Language and culture of each learner respected
Language	Embodied in transactions between individuals and social and natural context Not self-contained, ungrounded, ready-made code Activation of reader's linguistic-experiential reservoir Both primary language and English seen as funds of knowledge Also, texts in other languages and from other cultures	Acquired as it is used in meaningful communication contexts Not learned via rules of grammar and pronunciation Words given sense from context Role of primary language essential for learning English and academic achievement Home language of English learner valued and given high status
Teacher	Listens to students Invites students' personal responses to texts as meaning construction Learning from literature dependent on social and cultural context of students' lives	Focuses on meaning Comprehensible input: key is student background knowledge Context-embedded communication: students' lives are the context, basis for cognitively demanding learning Taps into students' prior knowledge
Classroom	Students' voices a prerequisite Silence while listening and thinking understood Responses to text a starting point Multiple and diverse responses expected Conversations among students encouraged and valued	Students' voices the goal Silent period expected Diversity celebrated Cooperative, collaborative atmosphere essential Utilizes funds of knowledge from students' home and community

In a reader-response type discussion, the atmosphere is more of a conversation with friends than an oral test. Responses that might be acceptable in a more reader-response type (e.g., "That turnip's no good") would not be in a more text-centered type. The point is that language development would not be inhibited because students lacked interest or confidence or the formal language or rhetoric necessary to answer analytical questions about a text.

Each student would respond in a unique way, no matter his or her level of English proficiency. Each should be allowed to respond in his or her native language or English or a combination of the two. What's important is that students are actively engaged, as explained in Piaget's constructivist theory (1973, 1977).

The Language

Drawing on the field of semiotics (Pierce, 1933, 1935), which explains the importance of the context of language, Rosenblatt maintains that language is "not . . . a self-contained, ungrounded, ready-made code of signifiers and signifieds, but as embodied in transactions between individuals and their social and natural context" (1986, p. 122). An essential idea in her transactional theory is that of the activation of the reader's "linguistic-experiential reservoir" as the means to construct new meanings and experiences while reading. This concept takes into account both the first and second language as funds of knowledge for the English learner, as well as reading texts in languages other than English or produced in other cultures. The emphasis here is on the unique, lived-through experience of each individual reader.

Second language theorists, such as Cummins and Krashen, who advocate a communicative approach maintain that acquisition of the target language emerges from students' own experiences or funds of knowledge, which should be the focus of language instruction, as opposed to language learning, with its focus on rules of grammar and pronunciation dispensed by a teacher.

Vygotsky, too, emphasizes both the social context and the individual's role in language development (1962). Words, like literary interpretations, acquire sense from the context in which they appear: the" "sense of a word . . . the sum of all the psychological events aroused in our consciousness by the word" (p. 46). Conversations about literature with a reader-response focus center around the student and encourage the student to draw on his or her own language, culture, and life experiences as a basis for language and literacy learning, rather than on the text itself or what might be learned from it. Both language and learning are centered in the student's own experiences, and home–school connections are supported.

The role of primary language, as described by Cummins and supported by research (August & Shanahan, 2006; Snow, et al., 1998), is important here. Providing primary language support will increase students' self-esteem and academic achievement, which in turn provide a supportive environment for learning English.

The Teacher

The teacher with a more reader-response orientation would invite students' personal responses to texts, encouraging the personal construction of meaning. This type of teaching reflects the belief that learning from literature is dependent on the social and cultural context of students' lives. Such a teacher would listen to students. An initial transaction with literature would become an invitation to the students to bring life experiences into the classroom. Not simply the text, but also students' responses to a literary text are the starting point for language and literacy experiences.

Ideas from second language theory parallel this perspective. One is Cummins's idea of *context-embedded instruction*. Students' lives, cultures, and language experiences constitute the context necessary for second language learning at a cognitively demanding level. Another is Krashen's idea of *comprehensible input*. This is a key to second language acquisition; the key to teachers providing this comprehensible input is tapping into students' background knowledge, which occurs naturally in student-centered instruction. From a sociocultural perspective, a teacher would also tap into a child's cultural and linguistic funds of knowledge and actively pursue home–school connections with students.

The Classroom

Reader-response theory suggests that student voice is essential to learning from literature in both a literal and a figurative sense. Response is individual and not tied to one agreed-upon meaning of a text. Silence while thinking about a text is understood. When they are expressed, students' responses to texts are the starting point, rather than ending point, for further discussion and language and literacy experiences. A student-centered classroom is an environment for rich discussions and exchanges between teachers and students, students and students, and students and texts. Multiple interactions are possible, creating a richly layered environment for experiencing literature and learning language. In such a classroom, you would not see a simple question–answer ratio of one teacher question to one student answer that could be verified by the text. Students might ask as many questions as the teacher. The teacher might share his or her own responses to the text and add personal life experiences to the mix. The atmosphere would be more like a warm, steamy, tangled, tropical rain forest than a cool, dry, formal English garden. Multiple and varied responses and interpretations of a text, rather than a single consensus, are expected. Above all, conversations among students are encouraged and valued.

In both a literal and a figurative sense, student voice is the goal in teaching English learners. A silent period is expected, however, and students are not forced to speak before they are ready. Listening and speaking are of primary importance; reading and writing come later. In transactional teaching, students are encouraged to talk about their responses to literature, a part of which is listening to others respond. Answers to efferent type questions ("What color shoes did Dorothy have on?") are neither forced nor the focus of a discussion. Reader-response theory emphasizes the importance of the reader's personal response. When the reader does speak, the teacher acknowledges and taps into student funds of knowledge and creates a classroom environment to make this happen. Cooperative, collaborative learning, such as student conversations when working in groups, is a part of the picture. Cultural and linguistic and personal diversity is expected and celebrated, and home–school connections are purposefully created.

EXPLORING IDEAS

1. Think about your own experiences with reading and literature while you were in Grades K through 12 or even in college. What literary theory or theories did the teaching of your various teachers reflect?

2. Think about a recent book or poem you have read or movie you have seen. On the basis of your thoughts, what was the stance you took toward this work: primarily efferent or primarily aesthetic? Why do you think so?

3. On the basis of your own experiences and the theory and research in this chapter, what do you think about the role of primary language support and tapping into cultural and linguistic funds of knowledge when teaching English learners?

4. Jot down a few ideas about any or all of the following that apply to any experience you may have had learning a language other than your home language:
   a. Learning English as a second language
   b. Learning a second language other than English in high school or college
   c. Learning a new language while visiting or living in another country
   d. Learning the language of your students if you are a native English speaker and they are native speakers of a language other than English

   Compare each of these in terms of how you actually learned to speak and use a new language for real purposes.

REFERENCES

August, D., & Shanahan, T. (Eds.). (2006). *Developing literacy in second-language learners: Report of the National Literacy Panel on Language-Minority Children and Youth*. Mahwah, NJ: Erlbaum.

Bloomfield, L. (1933). *Language*. New York: Henry Holt.

Brooks, C., & Warren, R. P. (1938). *Understanding poetry*. New York: Appleton Century.

Cazden, C. (1972). *Child language and education*. New York: Holt, Rinehart & Winston.

Chomsky, C. (1969). *The acquisition of syntax in children from 5 to 10* (Research Monograph No. 52). Cambridge, MA: MIT Press.

Chomsky, N. (1957). *Syntactic structures*. The Hague, The Netherlands: Mouton.

Chomsky, N. (1964). Review of B. F. Skinner's "Verbal Behavior." In J. A. Fodor and J. J. Katz (Eds.), *The structure of language*. Englewood Cliffs, NJ: Prentice Hall.

Chomsky, N. (1965). *Aspects of a theory of syntax*. Cambridge, MA: MIT Press.

Clifford, J. (Ed.). (1991). *The experience of reading: Louise Rosenblatt and reader-response theory*. Portsmouth, NH: Boynton/Cook.

Cook-Gumperz, J. (1979). Communicating with young children in the home. *Theory into Practice, 18,* 207–212.

Cox, C. (2008). *Teaching language arts: A student-centered classroom* (6th ed.). Boston: Pearson/Allyn & Bacon.

Cox, C., & Many, J. E. (1989, March). *Reader stance towards a literary work: Applying the transactional theory to children's responses*. Paper presented at the annual meeting of the American Educational Research Association, San Francisco, CA.

Cox, C., & Many, J. E. (1992a). Reader stance towards a literary work: Applying the transactional theory to children's responses. *Reading Psychology, 13* (1), 37–72.

Cox, C., & Many, J. E. (1992b). Beyond choosing: Emergent categories of efferent and aesthetic stance. In J. E. Many & C. Cox (Eds.), *Reader stance and literary understanding: Exploring the theories, research, and practice* (pp. 103–126). Norwood, NJ: Ablex.

Cox, C., & Zarrillo, J. (1993). *Teaching reading with children's literature.* Upper Saddle River, NJ: Merrill/Prentice Hall.

Crawford, J., & Krashen, S. (2007). *English learners in American Schools.* New York: Scholastic.

Cummins, J. (1981). The role of primary language development in promoting educational success for language-minority students. In *Schooling and language-minority students: A theorietical framework* (pp. 3–49). Los Angeles: California State University.

Cummins, J. (1984). *Bilingualism and special education: Issues in assessment and pedagogy.* San Diego: College-Hill.

Cummins, J. (1989). *Empowering minority students.* Sacramento: California Association for Bilingual Education.

Cummins, J. (1992). Language proficiency, bilingualism, and academic achievement. In P. A. Richard-Amato & M. A. Snow (Eds.), *The multicultural classroom: Readings for content-area teachers* (pp. 16–26). White Plains, NY: Longman.

Cummins, J. (2000). Beyond adversarial discourse: Searching for common ground in the education of bilingual students. In P. McLaren & C. J. Ovando (Eds.), *The politics of multiculturalism and bilingual educaton* (pp. 126–147). Boston: McGraw-Hill.

Cummins, J., et al. (2005). Affirming identity in multicultural classrooms. *Educational Leadership, 63,* 38–43.

Dewey, J. (1938). *Experience in education.* New York: Collier.

Duran, R. A. (1996). English immigrant language learners: Cultural accommodations and family literacy. In L. A. Benjamin & J. Lord (Eds.), *Family literacy: Directions in research and implications for practice* (pp. 25–30). Washington, DC: U.S. Department of Education, Office of Educational Research and Improvement.

Farrell, E. J., & Squire, J. R. (Eds.). (1990). *Transactions with literature.* Urbana, IL: National Council of Teachers of English.

Fries, C. (1945). *Teaching and learning English as a foreign language.* Ann Arbor: University of Michigan.

Gee, J. P. (1996). *Social linguistics and literacies: Ideology in discourses.* Britsol, PA: Taylor & Francis.

Gutierrez, K. D., & Rogoff, B. (2003). Cultural ways of learning: Individual traits or repertoires of practice. *Educational Researcher, 32* (5), 19–25.

Halliday, M. A. K. (1975). *Learning how to mean.* London, UK: Edward Arnold.

Heath, S. B. (1983). *Ways with words: Language, life, and work in communities and classrooms.* New York: Cambridge University Press.

Held, D. (1980). *Introduction to critical theory: Horkheimer to Habermas.* Berkeley: University of California Press.

Hunsberger, M., & Labercane, G. (Eds.). (2002). *Making meaning in the response-based classroom.* Boston: Allyn & Bacon.

Hymes, D. (1974). *Foundations in sociolinguistics: An ethnographic approach.* Philadelphia: University of Pennsylvania Press.

James, W. (1890). *The principles of psychology* (2 vols). New York: Henry Holt.

Karolides, N. J. (Ed.). (1992). *Reader response in the classroom: Evoking and interpreting meaning in literature*. White Plains, NY: Longman.

Karolides, N. J. (Ed.). (1997). *Reader response in elementary classrooms: Quest and discovery*. Mahwah, NJ: Erlbaum.

Krashen, S. D. (1981). *Second language acquisition and second language learning*. Oxford, UK: Pergamon.

Krashen, S. D. (1982). *Principles and practices in second language acquisition*. Oxford, UK: Pergamon.

Krashen, S. D. (1985a). *The input hypothesis: Issues and implications*. New York: Longman.

Krashen, S. D. (1985b). *Inquiries and insights: Essays in language teaching, bilingual education, and literacy*. Hayward, CA: Alemany.

Krashen, S. D. (2003). Three roles for reading for minority-language children. In G. Garcia (Ed.), *English learners: Reaching the highest level of literacy learning*. Newark, DE: International Reading Association.

Krashen, S. D. (2004). False claims about literacy development. *Educational Leadership, 61* (6), 18–21.

Krashen, S. D., & Terrell, T. D. (1983). *The natural approach: Language acquisition in the classroom*. Englewood Cliffs, NJ: Prentice Hall.

Larsen Freeman, D., & Long, M. H. (1991). *An introduction to second-language acquisition research*. White Plains, NY: Longman.

Lindfors, J. W. (1987). *Children's language and learning* (2nd ed.). Upper Saddle River, NJ: Merrill/Prentice Hall.

Many, J. E., & Cox, C. (Eds.) (1992). *Reader stance and literacy understanding: Exploring the theories, research, and practice*. Norwood, NJ: Ablex

Many, J. E. (1991). The effects of stance and age level on children's literary responses. *Journal of Reading Behavior, 21,* 61–85.

Many, J. E. (2004). The effect of reader stance on students' personal understanding of literature. In R. B. Ruddell & N. J. Unrau (Eds.), *Theoretical models and processes of reading* (5th ed., pp. 914–953). Newark, DE: International Reading Association.

Many, J. E., & Wiseman, D. (1992). The effect of teaching approach on third grade students' responses to literature. *Journal of Reading Behavior, 24,* 265–287.

McLaughlin, B. (1987). *Theories of second-language learning*. London: Edward Arnold.

Menyuk, P. (1963). Syntactic structures in the language of children. *Child Development, 34,* 407–422.

Moll, L. C. (Ed.). (1990). *Vygotsky and education: Instructional implications and applications of sociohistorical psychology*. Cambridge, UK: Cambridge University Press.

Moll, L. C. (1994). Literacy research in community and classrooms: A sociocultural approach. In R. B. Ruddell, M. R. Ruddell, & H. Singer (Eds.), *Theoretical models and processes of reading* (4th ed., pp. 179–207). Newark, DE: International Reading Association

Moll, L. C., Amanti, C., Neff, D., & Gonzalez, N. (1992). Funds of knowledge for teaching: Using a qualitative approach to connect homes and classrooms. *Theory Into Practice, 31,* 132–141.

Moll, L. C., & Greenberg, J. B. (1991). Creating zones of possibilities: Combining social contexts for instruction. In L. C. Moll (Ed.), *Vygotsky in education* (pp. 319–348). Cambridge, UK: Cambridge University Press.

Nagy, W. E., Garcia, G. E., Durgunoglu, A. Y., & Hancin-Bhatt, B. (1993). Spanish-English bilingual students' use of cognates in English reading. *Journal of Reading Behavior, 25* (3), 241–259.

Pflaum, S. W. (1986). *The development of language and literacy in young children.* Upper Saddle River, NJ: Merrill/Prentice Hall.

Piaget, J. (1973). *To understand is to invent: The future of education.* New York: Grossman.

Piaget, J. (1977). *The development of thought: Equilibration of cognitive structures* (A. Rosin, Trans.). New York: Viking.

Pierce, C. S. (1933, 1935). *Collected papers* (Vols. 3 and 6) (P. Weiss & C. Hartshorne, Eds.). Cambridge, MA: Harvard University Press.

Proctor, P., August, D., Carlo, M., & Snow, C. (2006). The intriguing role of Spanish language vocabulary knowledge in predicting English reading comprehension. *Journal of Educational Psychology, 98,* 159–169.

Richards, I. A. (1935). *Practical criticism: A study of literary judgment.* New York: Harcourt Brace.

Rodriguez-Brown, F. V. (2003). Family literacy in English language learning communities: Issues related to program development, implementation and practice. In A. De Bruin & B. Krol-Sinclair (Eds.), *Family literacy: From theory to practice* (pp. 126–146). Newark, DE: International Reading Association.

Rodriguez-Brown, F. V. (2004). Project FLAME: A parent support family literacy model. In B. Wasik (Ed.), *Handbook of family literacy* (pp. 213–229). Mahwah, NJ: Erlbaum.

Rosenblatt, L. M. (1982). The literary transaction: Evocation and response. *Theory into Practice, 21,* 268–277.

Rosenblatt, L. M. (1986). The aesthetic transaction. *Journal of Aesthetic Education, 20,* 122–128.

Rosenblatt, L. M. (1994). *The reader, the text, the poem: The transactional theory of the literary work.* Carbondale: Southern Illinois University Press. (Original work published 1978)

Rosenblatt, L. M. (1995). *Literature as exploration.* New York: Modern Language Association. (Original work published 1938)

Rosenblatt, L. M. (2004). The transactional theory of reading and writing. In R. B. Ruddell & N. J. Unrau (Eds.), *Theoretical models and processes of reading* (5th ed., pp. 1363–1398). Newark, DE: International Reading Association.

Snow, C. E., Burns, M. S., & Griffin, P. (Eds.). (1998). *Preventing reading difficulties in young children.* Washington, DC: National Academy Press.

Strickland, R. J. (1962). *The language of elementary school children* (Bulletin of the School of Education, No. 4). Bloomington: Indiana University.

Swain, M. (1986). Communicative competence: Some roles of comprehensible input and comprehensible output in its development. In J. Cummins & M. Swain (Eds.), *Bilingualism in education* (pp. 16–28). White Plains, NY: Longman.

Tough, J. (1977). *The development of meaning.* London, UK: Allen & Unwin.

Vygotsky, L. S. (1962). *Thought and language* (F. Hanmann & G. Vakar, Eds. & Trans.). Cambridge, MA: MIT Press.

Vygotsky, L. S. (1978). *Mind in society*. Cambridge, MA: Harvard University Press.

Vygotsky, L. S. (1986). *Thought and language*. Cambridge, MA: MIT Press.

Wellek, R., & Warren, R. (1949). *Theory of literature*. New York: Harcourt Brace.

Wells, G. (Ed.). (1981). *Learning through interaction: The study of language development*. London, UK: Cambridge University Press.

Zarrillo, J., & Cox, C. (1992). Efferent and aesthetic teaching. In J. Many & C. Cox (Eds.), *Reader stance and literary understanding: Exploring the theories, research, and practice* (pp. 235–249). Norwood, NJ: Ablex.

CHAPTER THREE

Bridging Theory and Research into Practice

In first grade a young reader named Anne listened as her teacher read aloud the excerpted book *Anna Banana and Me* from a commercial reading series and then told the students that "the story has a lot of messages." She said the people who made the reader wrote some questions for students to consider, which she had written on a piece of chart paper for them to answer. And Anne did this. In third grade Anne visited another room in her school as part of a rotation plan for students in different classes to get to know each other. It was a bilingual Spanish/English class, and the teacher asked her to join a Literature Circle and to read aloud the book *Encounter* by Jane Yolen (1992) to the other students in the group while he met with other groups. And Anne did this. When she finished, the teacher joined the group and said to the students, "Tell me about the book."

THE READER AND THE TEXT WHEN TEACHING WITH LITERATURE

Both of these teachers were considered excellent and effective, and Anne enjoyed being a student in both classes. Each of their approaches to guiding students' understanding of literature, however, reflected differences in orientation towards the relationship between the reader and the text, which ultimately made for differences in their practices. Teachers' basic assumptions underlying their practices when teaching with literature, whether those assumptions are conscious or not, can reflect a whole range of theoretical orientations on a continuum from more text-oriented to more reader-oriented. More reader-oriented approaches in elementary school often strive for a balance between the reader and the text—a reader-plus-text orientation. When teachers use a commercial reading series, as Anne's first-grade teacher did, it's likely that they will use a more text-oriented approach—following reading with prepared questions, activities, and assessments from the accompanying teacher's guide. When teachers use children's books and Literature Circles, as the teacher did in Anne's third-grade class, it's likely they will use a more reader-plus-text approach after reading, beginning with an open question to solicit students' responses to the book based on their personal experience of reading the text. Both orientations can incorporate teaching about story genre and structure, examining characters' motivations, comparing books by the same author or on the same topic, exploring theme or understanding how a conflict drives a story, making inferences, identifying the author's viewpoint, and learning about the authors and their craft, all of which lead to comprehension, interpretation, and deeper understanding of a text. However, a more reader-plus-text approach would begin by first engaging students with a question about how each student experienced the text and the personal connections she or he made, such as "Tell me about the book." Student responses then become the basis for rich, reader-oriented discussions of books in Literature Circles, deeper understanding of the stories, student reading and writing on self-selected topics of interest, and integrated teaching of literacy and the content areas.

Because this book is about engaging English learners through experiencing literature, this chapter will describe a more reader-plus-text approach, showing how to implement the transactional theory in the context of theories and research on learning English as a second language, social constructivism, and sociocultural perspectives when teaching English learners. You will read a summary of each of the underlying theories behind the more text-oriented approach used by Anne's first-grade teacher and the more reader-plus-text approach used by the teacher in third grade, and you will follow Anne's experience with a lesson in both classes. You have already read about these theories in Chapter 2, which explains how meaning can be determined in our experiences with literature. Ideas for engaging English learners through exploring literature, developing literacy, and differentiating instruction will also be described through the instructional model of a "ripple effect" of integrated teaching.

The Text

A more text-oriented approach to teaching with literature reflects the New Critical, formal analysis of a text. Emphasis is placed on explication of a text by considering such things as genre, the structure of the work, and the use of language, but the personal significance of the work to the reader is not stressed.

Materials include a set of readers and sets of selected paperback books for the whole class, as well as a teacher's guide with plot summaries, analyses of the stories, classification by genre (e.g., fables, myths, plays, or autobiographies), lesson plans, and step-by-step instructions for before and after reading, including questions that help students focus on analysis of the text. Elementary classrooms in which this approach dominates might make use of a commercial reading series with stories excerpted and adapted from children's literature and a teacher's guide. In middle and high school, literature anthologies might be used, and supplemental materials might include a student workbook with questions that students would respond to in writing. These materials are usually graded by level, and students participate in either a whole-class lesson directed by the teacher or a smaller group, often formed according to student ability. Students in a whole-class lesson or a small group usually read the same story. These series usually identify a range of strategies and skills to be learned by the students.

Student self-selected and independent reading can also be a part of the reading program, but the commercial series is the centerpiece. Reflecting the New Critical perspective, a commonly used student activity associated with reading a self-selected book independently is a book report, which requires a student to do a plot summary, analyze the structure of the story, and identify and describe the genre and literary elements or use of language. Although students might also be asked to write a personal response, the emphasis would be on their ability to analyze the text.

Let's look into the first of Anne's two classrooms, which reflect two different approaches to how children learn, develop language and literacy, and understand literature. Anne is the native English-speaking child you read about at the beginning of the chapter, and you will read more about her later in the "Case Study of Anne: The Native English Speaker." Her school has a high percentage of English learners, primarily native Spanish-speaking Mexican American children. In this first classroom, Anne was in first grade, and the teacher was using a commercial reading series with stories excerpted and adapted from literature. As you read, think about the theories and research on teaching with literature, learning, and language and literacy development, as well as how they are put into action in this classroom. Pay particular attention to who is doing the talking and what types of questions are used, two fundamental issues in both first and second language learning.

A More Text-Oriented Lesson from a Commercial Reading Series

Anne's first-grade teacher used a commercial reading series with excerpted and adapted selections of children's literature. The series provided a student anthology or reader, sets of paperback copies of selected stories for each child, a pupil response booklet with questions and prompts for student writing after reading, and a teacher's guide with ideas for teaching with literature provided by the publisher.

TEACHER ASKS QUESTIONS ABOUT *ANNA BANANA AND ME.*   The teacher begins the lesson by asking the question "Are any of you ever afraid when you try something new?" Students answer this question for a full 10 minutes, each child always responding to the teacher. Anne does not participate. Then the teacher says, "Today, we're going to learn something about a person who follows someone else's actions when the person was unsure and afraid. I think it's exciting to read about somebody who has some of the same feelings we do." She hands out paperback copies of the excerpted book *Anna Banana and Me*, which came with this reading series. First, she directs the students to look at the title and then asks a series of questions: "What does it say? What is she? How do you know she's friendly?" She tells them to notice that the author and the illustrator are related, which techniques the illustrator uses (black ink and watercolor), and what information the title page and dedication page give. Anne still says nothing.

After the teacher reads the book aloud, she says, "The story had a lot of messages." She tells the students that the people who made the reader wrote some questions for students and that she has written them on a sheet of chart paper. She reads them aloud and asks the students to answer each of them:

1. Where do you think the characters are?

2. What does Anna Banana say about feathers?

3. Why does the boy go home?

4. Why does she visit him?

5. What kind of building does he live in?

6. What is he doing?

7. Why does his voice echo?

8. How do you think the boy is feeling about Anna Banana? (The teacher points out that this questions doesn't have a right or wrong answer.)

9. What's something in the story that makes you think that?

Finally, the teacher asks what she calls a "thinking question": "How does the boy suddenly become brave?" The children offer many tentative answers to this question. Anne finally raises her hand and answers in a rather uncompromising way: "Because Anna Banana told him the feather was magic and made him brave." The teacher says, "Here is a big question. WAS IT MAGIC?" Anne answers: "Yes, because it really made him brave." The teacher says, "Anne says the feather was magic. What do the rest of you think?" Answers include (a) in the story, but not in real life; (b) sort of, not really; (c) sort of, but different; (d) I think that it's not real, but he thought it was, and then it was, but not really.

It seems the teacher wants the students to learn the difference between real and make-believe and to come to the consensus that magic could happen in a story but not real life. The students appear to sense that she is waiting for this answer. After no one disagrees that magic can't happen in real life, Anne speaks again: "I think he really believes that the feather is magic and it will make it happen. When I throw a coin into a wishing well, I believe my wish will come true." She says this in a rather uncompromising, even matter-of-fact, way. She apparently has not been swayed by the teacher's implied answer or the lack of support from other students. After this teacher-directed question-and-answer period, the teacher gives the students a writing prompt: "If the feather were really magic, I would . . . ." She tells them to go to their seats and write.

Box 3.1 Further explores Anne's experience with this more text-oriented lesson.

BOX 3.1   *Case Study of Anne: The Native English Speaker*

As you read the sections listed here in the case study about Anne, pp. 163–72, reflect on the theories and research regarding literacy and teaching with literature and Anne's experience in first grade during a lesson using literature. Jot down ideas in response to the following prompts:

▲ Consider each of the following areas of information about Anne in the context of the more text-oriented lesson you just read about:
1. Background and Home Influences
2. Language Development
3. Anne as a Student

For each area, note how well you think this lesson addressed Anne's strengths and needs as a reader and writer.

▲ Given what you know about Anne, jot down the things that you might retain or change in this lesson regarding her understanding of literature and her literacy development. Explain your ideas in terms of the different theories and research on literacy and teaching with literature.

▲   Create your own draft of a lesson plan for a story like this, and explain it in terms of the theories and research you have read about so far.

▲   Discuss Anne's frustration with reading in school in terms of the theories of teaching literature you have read about. What are some things you might do as her teacher to maintain her success in reading, as well as her love of it?

The Reader-Plus-Text

A more reader-plus-text-oriented approach to teaching with literature reflects an awareness of both the reader and the text during reading, as described in Rosenblatt's transactional theory (1994, 1995, 2005). Each reader draws on his or her own personal reservoir of linguistic and life experiences so that meaning is experienced between the reader and the text in a reciprocal relationship in which one conditions the other. Each reader also assumes a stance on a continuum from more efferent (i.e., based on factual information or analysis of the text) to more aesthetic (i.e., based on what the reader is experiencing while reading). A reader's stance may be a mix of aesthetic and efferent; many readings fall in the middle of this continuum as the reader ultimately evokes an understanding of the work for interpretation and evaluation.

Literature Circles are a way for a teacher to organize teaching with literature that reflects a more reader-plus-text orientation. Students can be joined together in groups and read a book of their choice according to interests and also learning in a content area. Different groups may read different books. Groups meet on a regularly scheduled basis to discuss literature, often during reading and writing workshop. Topics for discussion come from the students, and the discussion itself may be more like a conversation. The teacher facilitates by organizing the groups, finding books and other materials, and meeting with the groups on a rotating basis. Students may also take turns leading the groups themselves. More reading and writing by students develop as a result of meeting in Literature Circles and frequently extend across the curriculum so that students are learning in content areas as well as developing language and literacy.

Teacher questions and prompts generally are centered around the students' responses reflecting their transactions with literature and begin by asking students to draw on their own lives and experiences as a basis for understanding literature. Students may choose different topics for writing (e.g., writing about the story or writing another story, a poem, a play, or a song), drama and art making (e.g., producing a play or puppet show, illustrating their writing, making masks or puppets, making a book), or a project in a content area (e.g., an informational report, maps, models, or murals). Materials in the class would include many children's books of fiction and nonfiction and other types of texts: students' own writing, charts made by the teacher, magazines, newspapers, and electronic texts such as CDs, DVDs, and the Internet.

Now let's look into the second of Anne's two classrooms. As you may remember, the school has a high percentage of English learners, primarily native Spanish-speaking Mexican American children. In this second classroom, Anne was in third grade, and the teacher was using Literature Circles.

A More Reader-Plus-Text-Oriented Lesson in a Literature Circle

In third grade Anne spent time in Paul's classroom during a period of classroom rotations intended to let the children in this diverse school setting get to know each other. Paul was a bilingual Spanish/English teacher, but he and his students used only English during the rotation period when students who did not speak Spanish were guests in the room.

If you remember from Chapter 1, Paul made a shift from a more text-oriented approach using a commercial reading series to a more reader-plus-text approach using student-selected books and Literature Circles. He then read aloud from a wide range of both fiction and nonfiction and encouraged students to do self-selected, independent reading and to read and write together in Literature Circles. Frequently, books that students read and discussed and wrote about became a focal point for integrating literacy and content areas. Here is such a lesson.

STUDENTS RESPOND TO ENCOUNTER   One Literature Circle in Paul's class has been reading and learning about Puerto Rico. The librarian, who works closely with Paul by paying attention to what his students are reading and learning about, offers Antonio several books about the Caribbean. One book is *Encounter*, by Jane Yolen (1992), a story of Columbus's arrival and meeting of the Taino. The narrator's voice in the story is that of a Taino child.

This particular Literature Circle meets, and Antonio begins by telling them, "I went to the library and got this book and read it. It's a sad story about how Columbus brought disease to the Taino people. They wanted to get along with him, but he killed them off."

Paul approaches the group with Anne and asks whether she can join them. They agree. After asking them what they are doing, he asks whether Anne can read *Encounter* aloud to them because Antonio is very interested in the book, which is in English, and Anne is an "expert English user." (Paul wants Anne to feel like part of the group.) Anne reads it aloud; Antonio, Fabiola, Eddie, and Laura listen. Paul confers with another group and then moves about the room, conferring and interacting with other Literature Circle groups. He returns to this group when Anne finishes, suggesting they might all talk about the book. They begin an animated and lengthy discussion, pointing and referring to the dramatic and somber illustrations by David Shannon.

Paul: *Tell me about the book.*
Antonio: *He was little, a child. He was Taino, and Christopher Columbus was Italian, sent from Spain.*
Anne: *He took the Taino as slaves and came back for more.*
Paul: *What happened to the rest of the Taino?*
Antonio: *Many died. Only one survived in the story.*
Paul: *Why?*
Antonio: *Because . . .* (He reads part of the story and points to a picture with knives.)
Paul: *Tell me more about the boy.*
Anne: *He had a dream, and when he woke up . . .*
Antonio (finishing Anne's sentence): *. . . the boy saw them and thought their skin was funny* (points to picture of Columbus's crew), *but he was afraid.*

Paul and students discuss *Encounter* in a Literature Circle.

Paul: *Why do you think?*
Antonio: *'Cause he has his people and land taken away.*
Paul: *Have any of you ever had things taken away?*
Anne: *We were robbed. TV, VCR, my dad's tools, and our bikes.*
Eddie: *My mom was washing clothes and put them outside to dry, and they were taken. They stole my overalls.*
Laura (to Anne): *How did they get in your house?*
Anne: *Don't know.*

(Every student shares an experience of having something stolen.)

Paul: *So you've all been robbed, and the child in this book has been robbed.*
Anne: *Yeah. Of his own people.*
Antonio: *They took him away from his land.*
Paul: *Did he ever come back?*
Anne: *Let me read the last page* (pointing to picture of child as an old man, telling the story).
Paul: *What is he thinking?*
Eddie: *Of his people.*
Paul: *Tell me more.*
Laura: *He's wondering what they were doing* (pointing to picture of Columbus's ships drawn as huge birds of prey).
Anne: *His dream about the ships.*
Paul: *Look at the picture* (a white bird like a ship). *He is—he's dreaming of a ship.*

Anne: *My favorite picture is his dream of flying ships.*
Fabiola: *They look like parrots. My favorite picture is this one.*
Paul: *Do you ever have dreams?*

The discussion continues, with students sharing their dreams, especially bad ones. The talk shifts to books with dreams, such as *There's a Nightmare in My Closet* (Mayer, 1968), *There's an Alligator Under My Bed* (Mayer, 1987), and *The Wreck of the Zephyr* (Van Allsburg, 1983). Paul says, "We should write about our dreams." They also talk about the picture of the bird/boats in the boy's dream in *Encounter* and about old horror movies, and Antonio talks at length about a story he heard in Mexico about being thrown into a hole with fire if you said a bad word.

Paul suggests that they think about their discussion and something they could do in their Literature Circle, perhaps about Christopher Columbus or dreams. Paul lists, on a sheet of chart paper, ideas they generate:

1. Make a story about what happened.

2. Do it on the computer like a book.

3. Make a musical play with songs.

4. Write poems about dreams of boats or dreams or boats.

5. Get some biographies of Christopher Columbus, and read them.

    This is what the students actually did:

1. Read other books about Christopher Columbus (see examples in Box 3.2).

BOX 3.2   *Comparing Cultural Perspectives Through Literature*

For stories, interviews, and teaching ideas that re-evaluate the legacy of Columbus in the Americas, see *Rethinking Columbus: The Next 500 Years* (Bigelow & Peterson, 1998) and books for children from the European perspective, Columbus's perspective, and the Taino perspective.

European Perspective

▲ *Columbus* by Ingri and Edgar Parin d'Aulaire (1955)—This well-illustrated picture book biography portrays the native Taino people as simple "heathens," who worshipped Columbus and his men as gods. The book also shows Columbus's intentions to convert the Taino to Christianity and to teach them Spanish. This book doesn't tell readers that the Taino virtually ceased to exist as a people after Columbus landed.

▲ *The Columbus Story* by Alice Dalgliesh (1955)—This is another well-illustrated picture biography. Its only mention of the Taino says that Columbus "took with him some Indians."

Columbus's Perspective

▲ *I, Columbus: My Journal, 1492–1493,* edited by Peter and Connie Roop (1990)— Adapted from a copy of Columbus's log, this book shows that he wanted the native people to develop a friendly attitude so they could be converted to Christianity, as they seemed to have no religions. Columbus wanted to take them to Spain so they could learn Spanish, even though he recognized that they had their own culture and language.

▲ *The Log of Christopher Columbus* by Christopher Columbus, selections by Steve Lowe (1992)—In this picture book, also adapted from Columbus's log, the explorer mentions meeting friendly native people on arrival in San Salvador, which is where the book ends.

Taino Perspective

▲ *Encounter* by Jane Yolen (1992) and *Encuentro* (1996), the Spanish version—This dramatically illustrated historical fiction picture book shows that Columbus encountered native people who had an established culture and civilization. Events are seen through the eyes of a Taino boy, who escapes from Columbus's ship (which is taking his people to Spain) and lives to old age. During his life, he sees colonization by the Spanish result in the loss of his land, religion, language, and people. The boy is represented as the last Taino.

▲ *Morning Girl* by Michael Dorris (1992)—This short novel gives a historical fictional perspective about what the community of Taino people that Columbus met in the 15th century might have been like. Readers meet Morning Girl and her family and see that they live in a community striving to coexist with the natural world. The community also expects visitors to be friendly, not dangerous. The book ends with the arrival of Columbus.

Other books about Columbus

▲ *The First Voyage of Christopher Columbus, 1492* (Smith, 1992).

▲ *Follow the Dream: The Story of Christopher Columbus* (Sis, 1991).

▲ *Pedro's Journal: A Voyage with Christopher Columbus, (August 3, 1492–February 14, 1493)* (Conrad, 1991)

▲ *A Picture Book of Christopher Columbus* (Adler, 1991a)

▲ *Un libro illustrado sobre Cristóbal Colón* (Adler, 1991b)

▲ *Where Do You Think You're Going, Christopher Columbus?* (Fritz, 1980)

▲ *Who Was First? Discovering the Americas* (Freedman, 2007)

---

2. Made a comparison chart of several books about Christopher Columbus and his meeting the Taino people because the students found these books had very different perspectives (see Figure 3.1).

FIGURE 3.1 A Comparison Chart Made by Students and Teacher

What happened to the Taino people when Columbus came to the Americas?

In *Encounter* by Jane Yolen	In *Columbus* by the d'Aulaires
▲ Taino welcomed Columbus with a feast.	▲ Didn't mind being treated like a god.
▲ Took Taino's gold and gave them beads.	▲ Thought gold was his to take.
▲ Took Taino as slaves to Spain.	▲ Thought Taino should be converted.
▲ He lied to them.	▲ They were cold in Spain.
▲ They lost land, language, and religion.	▲ Doesn't say what happened to them.
▲ 300,000 Taino in 1492—only a few today.	▲ Taino didn't seem important to them.

3. Invited a teacher in the school who had studied in Puerto Rico to talk to the class about the Taino and other native people of Puerto Rico.

4. Did a play of *Encounter* (Antonio played Christopher Columbus with mixed feelings. He had the lead part, but with Richard III overtones.)

5. Wrote poems about dreams, loneliness, boats, and the ocean (See photo, Antonio's poem about the ocean "The Different Waves" written after reading and discussing *Encounter* in a Literature Circle.)

Here is a group poem written by Anne, Fabiola, and Laura that came from their discussions of the old man at the end of the story *Encounter*. Even the children realized he was alone and the last of the Taino people. The poem is an example of rich engagement into literature and meaning-making experiences with reading.

Loneliness

By Anne, Fabiola, and Laura
Everything was quiet
The sea was calm
The sun was hiding behind dark clouds
The seagulls were silent
The wind was blowing like a silent song
You could not even hear a whale splash
This looks like loneliness and that's what it was

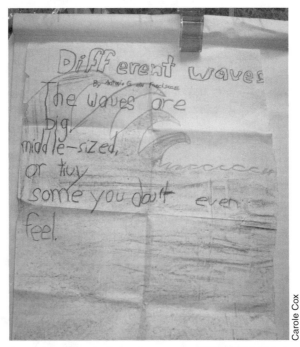

Carole Cox

Antonio's poem about the ocean "The Different Waves," written after reading and discussing *Encounter* in a Literature Circle.

BOX 3.3   *Case Study of Anne: The Native English Speaker*

Read the section "Anne's Response Style: Challenges the Text," pp. 169–72, and consider the following prompts. Jot down your ideas about them:

▲ Compare Anne's reading experiences in her first-grade classroom and in Paul's third-grade classroom of English learners with regard to
    1. Anne's role as a reader in the classroom
    2. The role of the teacher in each classroom
    3. Anne's response style

▲ Describe how you think each of the two teachers viewed Anne in the context of a lesson using literature.

▲ Draft a Literature Circle plan for one of the books that I read to Anne with ideas for language and literacy activities, based on her responses to the book.

Comparison of Two Classrooms

Keep these two classrooms in mind as you consider a comparison of the roles of the teacher and the students in a more text-oriented approach and a more reader-plus-text approach (see Table 3.1). Think about the conceptual differences with regard to teaching with literature and English language and literacy development.

TABLE 3.1 A comparison of two approaches

The Teacher

More Text-Oriented Approach

Makes most decisions for what is to be learned
Uses commercial reading series
Follows teacher's guide for series
Follows a sequence of stories and skills to be mastered

Reader-Plus-Text Approach

Provides opportunities for independent learning
Uses children's literature and student writing
Listen to students; honors student voice
Uses ideas/interests of students to generate thematic learning

The Students

More Text-Oriented Approach

Guided by what teacher has modeled
Follow directions of teacher from teacher's guide or student workbook
Do the same assignments as other students
Often are grouped by ability

Reader-Plus-Text Approach

Make choices: what to read, how to respond, what to learn
Work in groups; discover things on their own
Interact, cooperate, collaborate, plan on their own
Are grouped by interests and compatibility

Transactional teaching with a reader-plus-text orientation to literature is a powerful means to actively engage English learners in experiences with literature and reading, to focus on the personal construction of meaning, and to integrate the curriculum. Teachers of English learners in a student-centered classroom focus on children's responses, rather than on the teachers' predetermined ideas or those found in a teacher's guide for a commercial reading series. These teachers encourage their students to respond openly, drawing on their own experiences and funds of knowledge, and consider a sociocultural perspective when teaching. They begin by asking open questions—"Tell me about the book"—thereby directing children to take an aesthetic stance towards literature. They are aware of each English learner's level of proficiency in English and know how to assess it as a basis for differentiating language and literacy learning. They are also mindful of the many things that make each child unique.

Language is just one of the things that characterizes an English learner. Engaging English learners means focusing on their unique ideas and responses to literature and life. Think back to the English learners you have read about so far in this book: Javier, the turnip expert and sometimes behavior problem in Chapter 1; Juan, the beginning English learner who makes personal connections to literature in Chapter 2; Antonio in this chapter, who along with Anne and other English learners and their teacher Paul engaged in a philosophical, metaphorical discussion about what loss and dreams mean in our lives, from his own personal losses and dreams to those of the Taino people described in the book *Encounter*.

Let's continue to look at how to engage English learners and put the theories and research into practice by exploring literature, developing literacy, and differentiating instruction. In Chapters 4 and 5 you will see how Paul did this in his third-grade classroom of English learners.

Exploring Literature: The Ripple Effect

Like the experiences of famous explorers in history, each child's experience with literature as exploration will be different. Each will be a unique journey. Just as the early Polynesians who sailed to Easter Island or the Vikings to North America or Columbus to the Caribbean—just as these explorers set out at different times, from different ports, seeing different seascapes and landscapes along the way, different children will experience the same book in different ways, depending on their own unique personal, cultural, and linguistic reservoir of memories and thoughts.

Remember Javier from Chapter 1? The focus of his attention while reading the story *The Rabbit and the Turnip* was on what was wrong with the way the illustrator drew the turnip, because he had seen real turnips on his grandfather's ranch in Mexico, and they were different. This led to his questioning of other aspects of the story, based on his life experiences. This approach doesn't mean that readers will never reach any consensus on meaning in a story. Remember Anne and Antonio and other English learners in Paul's class as they discussed the book *Encounter* in this chapter? Even though they had different experiences with being robbed themselves, they all agreed the Taino had indeed been robbed of their lives and history and future by the impact of Columbus landing on their island. These real children reflect Rosenblatt's transactional model of reading.

But how do you put this model into practice in the classroom, particularly when teaching English learners? First, student-centered classrooms, just like students, do not all look the same, but many share a social constructivist view of learning and the transactional model of the reading process. Second, teachers of English learners take into account the unique cultural, linguistic, and experiential funds of knowledge of each of their students, valuing their home language and giving it high status, reflecting a sociocultural perspective on learning and teaching.

Such classrooms are organized to provide time, opportunities, and an environment for students to explore literature as they read, respond, and ripple—developing further language and learning experiences across the curriculum. I have called this a "ripple effect" of integrated teaching (Cox, 2008) because I know it is not totally planned in advance by the teacher. It is like a pebble thrown into a pond, which sends out many concentric waves that can ripple out and extend across the curriculum, depending on the ideas, interests, and experiences of the students. For example, when Paul formed a Literature Circle with students who were reading the book *Encounter,* they continued to read, listen, think, talk, write, research, and act out their ideas about the book, Columbus, the Taino people, and their own experiences with dreams. This concept of a ripple effect can be broken down into three parts: read, respond, and ripple.

Read

First, children must have books, time, and models for reading. A student-centered classroom in which children can explore literature requires creating a room environment, a classroom library, and a schedule that provides time and many opportunities to read. Classroom reading corners or libraries have designated spaces for shelves and book displays, tables, comfortable chairs (or floor pillows, beanbag chairs, or mats), or a rocker for the teacher to use to read aloud—or a child to use to read and rock in.

Time for reading can be built into the schedule throughout the day. The teacher or other students reading aloud can happen several times a day—with the whole class or a group, using picture books or chapter books or the newspaper, for the purpose of sheer enjoyment or curiosity or in connection with a ripple effect, such as that with Christopher Columbus and the Taino people in *Encounter*. Students participate in reading by following along in their own copy of a chapter book or by reading the text of a Big Book, guided by the teacher, or by reading a teacher-made chart of poems or songs, which can also be written on sentence strips and used in a pocket chart. Students can read with a buddy, in pairs, or in a small group. One child can read to others, as Paul had Anne do when she visited his class during a rotation of students in the school. Students may be reading for information to use for a project they are working on, such as comparing different perspectives on Columbus or putting on a play of the book *Encounter*, or simply because they like the same book and each other or because one wants to share a favorite book with a friend.

Sustained silent reading means everyone reads at the same time, silently. Students may self-select books and read for pleasure, or they may be reading widely on a topic of interest. Much wide independent reading occurs when students work in Literature Circles during blocks of time for reading and language arts.

Respond

The first step in responding to literature in the classroom comes through discussions and conversations about a book, occurring with the teacher and with other students. Teachers provide time and opportunities for children to talk—in a whole-class discussion, Literature Circles, conferences with the teacher in Literature Circles, conferences one-on-one with the teacher, or a child talking to another child. This time to talk and respond to literature is the beginning of a journey of exploration of literature. It provides the rich source of ideas and inquiries that can lead to learning and teaching across the curriculum, in a ripple effect of integrated teaching. This is some of the richest time for children to reflect on their own unique responses as a basis for further student-centered experiences with literature (Cox, 1997, 1998 ; Eeds & Wells, 1989; Sipe 1998).

When asking children to respond to literature, simple but powerful teaching tools are the questions and prompts teachers use that can clearly reflect their orientation towards teaching with literature. From a reader-response orientation, a teacher would first ask an open question—"Tell me about the story" or Paul's phrase "Talk to me"—to allow the children to tap into their personal experience of the story.

QUESTIONS AND PROMPTS FOR LITERATURE DISCUSSIONS: AESTHETIC AND EFFERENT. Rosenblatt argues that for experiences with literature, teachers should first direct children to take an aesthetic stance. Included here are aesthetic questions and prompts based on my own research of children's responses to literature (Cox, 1997, 1998), which I turned into questions and prompts that teachers can use. It's important to note that in my 6-year longitudinal study of children's responses to literature (Cox, 1998), I found that children predominantly took an aesthetic stance, that these responses were much more extensive than those that were predominantly efferent, and that efferent understandings of a story—such as explanations, print and language, content, and analysis—were always part of a broader aesthetic response. The efferent emerged from the aesthetic. The more aesthetic questions here direct students to focus on their personal experience with a text; the more efferent questions focus on the text itself. You start with the aesthetic, and listen for the efferent, which is usually embedded within the aesthetic.

Aesthetic Questions and Prompts

What do you think about the story?
Tell anything you want about the story.
Was there anything you wondered about? Tell about it.

What was your favorite part? Tell about it.

Has anything like this ever happened to you? Tell about it.

Does the story remind you of anything? Tell about it.

Is there anything you would change in the story? What would that be?

What else do you think might happen in the story?

What would you say or do or how would you act if you were a character in the story?

Efferent Questions and Prompts

Explain the main idea, problem, or character's actions in the story.

Why did the characters behave as they did?

How did the author solve the problem in the story?

Were there any words or phrases you didn't understand? What were they?

What was the story about? Retell it.

Describe the setting, characters, and plot of the story.

Tell the order of events in the story.

Is the story fact or fiction?

What other stories are like this one? Compare and contrast them.

WRITTEN RESPONSES TO LITERATURE.   Children may also write in response to literature. Keeping a literature journal is a natural way to do this. These journals can also be brought to Literature Circles and shared in discussions. Double-entry journals are a variation on literature journals: Each page is divided down the middle, and students note a part of the book that attracted their attention on the left and a personal response to it on the right. If you do use journals, you can use the questions and prompts in the preceding section if you feel they are necessary.

Although some students enjoy journal writing, be mindful that not all of them want to stop while reading a book and write a response. In the Case Study of Anne, remember her frustration with a lot of written work associated with reading: "You have to write down the stupid thing. [She sounds very frustrated and is practically crying.] I hate that. You gotta write down everything you do. I don't get how that is reading." You should observe your students, and if they are engaged in reading, literally lost in a book, and they participate in discussions in Literature Circles, then perhaps journals are not appropriate for them.

On the other hand, writing is a natural outcome of reading and responding to literature, especially as part of a ripple effect of integrated teaching that begins with literature. And there are many ways for students to respond in writing, as well as through drama, art, and media.

MANY WAYS TO RESPOND.   You've already read about some of the ways children can respond to literature in the descriptions of Literature Circles in Paul's class in chapter 1 when his students read *The Rabbit and the Turnip* (Sadler, 1968) and *Curious George* (Rey, 1973), and in this chapter when his students and Anne read *Encounter* (Yolen, 1992). In Chapters 4 and 5 you will read about many of the real experiences Paul's students had responding to many other books. See Figure 3.2 for numerous response ideas at a glance.

Carole Cox

Student's in Paul's class write in literature journals.

BOX 3.4   *Case Study of Eduardo: The Intermediate/Advanced English Learner*

Read "Meet Eduardo," "Background and Home Influences," and "Eduardo's Response Style," p. 173–183. As you read these sections of this case study, consider the following questions and prompts:

▲ Compare Eduardo to Juan and Anne in terms of their personal response styles. What implications would this have for you as a teacher as you guided each of them through exploring literature in Literature Circles?

▲ How would you guide Eduardo's writing development, based on his response style and his actual responses to books as described in the case study?

▲ Since Eduardo consistently breaks through the boundaries of the text in discussions, list some response options you think would be meaningful for him and other students like him. How would you also check for their understanding of a story?

FIGURE 3.2 Ways to respond to literature

Advertisements	Interviews with story	Posters
Bookmaking	characters	Powerpoint presentation
Cartoons	Letters	Props for plays or storytelling
Collage	Literature as a model for	Puppets
Constructions	writing	Read another book
Dance	Magazines	Reader's theatre
Debate	Maps of a story world	Role playing
Demonstration	Murals	Scripts for drama
Dioramas	Museum-type display	Songwriting
Drama	Musical theater	Story dramatization
E-mail dialogues	Newspaper	Storytelling
Games	Photo-essay	Videotaped dramatizations
Illustrations and captions	Plays	Web pages
	Poetry	WebQuest

Ripple

The power of literature is to capture the imagination for a moment, to take it where it's never been before—to other times and places and even to other worlds. By exploring literature, we can empathize with others and discover their needs and pleasures, joys and fears—not unlike our own. And above all, through literature we can feel, see, and understand things that would otherwise have remained unknown—about ourselves and the world.

In a classroom of English learners, literature extends students' interests and develops listening, thinking, speaking, reading, and writing. It also extends students' reading and learning on a wide variety of subjects of interest to them. Finally, it extends language learning across the curriculum, integrating language and literacy with the content areas. That's the ripple effect. Figure 3.3 shows a graphic depiction of a ripple effect with English learners that you read about earlier in the chapter.

Literature Circles

Literature Circles are one way to organize teaching with literature that often leads to a ripple effect of learning across the curriculum. Literature Circles form when students have a shared interest in a book or a topic or they like to work together. The basic idea behind this approach is that children form small groups to read, discuss, and possibly develop projects related to a single book, author, genre, topic, or a combination of these. Literature Circles have been widely used in literacy instruction. Martinez-Roldan and Lopez-Robertson (2000) reported on their use in a first-grade class of English learners and concluded that "young bilingual children, no matter their linguistic background, are able to have rich discussions if they have regular opportunities to engage with books from a transactional perspective." While Literature Circles can take many forms, they usually share the same characteristics described by Daniels (2002):

▲ Children choose the books they will read.

▲ Small, temporary groups are formed around these book choices.

FIGURE 3.3 The Ripple Effect of Integrated Teaching

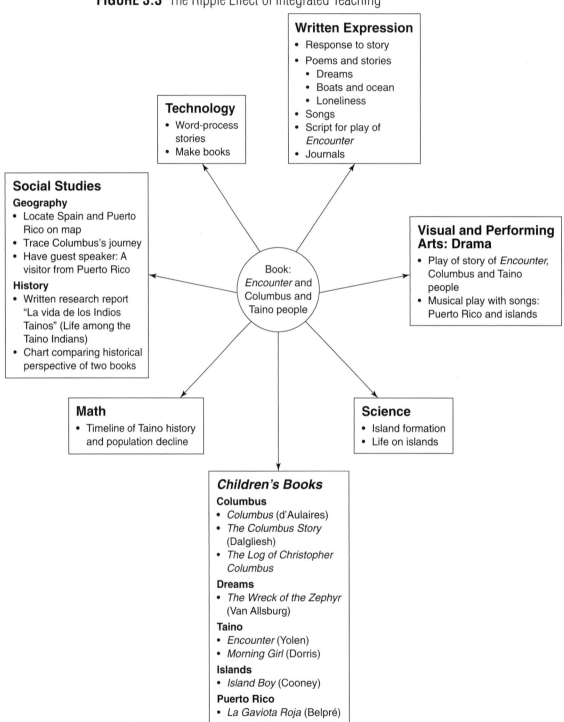

Written Expression
- Response to story
- Poems and stories
  - Dreams
  - Boats and ocean
  - Loneliness
- Songs
- Script for play of *Encounter*
- Journals

Technology
- Word-process stories
- Make books

Social Studies
Geography
- Locate Spain and Puerto Rico on map
- Trace Columbus's journey
- Have guest speaker: A visitor from Puerto Rico

History
- Written research report "La vida de los Indios Tainos" (Life among the Taino Indians)
- Chart comparing historical perspective of two books

Book: *Encounter* and Columbus and Taino people

Visual and Performing Arts: Drama
- Play of story of *Encounter,* Columbus and Taino people
- Musical play with songs: Puerto Rico and islands

Math
- Timeline of Taino history and population decline

Science
- Island formation
- Life on islands

Children's Books
Columbus
- *Columbus* (d'Aulaires)
- *The Columbus Story* (Dalgliesh)
- *The Log of Christopher Columbus*

Dreams
- *The Wreck of the Zephyr* (Van Allsburg)

Taino
- *Encounter* (Yolen)
- *Morning Girl* (Dorris)

Islands
- *Island Boy* (Cooney)

Puerto Rico
- *La Gaviota Roja* (Belpré)

▲ Different groups read different books.

▲ Groups meet to discuss their reading on a regularly scheduled basis.

▲ Children write in journals and share these written notes in their groups.

▲ Topics and questions for discussion come from the children.

▲ Discussions are open, natural conversations centered around children's responses to, questions about, and personal connections to books.

▲ The teacher meets with groups on a rotating basis but serves as facilitator rather than as a group member or instructor.

▲ Children may assume different roles.

Daniels describes six roles children can take. The teacher can use these as needed, and other roles may emerge from the Literature Circle depending on what experiences are planned.

1. *Discussion director:* Keeps things moving along

2. *Connector:* Makes connections to personal experiences or other books

3. *Word wizard:* Notes the author's specific word choices

4. *Illustrator:* Creates an illustration of a significant event in the book

5. *Passage picker:* Chooses and reads aloud a special passage, explaining why it was picked

6. *Summarizer:* Summarizes the text and the Literature Circle discussion

These roles also offer a way to differentiate instruction for English learners because some require more English proficiency than others. For example, a beginning English learner like Juan could participate as the illustrator, while an intermediate/advanced English learner like Eduardo could be the discussion director. Literature Circles are good for English learners for other reasons. They use context-embedded instruction as described by Cummins (1992). It's essential to tap into students' prior experience and funds of knowledge from a sociocultural perspective. Reading is done in groups with peer support where primary language support can be provided as well. The teacher or more proficient English speakers can read aloud, as Anne did in the Literature Circle for *Encounter* in Paul's class. Graphic organizers such as a cluster of ideas can be used by the teacher or another student, as Javier did with *The Rabbit and the Turnip* in Chapter 1, using visuals to support English development.

Integrated Teaching of Literacy and the Content Areas with English Learners in Sr. B.B.'s Class

To make the concept of the ripple effect of integrated teaching come alive, read "A Thought from Paul" below on his experiences with content area teaching that emerged from Literature Circles in his class of English learners.

A Thought from Paul ⎯⎯⎯⎯⎯⎯⎯⎯⎯⎯⎯⎯⎯⎯⎯⎯

Content instruction in mathematics, social studies, and science can be integrated quite naturally with literature-based instruction. It is not a substitute for daily, systematic instruction. The rule of thumb, however, is not to force the subject area into the story; rather, let the story dictate what concepts may emerge. Forcing content instruction into a discussion of a story is more of a distraction from a good story than helpful instruction. Additionally, drawing story characters on worksheets in an attempt to tie a story to student work in other subject areas is no more than a superficial connection between dubious teaching and literature-based instruction. Nevertheless, mathematics, social studies, and science content can be meaningfully integrated with literature-based instruction in numerous ways. The following examples of integration are actual occurrences from my classroom, along with suggestions for successful instruction.

Mathematics

▲   Do not force mathematics into a story; maintain daily systematic mathematics instruction.

▲   Let the story and the subsequent student discussion dictate the mathematics concepts to explore.

▲   When students are writing their own versions of a story, ask for details that involve mathematics: How many? How much? What size? What is the average? How much time did it take?

▲   When a student expresses an opinion about what "most people think," ask him or her to test that opinion with a survey.

▲   Look for opportunities to measure dimensions by creating sets and props for plays, life-size animal creations, or mapped-out distances.

EXAMPLES

A. *Robbery, Money, and Math:* Two students, Carmina and Rosalinda, were reading one of the Encyclopedia Brown stories in which he solved a robbery case. The girls wanted to write their own version of the story, so I suggested that they keep a detailed record of the money involved.

What they wrote opened with a fast-food business that began the day with $75.45 in the cash register. Before the robbers arrived on the scene of the crime, 12 customers had come to purchase food. To know how much money the fast-food business had made to that point, the students created a menu, priced the items, itemized what was purchased by the customers, and added the total sales to the starting amount.

The girls figured that the robbers would be too hurried to deal with the coins in the till, so they figured the amount stolen on the basis of bills. They also included that, prior to being captured, the robbers spent some of the money to purchase a Christmas tree and decorations; the girls subtracted this amount from the total.

Figuring out how much money the fast-food business recovered at the end of the story turned into a complex series of calculations. The students' version of a robbery was not only an entertaining story but also included detailed information of how much money was made, lost, and recovered in an adventurous day. The students authentically responded to the story, integrated mathematics concepts, and developed written language.

B. *Mathematics as the Language of Inquiry:* A natural way to incorporate mathematics concepts with literature-based instruction is to ask students to conduct an opinion survey related to a story. One such example grew out of a discussion of *Henry Huggins* by Beverly Cleary (1950). While discussing the story about Henry's adventures with various pets such as the dog Ribsy or the fish, José and Johnny speculated what most people would like to have as a pet. This comment opened the way for conducting a 7-step opinion survey:

1. Form research question (What is your favorite pet?).
2. Hypothesize the outcome.
  a. Limit the range of choices to five or six pets plus "other" for an open choice.
  b. Estimate which pet will be the class favorite.
3. Collect the data.
  a. Devise a way to record responses.
  b. Start asking the question.
4. Organize the data.
  a. Use a table.
  b. Represent the data on a graph.
5. Write down observations.
  a. Record what the graph tells you in sentence form.
  b. Notice any interesting information.
6. Interpret the data.
  a. Calculate the percentages for each pet. Use this formula: (# of votes in a category/Total # of responses) $\times 100 =$ ____%.
  b. Compare your results with your original hypothesis. Were you on the mark? How far off was the hypothesis? Why?
7. Report the findings to the class in writing.

The entire inquiry process is a systematic way to naturally integrate dealing with data with literature-based instruction. The process has several instructional benefits: (a) It maintains the integrity of the story of Henry Huggins, (b) written language is developed, and (c) the students learn an open-ended research technique they can apply to numerous Inquiry situations.

C. *Measurement and Animals:* While studying Lynne Cherry's *The Great Kapok Tree* (1991), I suggested that the students re-create a life-size version of the different animals in the story. Eduardo's group selected the boa constrictor. They went to the library to research the actual length of an adult boa constrictor and found that the snake ranged in size from 10- to 15-meters in length.

Initially, Eduardo was not impressed by such small numbers. He said, "Oh, that's not very long." So I replied by asking him to take hold of one end of a string. With a meterstick and pieces of masking tape, we marked off each meter. As the string lengthened, Eduardo stepped back until he wound up outside the classroom and down the hall a way. He finally realized the dimensions of this great snake. It was remarkable to see the light bulb go on with use of string and tape as a concrete manipulative.

This concrete way of measuring the length of the boa constrictor in meters had the benefits of building mathematical understanding and giving the students a metered string to accurately measure butcher paper to paint a life-size boa constrictor.

Social Studies

▲ Social studies begins with the story of our lives. Look to touch students' experience with story.

▲ Compare and contrast opposing stories of the same individual or event.

▲ Challenge the author. Question the sources for the author's information.

▲ Interview any knowledgeable person as an expert on his or her own story.

▲ Validate the life story that each child brings by making his or her life the object of writing and study in the class.

EXAMPLES

A. *Biographical Research:* When reading historically based literature, a natural way to incorporate social studies is to research and record the biography of a character in the story. In my classroom, one group of students read Ingri and Edgar d'Aulaire's (1995) book *Columbus;* another selected Jane Yolen's (1992) book *Encounter.* The two groups came up with radically different perceptions of Christopher Columbus. The polarization provided a unique opportunity to take a second look at the story of Christopher Columbus.

B. *Interviewing an Expert:* While reading Pura Belpré's (1987) story based in Puerto Rico, "La Gaviota Roja," I remembered that one teacher in the school was Puerto Rican. I mentioned that fact to the students, who in turn invited her to speak to the class. The students formulated questions about the island and its history, took notes during the interview, and wrote up the information in the form of a Big Book.

C. *Recording Your Story:* Whenever possible, I asked students to record their own stories as they related to the text. This involved interviewing family members or relating a personal account and capturing the story in written form.

Science

▲ Focus on the processes of science, and look for ways to apply those processes where appropriate.

▲ Combine illustrations with writing to provide for comprehensible input.

▲ When a story exhibits a wide variety of objects or life forms, allow the scientist inside each child to order them with classification.

▲ Bring real-life objects or life forms to the classroom whenever possible.

▲ Encourage detailed observation in the form of drawings and written expression.

▲ Keep reference material at the ready, such as field guides.

▲ Compare and contrast examples of objects and life forms in their appearance and/or life cycles.

EXAMPLES

A. *Classification:* Barbara Cooney's *Island Boy* (1998) provided Baudelio and Carmen a wonderful opportunity to identify and classify East Coast sea birds as they tried to understand which birds were cormorants in the story. They used a bird watcher's guide as a reference tool and created a poster with the various birds grouped according to their unique characteristics.

B. *Detailed Observation:* Sylvia and Laura started reading *Top Secret* by John Reynolds Gardiner (1985), the hilarious story of a boy who invented "human photosynthesis" for a science project. He eventually turns his skeptical teacher, Mrs. Green, into a tree. I suggested that the girls take a closer look at leaves through the microscope to detail the components of leaves that photosynthesize. They drew pictures of the leaves from the microscope observations and labeled the significant parts.

C. *Recording Life Cycles:* The cycle of birth, change, and death is recorded in a myriad of ways in children's literature, whether it is Eric Carle's *The Very Hungry Caterpillar* (1969), the family on Tibbets Island in Barbara Cooney's *Island Boy* (1988), or plant life in Brenda Guiberson's *Cactus Hotel* (1991). Recording that cycle can take the form of creating a Big Book accompanied by illustrations. A unique way to document the cycle in the story is to begin with a large tagboard circle (18 inches in diameter). Cut a doughnut hole in the middle of the circle (approximately 1 inch in diameter). Identify the number of stages in the cycle, add one extra for a title page, and cut the circle into corresponding equal parts. Draw the animal or plant at each stage of the cycle on the pieces of the circle. Label each stage, write an explanation of each stage on a separate card, and glue it to the appropriate segment of the circle. Reattach each segment, in order, with cloth tape, allowing for a half-inch space between segments. Accordian fold the pieces so that the title page segment is on top. The final product documents the life cycle.

Developing Literacy

Exploring literature through the ripple effects of integrated teaching and Literature Circles provides an instructional framework within which to develop literacy for English learners (Vardell, Hadaway, & Young, 2006). Research on developing literacy for English learners confirms the importance of language interactions in both English and a child's home language as a basis for learning to read and write, which occurs naturally in student-centered discussions in Literature Circles (Hudelson, Poynor, & Wolfe, 2003). In particular, teachers can support such learning by doing the following:

1. Creating an environment that both acknowledges and respects the language and literacy development of the child's home and community;
2. Providing multiple opportunities for language interactions that include oral and written experiences with both the teacher and classmates;
3. Observing children's language interactions and planning instructional activities that reflect the reality of idiosyncratic nature of literacy development in children; and

4.   Allowing and valuing the use of the first language in the language and literacy development of the second language. (pp. 428–429)

Research has also suggested that the development of literacy for English learners is a social process, and children need many opportunities to talk, share, and collaborate with others in groups (Dworin, 2006). In addition, English learners need multiple opportunities to use both their home language and English in authentic contexts connected with their own lives through speaking, reading, and writing (Hudelson et al., 2003; International Reading Association, 2001; Rubin & Carlan, 2005). The importance of home–school connections is also well documented (Ortiz & Ordonez-Jasis, 2005). Studies have shown the importance of teaching young children to read and write in their native language—the language they already know— rather than in a language they don't know well (Lenters, 2005; Snow, Burns, & Griffin, 1998).

Key conclusions and recommendations from *Developing Literacy in Second-Language Learners: Report of the National Literacy Panel on Language-Minority Children and Youth* (August & Shanahan, 2006) can be met by teachers exploring literature through Literature Circles and the ripple effects of integrated teaching with English learners. This report recommends that teachers develop more thorough discussion of reading material and literature and that English language material be read by students beyond the instructional day, in order to build vocabulary and comprehension. The report also notes that well-developed oral language skills (vocabulary, grammatical knowledge, phonological memory) are related to writing quality. The acquisition of proficient writing skills entails spelling skills, decontextualized language skills, use of cohesive devices such as temporal references and conjunctions, metacognition such as audience awareness, familiarity with written genres and subjects, and opportunities to practice writing. All of these can occur naturally when exploring literature.

BOX 3.5   *Case Study of Eduardo: The Intermediate/Advanced English Learner*

Review "Language Development" and "Eduardo as a Student," pp. 175–79. As you read these sections of Eduardo's case study, consider the following questions and prompts:

▲   What are some ways you could create meaningful home–school connections with Eduardo's mother to support his literacy development? Why would this be important?

▲   Describe some key strategies you would use as you planned for Eduardo's experiences with literature and literacy development, based on his level of English development and past performance as a student. How do theory and research on English learners support your ideas?

Differentiating Instruction

You have read about several children so far in this book—Javier, Anne, Antonio, Juan, and Eduardo—and you will read about more in Chapters 4 and 5. They are all different in many ways, in addition to being English learners at different stages of English development or a native English speaker in Anne's case. For example, they have different learning styles—the ways they think and learn. We each have our own ways, irrespective of our home language or ability in English. Howard Gardner (1983) has characterized learning styles in his theory of multiple intelligences. He describes eight ways we can be smart:

1. *Verbal/linguistic:* reading, writing, speaking, listening

2. *Logical/mathematical:* working with numbers and abstract patterns

3. *Visual/spatial:* working with images, mind mapping, visualizing, drawing

4. *Musical/rhythmic:* using rhythm, melody, patterned sound, song, dance

5. *Bodily/kinesthetic:* processing information through touch, movement, dramatics

6. *Interpersonal:* sharing, cooperating, interviewing, relating

7. *Intrapersonal:* working alone, self-paced instruction, individualized projects

8. *Naturalist:* spending time outdoors, sorting, classifying, noticing patterns

Others have characterized the way we think and learn with other classification systems (Dunn & Dunn, 1987; Kolb, 1984; Silver, Strong, & Perini, 2000), but however you label the differences, theory and research in this area suggest to teachers that instruction must be differentiated. According to Carol Tomlinson (2001), "In a differentiated classroom, the teacher proactively plans and carries out varied approaches to content, process, and product in anticipation of and response to student differences in readiness, interest, and learning needs." (p. 7). She also tells us what differentiated instruction looks like:

1. *Proactive:* The teacher is proactive in planning a variety of approaches tailored to the way individual children learn, rather than using a single approach and retroactively adjusting when it becomes clear it's not working for some students.

2. *More qualitative than quantitative:* The teacher adjusts the nature of the assignment, rather than simply giving an advanced student more of the same work or a struggling student less.

3. *Rooted in assessment:* The teacher wants to know as much as possible about students to plan their instruction, rather than assessing after teaching to find out if they "got it."

4. *Providing multiple approaches to content, process, and product:* The teacher deals with three curricular elements: (a) content—what they learn; (b) process—how they make sense of it; and (c) product—how they demonstrate it. Teachers can take different approaches to varying each element.

5. *Student-centered:* The teacher knows that to be effective, learning experiences must be engaging, relevant, and interesting and must be built on each student's previous learning. What some find simple, others find challenging. Students must also take responsibility for their own learning.

6. *Organic:* The teacher collaborates with students, continually monitoring them, draws on a range of strategies and resources, and sees differentiation as a way of life in the classroom.

I especially like the way Tomlinson demythologizes the idea of differentiating instruction by describing what it is *not.* It is not simply "individualized instruction," or doing something different for every child. It is not chaotic. Teachers who differentiate exert more leadership, in that they are constantly choreographing what goes on in the classroom. They also expect children to learn to take responsibility for their own behavior. Further, differentiation is not homogeneous grouping based on ability, which is only one of the characteristics of a learner, nor does it mean simply making the same assignment harder for some and easier for others.

With regard to English learners, a key conclusion and recommendation from *Developing Literacy in Second-Language Learners: Report of the National Literacy Panel on Language-Minority Children and Youth* (August & Shanahan, 2006) is that English learners are a heterogeneous group and attention must be paid to individual differences. Factors that influence second language reading comprehension include background knowledge, motivation, story structure, and home literacy, and these need to be taken into consideration when planning literacy instruction for each child. Teaching with literature and using Literature Circles are excellent ways to differentiate instruction for English learners.

In his book *Differentiated Early Literacy for English Language Learners: Practical Strategies* (2006), Paul describes the first step in differentiating instruction for English learners: "Prior to selecting appropriate English language development (ELD) strategies and activities, it is vital to identify the level of language proficiency the student has achieved in order to provide matching instructional strategies (p. 7)." Paul emphasizes the importance of standards-based instruction for English learners, using as a framework the goals and standards of Teaching English to Speakers of Other Languages (TESOL, 2006), in addition to national or state content standards. (For the TESOL PreK–12 English Language Proficiency Standards, go to www.tesol.org.) Paul also reminds us of importance of each child's personal perspective from reader-response theory.

Second language learners move through stages of language proficiency from Beginning to Early Intermediate and Intermediate and on to Early Advanced and Advanced. There may be a silent period at the beginning, sometimes called *pre-production*, when students are focusing on listening and understanding but not yet speaking. You should be aware of the characteristics of each stage as you plan to assess and differentiate instruction for English learners. Remember that you are not teaching a beginning English learner less—the content standards are the same for all children—but you are adapting activities for the child based on his or her stage, in order to meet the standards. Paul will show you how to do this in Chapter 4.

BOX 3.6

Case Study of Juan: The Beginning English Learner
Case Study of Anne: The Native English Speaker
Case Study of Eduardo: The Intermediate/Advanced English Learner

Think about what you read in the case studies of these two English learners and one native English speaker, and respond to the following questions and prompts:

▲ Choose one grade from kindergarten to fifth and compare Juan and Eduardo in that grade with regard to English language development and as students. Describe how you would differentiate instruction for each of them when exploring literature and developing literacy in Literature Circles.

▲ Compare the literacy development needs of both Juan and Eduardo with those of Anne, considering each child's background and home influences. How are they the same, and how are they different?

▲ Using Gardner's theory of multiple intelligences, how would you characterize Anne, Juan, and Eduardo? Considering Tomlinson's description of differentiated instruction, how would you use this information as you guided them through exploring literature and developing literacy?

A Thought from Carole

When I was an elementary school teacher, one of the things I discovered was that I was really teaching each child rather than a curriculum. And each child was different in some ways from all the others. This was both a challenge and a rush. When a pebble of ideas or interests would hit the pond and a ripple effect of inquiries and experiences would start to spread through the classroom and across the curriculum, I often felt as if I should buckle my seat belt as the journey started. I wasn't sure where it would lead, but I trusted that I could teach and that my children could learn. I often had the feeling I was on the deck of the starship *Enterprise,* considering its mission statement: "To go where no [person] has gone before." Did this mean I had no idea what to do? To the contrary, I drew on my observations of children and how they learn, my knowledge about how to organize a classroom, my own experiences with all kinds of texts from literature to television to film and other art forms, content area knowledge gained in 16 years of schooling and living in another country and learning another language, and so on. But the single most important thing was what my students brought to the classroom. My job was to discover what it was and center my teaching around it. The result? A student-centered classroom. In today's classroom with many English learners, knowledge of your students—including, but not limited to, home language and level of English proficiency—is the place where the journey begins.

EXPLORING IDEAS

1. Think about how your teachers taught with literature when you were in elementary school. Which theoretical models did their teaching reflect? Why?

2. What do you think the role of literature should be in second language education? Compare your ideas with the research on how literature is used and reading is taught, explained in this chapter, and the context of your own experience.

3. Observe a class with a majority of English learners during time when the teacher is teaching with literature. Take notes and analyze them according to the teacher's approach. What do you think about it? How do you think you will teach with literature?

4. Read the children's book *Encounter*. Read the description of what happened in Paul's class when a literature group formed around the book, and brainstorm some of your own ideas for using this book with a response-centered approach. Try some of them out with a group of English learners, or use any good children's book and a response-centered teaching approach.

CHILDREN'S BOOKS

Adler, D. A. (1991a). *A picture book of Christopher Columbus*. New York: Holiday House.

Adler, D. A. (1991b). *Un libro illustrado sobre Cristóbal Colón* (traducción de Teresa Mlawer). Madrid, Spain: Editorial Everest.

Belpré, P. (1987). "La gaviota roja." In *Campanitas de oro* (pp. 121–135). New York: Macmillan.

Carle, E. (1969). *The very hungry caterpillar*. New York: Philomel.

Cherry, L. (1991). *The great kapok tree*. New York: Harcourt.

Cleary, B. (1950). *Henry Huggins*. New York: Morrow.

Columbus, C. (1992). *The log of Christopher Columbus* (selections by S. Lowe). New York: Philomel.

Conrad, P. (1991). *Pedro's journal: A voyage with Christopher Columbus (August 3, 1492–February 14, 1493)*. Honesdale, PA: Boyds Mills Press.

Cooney, B. (1988). *Island boy*. New York: Viking.

Dalgliesh, A. (1955). *The Columbus story*. New York: Scribner.

d'Aulaire, I., & d'Aulaire, E. P. (1955). *Columbus*. New York: Doubleday.

Dorris, M. (1992). *Morning girl*. New York: Hyperion.

Fritz, J. (1980). *Where do you think you're going, Christopher Columbus?* New York: Putnam.

Freedman, R. (2007). *Who was first? Discovering the Americas*. New York: Clarion.

Gardiner, J. R. (1985). *Top secret*. Boston: Little Brown.

Guiberson, B. (1991). *Cactus hotel*. New York: Henry Holt.

Mayer, M. (1968). *There's a nightmare in my closet*. New York: Dial.

Mayer, M. (1987). *There's an alligator under my bed*. New York: Dial.

Rey, H.A. (1973). *Curious George.* New York: Houghton Mifflin.

Roop, P., & Roop, C. (Eds.). (1990). *I, Columbus: My journal, 1492–1493.* New York: Avon.

Sadler, R. (1968). *The Rabbit and the Turnip.* London: Richard Sadler Ltd.

Sis, P. (1991). *Follow the dream: The story of Christopher Columbus.* New York: Knopf.

Smith, B. (1992). *The first voyage of Christopher Columbus, 1492.* New York: Viking Penguin.

Van Allsburg, C. (1983). *The wreck of the Zephyr.* New York: Houghton Mifflin.

Yolen, J. (1992). *Encounter.* New York: Harcourt Brace.

Yolen, J. (1996). *Encuentro.* San Diego, CA: Harcourt Brace.

REFERENCES

August, D., & Shanahan, T. (Eds.). (2006). *Developing literacy in second-language learners: Report of the National Literacy Panel on Language-Minority Children and Youth.* Mahwah, NJ: Erlbaum.

Bigelow, W., Peterson, R. (Eds.). (1998). *Rethinking Columbus: The next 500 years* (2nd ed.). Milwaukee, WI: Rethinking Schools.

Boyd-Batstone, P. (2006). *Differentiated early literacy for English language learners: Practical strategies.* Boston: Allyn & Bacon/Pearson.

Cox, C. (1997). Literature-based teaching: A student response-centered classroom. In N. Karolides (Ed.), *Reader response in elementary classrooms: Quest and discovery* (pp. 29–49). Mahwah, NJ: Erlbaum.

Cox, C. (1998, April). *Children's stance towards literature: A longitudinal study, K–5.* Paper presented at the annual meeting of the American Educational Research Association, San Diego, CA.

Cox, C. (2008). *Teaching language arts: A student-centered classroom* (6th ed.). Boston: Pearson/Allyn & Bacon.

Cummins, J. (1992). Language proficiency, bilingualism, and academic achievement. In P. A. Richard-Amate &; M. A. Snow (Eds.), *The multicultural classroom: Readings for content-area teachers* (pp. 16–26). White Plains, NY: Longman.

Daniels, H. (2002). *Literature circles: Voice and choice in book clubs and reading groups* (2nd ed.). Portland, ME: Stenhouse.

Dunn, K., & Dunn, R. (1987). *Bringing out the giftedness in your child.* New York: John Wiley.

Dworin, J. E. (2006). The Family Stories Project: Using funds of knowledge for writing. *The Reading Teacher, 59*(6), 510–520.

Eeds, M., & Wells, D. (1989). Grand conversations: An exploration of meaning construction in literature study groups. *Research in the Teaching of English, 23,* 4–29.

Gardner, H. (1983). *Multiple intelligences: The theory in practice.* New York: Basic Books.

Hudelson, S., Poynor, L., & Wolfe, P. (2003). Teaching bilingual and ESL children and adolescents. In J. Flood, D. Lapp, J. R. Squire, & J. M. Jensen (Eds.), *Handbook of research on teaching the English language arts* (3rd ed.). Mahwah, NJ: Erlbaum.

International Reading Association (IRA). (2001). *Second-language literacy: A position statement of the International Reading Association.* Newark, DE: IRA.

Kolb, D. (1984). *Experiential learning: Experience as the source of learning and development.* Englewood Cliffs, NJ: Prentice Hall.

Lenters, K. (2005). No half measures: Reading instruction for young second-language learners. *The Reading Teacher, 58*(4), 328–336.

Martinez-Roldan, C., & Lopez-Robertson, J. (2000). Initiating literature circles in a first grade bilingual classroom. *The Reading Teacher, 52,* 270–281.

Ortiz, R. W., & Ordonez-Jasis, R. (2005). Leyendo juntos (reading together): New directions for Latino parents' early literacy involvement. *The Reading Teacher, 59*(2), 110–121.

Rosenblatt, L. M. (1994). *The reader, the text, the poem: The transactional theory of the literary work.* Carbondale: Southern Illinois University Press. (Original work published 1978)

Rosenblatt, L. M. (1995). *Literature as exploration.* New York: Modern Language Association. (Original work published 1938)

Rosenblatt, L. M. (2005). *Making meaning with texts: Selected essays.* Portsmouth, NH: Heinemann.

Rubin, R., & Carlan, V. G. (2005). Using writing to understand bilingual children's literacy development. *The Reading Teacher, 58*(8), 728–739.

Silver, H., Strong, R., Perini, M. (2000). *So each may learn: Integrating learning styles and multiple intelligences.* Alexandria, VA: Association for Supervision and Curriculum Development.

Sipe, L. (1998). The construction of literary understanding by first and second graders in response to picture storybook read-alouds. *Reading Research Quarterly, 33*(4), 376–378.

Snow, C. E., Burns, M. S., & Griffin, P. (Eds.). (1998). *Preventing reading difficulties in young children.* Washington, DC: National Academy Press.

TESOL. (2006). *PreK–12 English Language Proficiency Standards.* Alexandria, VA: TESOL.

Tomlinson, C. (2001). *How to differentiate instruction in mixed-ability classrooms* (2nd ed.). Alexandria, VA: Association for Supervision and Curriculum Development.

Vardell, S. M., Hadaway, N. L., & Young, T. A. (2006). Matching books and readers: Selecting literature for English learners. *The Reading Teacher, 59*(8), 741–743.

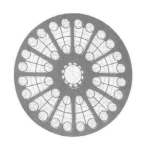

CHAPTER FOUR

Components of Student-Centered Instruction

The Fearsome Crowned Eagle
by Jackie Hernandez

The crowned eagle weighs about 9 pounds and is about 3 feet long. It gets its name from the big crest of feathers on its head. Village chiefs once used the feathers in their head dresses. Crowned eagles have to be fast to catch monkeys in the trees.

If I would be a eagle I would be happi because I will flie. I would have blak talons. I will dill my prey with my talons. I will haf feathers bown, blak, white. I will haf feathers and orange beek. I would eet Rats, Birds, Snakes.

They will kill their prey whith hug talons.

KNOWING THE ENGLISH LEARNER FOR DIFFERENTIATED INSTRUCTION

Knowing the English learner is a key to differentiating instruction in Literature Circles. English learners are a heterogeneous group; one-size-fits-all approaches to teaching are inadequate to meet their needs. This was affirmed by the report of the National Literacy Panel on Language-Minority Children and Youth (August & Shanahan 2006), which reviewed hundreds of research studies on the subject. The report's first recommendation for professional development for all teachers was differentiated instruction. Differentiated approaches to instruction take into account sociocultural and developmental factors that students bring to school; they use standardized and authentic assessment to inform and accommodate daily instruction based on the students' language proficiency levels as well as their strengths and needs.

In the context of reader-response theory, the text and differentiation takes place in the exchange between the English learner, the text, and the teacher. The kinds of questions the teacher uses are based on the English learner's level of oral language proficiency. For example, a newly arrived immigrant that knows very little English will respond more readily to yes/no, closed-ended, and either/or questions, whereas a more experienced English learner would be able to respond to simple open-ended questions, like "What were you thinking?" and a more advanced English learner could respond more freely to speculative what-if type questions that probe the imagination to a deeper degree.

Differentiation takes place in the context of reader-response theory in other ways, such as the kinds of strategies English learners use in response to reading a story. Research on the use of strategies by English learners (Chamot, Barnhardt, El-Dinary, & Robbins, 1999; Gu, Hu, & Zhang 2003) suggests that academically successful English learners orchestrate a wide range of learning strategies. They not only use a variety of strategies, but they monitor and select which ones are most useful for a given situation.

Getting to know the English learner requires a baseline assessment of language level. Often, an English learner is placed in a classroom without current assessment data being provided. Therefore, I developed a Quick Assessment Scale of Oral English Language Development (ELD) to measure basic proficiency levels (Boyd-Batstone, 2006). The scale was made by synthesizing the ELD stages and descriptors of student behaviors at each level of language proficiency, as found in the California Standards for English Language Development (1999). The scale (see Table 4.1) allows the teacher, via a brief conversation with the child, to quickly assess his or her language level by comparing the descriptors of student behaviors to the spoken language of the English learner. The scale also includes the estimated duration of each stage, the time one would expect the English learner to remain at a given level. This information can indicate normal progression through the stages or can signal a problem, such as language processing, that should be looked into.

The case studies that Carole examined included one native English speaker, Anne, and two English learners, Juan and Eduardo. The following is a quick assessment of the two English learners, using this scale as a tool:

▲ In kindergarten, Juan was very much in the Beginning stage of language development, as characterized by his silence and one- or two-word utterances. As his language developed, he began to speak in simple sentences, respond to questions, and share his own experiences. This placed him clearly in the Early Intermediate Stage. His use of vocabulary remained simple, and his speech and reading had frequent errors.

▲ Eduardo was much more fluent in his speech and freely used more descriptive vocabulary. His retelling of stories noted details that were freely compared to other events and personal experiences. However, sometimes a high level of oral fluency can be deceptive. The reason that Eduardo was not classified as Early Advanced was that his use of English remained limited to personal accounts and did not include academic vocabulary or subject-specific terminology. Further, he was still below grade level in his writing.

Table 4.2 shows that the recommended teacher strategies for both students are quite similar. The difference takes place at the student activity level. The teacher in both cases will teach vocabulary and help the students organize their ideas into written form. However, the teacher will extend vocabulary instruction for Eduardo, use a greater variety of graphic organizers, and demonstrate outlining. Juan's vocabulary development activities will involve the use of real objects and visuals, creating an illustrated thesaurus, and organizing simple paragraph writing.

TABLE 4.1 Quick Assessment Scale of Oral ELD

Level	Stage	Duration	Descriptors of Student Behaviors
1	Beginning	< 6 months	▲ May remain silent/active listening ▲ Uses gestures to convey a message ▲ Yes/no responses predominantly ▲ Speaks 1–2 word phrases ▲ Follows oral directions when modeled
2	Early Intermediate	3 months to 1 year	▲ Speaks simple sentences (limited to simple present and past tense) ▲ Responds to an open-ended question ▲ Retells events (from personal experience or in stories) ▲ Reads basic vocabulary ▲ May read simple sentences ▲ Frequent grammatical errors in speech (confuses he/she and him/her; infrequent use of irregular verb tenses)
3	Intermediate	2 to 3 years	▲ Retells events using descriptive vocabulary ▲ Summarizes narrative accounts ▲ Identifies main ideas ▲ Provides details orally ▲ Makes comparisons ▲ Identifies and defines new vocabulary orally ▲ Relies on illustrations for context clues in reading
4	Early Advanced	3 to 4 years	▲ Appears to be orally fluent ▲ Uses discipline-specific academic terminology (e.g., mathematics: numerator/denominator) ▲ Near grade-level proficiency in academic areas
5	Advanced	> 3 years	▲ Paraphrases/synthesizes content material ▲ Generates discussions ▲ Socially comfortable ▲ Understands jokes/ plays on words ▲ Grade-level proficiency in academic areas

(Boyd-Batstone, 2006)

Jackie's Experience as an Intermediate English Learner

Jackie, a third grader whose writing appeared at the beginning of this chapter, also fit the Intermediate stage of proficiency. She retold events using descriptive vocabulary, summarized narrative accounts, identified main ideas, provided details orally, made comparisons, identified and defined new vocabulary orally, and relied on illustrations for context clues in reading.

Jackie drafted "The Fearsome Crowned Eagle" (see Figures 4.1 and 4.2) as a response to her reading about animals in tropical rain forests. Her writing was then turned into a book, which she illustrated, bound, and donated to the school library for

TABLE 4.2 Quick Assessment of Two English Learners: Juan and Eduardo

	Juan *Early Intermediate*	Eduardo *Intermediate*
Descriptors of Student Behaviors	▲ Speaks simple sentences (limited to simple present and past tense) ▲ Responds to an open-ended question ▲ Retells events (from personal experience or in stories) ▲ Reads basic vocabulary ▲ May read simple sentences ▲ Frequent grammatical errors in speech (confuses he/she and him/her; infrequent use of irregular verb tenses)	▲ Retells events using descriptive vocabulary ▲ Summarizes narrative accounts ▲ Identifies main ideas ▲ Provides details orally ▲ Makes comparisons
Recommended Teacher Strategies	▲ Preteach key vocabulary in stories prior to reading, using real objects and visuals ▲ Guide process writing in response to stories with prewriting, clustering ideas to form a simple paragraph	▲ Explore multiple ways to express the same ideas using expanded vocabulary ▲ Use a variety of graphic organizers to encourage making comparisons ▲ Demonstrate outlining techniques
Recommended Student Activities	▲ Identify and illustrate key vocabulary in stories ▲ Create an illustrated thesaurus, use word webs with a key word at the center and similar words and illustrations surrounding it ▲ Use teacher-guided charts of prewriting to write a simple 3–4 sentence paragraph in response to a story	▲ Develop and maintain an individual thesaurus ▲ Write multiple-paragraph comparisons of characters, personal associations, or contrast two or more stories ▲ Use graphic organizers to create an outline with a logical flow

other students to check out. The student-made book was not the only product of her work; she also developed her language and literacy. The numerous experiences of listening, speaking, reading, and writing, as well as drawing, painting, and word processing, all contributed to developing her language and literacy (Gallas, 1994). Her work was part of a Literature Circle sequence that involved reading, conversing with others in a conference, and working in collaboration with classmates in a small group.

FIGURE 4.1 Jackie's Cluster of the Fearsome Crowned Eagle. Note the efferent reading.

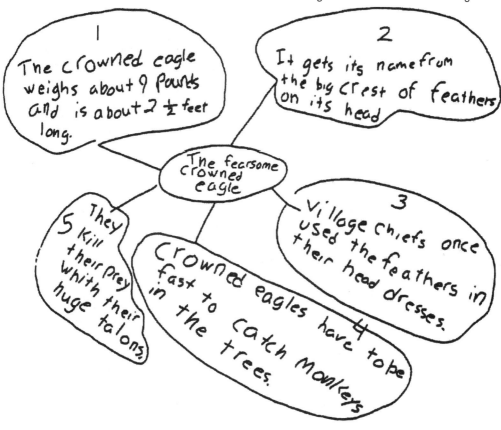

FIGURE 4.2 Jackie's Second Cluster of the Fearsome Crowned Eagle. Note the aesthetic reading.

Jackie's experience took place in a student-centered classroom environment structured for students to read quality literature, discuss ideas with students and teacher, and respond creatively to their thinking. Jackie's responses emerged out of her own experience and out of the multiple worlds she inhabited as a child growing and learning in two languages. Differentiated instruction demands that the teacher be prepared to respond to guide students through dialogue, act on their aesthetic responses (Rosenblatt, 1986), develop their language and literacy, and organize the presentation of their work for other students and parents. In broad terms, the components of Literature Circles with English learners involve (a) planning, (b) grouping, (c) conferencing, (d) developing a Literature Circle outline, and (e) differentiating instruction and assessment.

Included under these broad categories are practical concerns of the classroom teacher, such as establishing calendars and schedules, determining what literacy options the teacher must have at-the-ready to develop primary and second language and literacy, identifying what essential materials must be on hand, judging what computer software is useful for student authors, choosing and using quality literature, conducting initial literature conferences, using open-ended questions strategically, tugging at metaphors, generating writing with collaborative color maps, conducting subsequent literature conferences, coordinating group presentations, and assessing student work.

Jackie and her classmates engaged their minds in a wide range of experiences with reading, writing, and creative projects. They explored their imaginations and expressed their ideas about their reading. As their teacher, I did not take a back seat in the process but played multiple roles in the classroom: co-researcher, editor, project consultant, and at times mediator of disputes. My role as teacher was fluid, however, so I could move off-center and share these roles with my students. Conventional classrooms, characterized by teachers following scripted guides, cannot allow for this kind of flexibility and power sharing. Student-centered classrooms make teachers and students authors of their own literacy development as they choose their reading, generate ideas and create imaginative projects in a literature conference, write to express themselves, and finally make a presentation to classmates and parents.

LITERATURE CIRCLES WITH ENGLISH LEARNERS

All Literature Circles involve instructional schedules that progressively increase self-direction. However, in Literature Circles with English learners, the degree of that self-direction is influenced by the language level of the individual child. Other differences in such areas as management and conferencing techniques are also discussed here.

Scheduling

Planning for Literature Circles consists of scheduling and preparing for management of the entire process. Here you will find three kinds of schedules that range from an academic-year scope and sequence for long-term direction, to a 6-week Literature Circle planner, to a week-long schedule.

Academic-Year Scope and Sequence

The academic-year scope and sequence provided in Table 4.3 divides the school year into five phases. Note that specific calendar dates are not written into the scope and

TABLE 4.3 The Academic-Year Scape and Sequence

Round	Duration	Teacher Role	Student Role
1	3–4 weeks	▲ Select one book with multiple copies for each student to read ▲ Assign student to three small groups ▲ Conduct conferences with each group, using open-ended questions about the book	▲ Read the same book as others in group ▲ Produce two process-writing pieces, a group poem, and a painting based on the book ▲ Present finished work to classmates
2	3–4 weeks	▲ Select three books for students to choose to read ▲ Negotiate the groups so that the numbers are manageable in each group ▲ Conduct conferences with each group ▲ Organize rotation for presentation	▲ Choose to read one of three books ▲ Select related books for additional reading ▲ Form groups according to selection ▲ Produce two to three process-writing pieces, poetry, and an open-ended creative project ▲ Present to classmates
3	6 weeks	▲ Limit to four to six groups ▲ Establish a classroom criterion for forming groups (e.g., ratio of boys and girls) ▲ Conduct conferences ▲ Coordinate presentations	▲ Vote on what books are to be read ▲ Choose additional reading ▲ Negotiate the formation of groups around the books selected ▲ Present work to classmates and parents
4	6 weeks	▲ Limit to six groups ▲ Maintain grouping criteria ▲ Conduct conferences ▲ Coordinate presentations	▲ Nominate and vote on books ▲ Select related reading ▲ Negotiate small groups ▲ Produce four process-writing pieces, two poems or songs, and two or three creative projects ▲ Present work to classmates and parents
5 and beyond	6 weeks	▲ Turn over self-selection and grouping to students ▲ Consult with students in conferences ▲ Assist in coordinating the presentations	▲ Self-select books ▲ Negotiate groups around common Interest in books individuals may choose not to be part of a group and work by themselves ▲ Produce own literature plan with a minimum of three written pieces, two poems or songs, and a creative project may appear to be requiring less than the previous round, but projects tend to be more involved and lengthier at this point ▲ Present work in the school auditorium for parents and other classes

sequence and the total number of weeks does not add up to a complete academic year. There is an element of flexibility built into this scope and sequence because each school has its own unique scheduling issues. It was generally my experience as a classroom teacher that the first 2 to 3 weeks of a school year were settling-in times for stabilizing enrollments, establishing routines, and creating a classroom community. The scope and sequence would not begin until that settling-in period is over. Additionally, holiday planning and winter and spring breaks need to be taken into account to match the school calendar. And the final weeks of a school year usually are comprised of special activities that may preclude Literature Circles.

The reason for a scope and sequence is to move the students to an ever-increasing level of responsibility for self-direction. For example, you will see that in the first two phases the book selection and grouping of students are directly controlled by the teacher. In Phases 3 and 4, the teacher coordinates the selection and grouping processes, while in Phase 5 and beyond, the teacher assists and acts as a resource for the Literature Circles.

The 6-Week Planner

The 6-week planner in Table 4.4 gives a detailed look at one phase of the Literature Circle's scope and sequence. Week 1 is crucial for selecting titles for reading, forming small groups, assigning roles within the groups, creating organizing materials, and conducting that crucial first small-group conference that sets the Literature Circle in motion. Weeks 2 to 4 are the heart of the Literature Circle, in which students engage in discussion with regular conferences, think creatively, write in response to their story, and develop their small group's Literature Circle plan. Week 5 is a time for finishing teacher- and student-initiated projects and planning for presenting completed work. Week 6 is a celebration of student work and ideas with small-group and whole-group presentations. Family members are invited to attend, and students assess their own work as well as that of their classmates.

The Week-Long Schedule

The week-long schedule provided in Table 4.5 gives an example of a typical week in my classroom. You will see that the morning was prime time for instruction with Literature Circles. I found that if I planned instruction by the week in alignment with the 6-week planner and the academic-year scope and sequence, I planned much more efficiently than if I attempted to stay a day ahead of my classroom. The subject areas in the week-long planner are purposefully general in order to allow for rearranging the schedule. For example, I would conduct whole-group teacher-directed instruction to address specific skills required by state standards or by the observed needs of the students. Individual needs are better addressed in small-group conferences.

Management

Management styles differ from classroom to classroom. In keeping with a spirit of discovery and self-direction, I strove to develop a system that gave progressively more responsibility to the students.

TABLE 4.4 6-Week Planner

Week 1	▲ Students select books or stories in consultation with teacher. ▲ Students and teacher form literature groups around selected books or stories. ▲ Students choose a liaison for each group.	▲ Students make folders. ▲ Teacher provides reading journals.	▲ Teacher meets with each group to start first writing assignment. ▲ Teacher makes color map for collaborative writing.
Weeks 2–4	*Writing* ▲ Teacher conducts whole-group lesson on peer editing. ▲ Students engage in peer editing of first drafts. ▲ Teacher reviews writing, grades final drafts, records in grade book and on reader's folder. ▲ Students produce three or four pieces of written expression.	*Poetry/Music* ▲ Students select appropriate poetry or music to accompany the book or story they are reading. ▲ Students reproduce poetry or music artistically for display and/or performance. ▲ Students individually, collaboratively, or with the teacher compose one or two original pieces of music or poetry.	*Creative Ideas* ▲ Students develop a creative project to express the story within the realm of the visual/performing arts (e.g., painting, sculpture, drama, dance). ▲ Students create a project to connect the story to other areas of the curriculum such as science, social studies, or mathematics in consultation with teacher. ▲ Students and teacher develop computer hypertext versions of the story.
Week 5	▲ Teacher and students plan presentation. ▲ Students assign roles and responsibilities. ▲ Teacher schedules order of group presentations.	▲ Students finish writing, poetry, music, creative ideas. ▲ Students organize folder of completed work.	▲ Students write an invitation to parents. ▲ Teacher sends home parent invitations. ▲ Student literature groups conduct rehearsals.
Week 6	▲ Teacher sets up classroom in stations for group presentations. ▲ Teacher checks to make sure all groups have necessary props and materials to conduct their presentations.	▲ Students conduct group presentations. ▲ Students read individual written work in rotations. ▲ Students conduct whole-group collaborative presentations of artwork and creative projects.	▲ Students evaluate group presentation (self-assessment and/or group evaluation). ▲ Teacher conducts oral whole-group discussion. ▲ Students complete written evaluations of all presentations. ▲ Teacher and students select work for portfolios—one or two pieces that reflect academic progress.

TABLE 4.5 Week-Long Schedule in a Third-Grade Classroom

Time	Monday	Tuesday	Wednesday	Thursday	Friday
8:30–8:45	Opening/ roll	Opening/ roll	Opening/ roll	Opening/ roll	Opening/ roll
8:45–9:40	Read aloud	Read aloud	Read aloud	Read aloud	Read aloud
9:40–10:10	Journals/ shared reading	Journals/ shared reading	Journals/ shared reading	Journals/ shared reading	Journals/ shared reading
10:10–10:25	Recess ——→				
10:25–12:00	Literature conferences, collaborative color mapping	Literature conferences, collaborative color mapping	Literature conferences, editing and revising	Literature conferences, editing and revising	Literature conferences, exploring creative ideas
12:00–12:40	Lunch ———→				
12:40–1:40	Math/science Instruction	Social studies Instruction	Math/science Instruction	Social studies Instruction	Math/science Instruction
1:40–2:00	Recess ——→				
2:00–2:45	Math/science Instruction	Physical education	Math/science Instruction	Physical education	Math/science Instruction

Fostering Self-Direction

Managing Literature Circles in which instruction is differentiated necessitates fostering self-direction and providing materials for students to organize their work. For most teachers, the thought of elementary students selecting their own books to read suggests confusion and chaos. Trying to manage more than three reading groups is nightmarish for teachers in conventional classrooms; the last thing teachers want to give up is classroom control. In conventional classrooms, students are rewarded for compliance, rather than for self-direction and intrinsic motivation. Generally, students are trained to wait for the teacher's direction before proceeding. As a result, a process of unlearning must take place before students can accept the responsibility of self-direction. However, this responsibility can be easily fostered in such a way as to lessen the stress of the teacher as well. During each round of Literature Circles, I incrementally relinquished more control to the students (see again Table 4.3). But if I needed to step in and take back control, I did.

CHOOSING AND USING LITERATURE   Choosing and using literature implies that the students have available to them a vast array of engaging books. It is vital that the books capture the students' imaginations. Self-selection is key to the beginning of a literature group because it acknowledges the student as an active participant in the learning. Furthermore, students given the opportunity to choose their own literature develop an intrinsic motivation toward their schoolwork. Allowing students to self-select their own reading is an act of trust that builds a student-centered learning environment. It says to the students that their choices can be very good ones for themselves and that their ideas are valuable as well.

In the past, I took all the initiative in forming groups according to ability levels and the stories as sequenced in the literary readers. I planned the projects and activities the students were required to do. But I also spent an inordinate amount of time managing the behaviors of students expressing resistance to my own "neat" ideas. They forced me to rethink the underlying assumptions of my transmission mode of teaching and showed me that their ideas and interests were advancing the goals of language and academic content development. As I began to look to the students' interests in their reading, I found myself questioning the arbitrariness of my criteria for grouping. And as the students demonstrated that I could trust their judgment, I progressively turned over much of the decision process to them.

HOLDING STUDENT COURT.   Frequently in classrooms of English learners, disputes arise because of misunderstood language and/or cultural transgressions. This is normal, but without a system to safely address differing opinions, chaos can ensue. Classrooms function best when students take responsibility for their own learning behaviors. Therefore, I developed a student court that convened once a week for about 30 minutes to address any and all issues that arose in class. Over time the court evolved into an entire classroom management system that utilized listening, speaking, reading, and writing. The court had a community-building effect because it also became a safe way for boys and girls to compliment and thank one another for good work or assistance. Through the court, for example, a boy could write a thank-you note to a girl or boy who had helped him with his work. It would be read aloud by the elected judges so that the student that provided the helping hand would be acknowledged. And there would not be any reprisals for saying a nice word to a classmate of a different gender.

A typical student court session would go as follows: During the course of the week students would write down on half sheets of paper their compliments or complaints. They were encouraged to compliment or complain about anything or anyone, including the teacher and the administration. They simply had to put it in writing. (This technique eliminated tattletales in my classroom.) Once the compliment or complaint was written, the student would draw a happy face on the compliment or a sad face on the complaint and would give it to the judge with a two-pocket folder for safekeeping until court was in session.

The judge with the folder would begin a court session by reading the compliments. All four judges would decide whether the compliments merited more than group acknowledgment. In some cases, the judges would ask me to write a note to the parents of a particularly thoughtful student. The compliments were followed by a reading of the complaints. After each complaint was read, two other judges would ask questions like "When/where did this take place?" "Were there any witnesses?" "What did you do?" The fourth judge would monitor the discussion and say whose turn it was to speak. When the discussion seemed to have taken its course, I would intervene and ask the judges, "Do you need more information?" If the answer was yes, I would help them form questions to get the needed information. If the answer was no, I would say, "OK, judges, make a decision." They had the authority to give a warning, require time out, take away a recess, add points to the classroom behavior chart, request that the teacher write a note to parents, and even send a student to the office to meet with the principal.

I knew the system was working when students mustered up the courage to take me, the teacher, to court. In fact, I was summoned to court regularly for raising my voice unnecessarily or for overstepping my authority as a teacher. When I was taken to court, the judges would have me put my head down during recess, which in all honesty I enjoyed. Sometimes, they would write notes to my wife, Nancy, which she particularly enjoyed responding to. She would tell the students that she gave me a stern talking to and sent me to bed early that night and that if the problem happened again, they should feel free to contact her. Although this sounds lighthearted, it had a miraculous effect on the classroom. It freed me to teach and put the responsibility on us all to behave.

For English learners, the student court had wonderful benefits. Students were required to write authentically. If the compliment or complaint was illegible, the court would throw it out. So it was common for students to help each other with grammar and spelling as they wrote their submissions to the court. Another benefit for English learners was that the court gave them a safe way to respond to perceived insults or disrespect due to differences in language or culture. Rather than reacting in the moment, students developed the habit of saying, "I'm taking you to court." It gave them space to get out of a potentially heated situation by writing about it, and often it allowed the perpetrator to rectify the situation by clarifying the words or apologizing for an unintended offense. It was very common in court to hear the judge begin to read a complaint and have the author of the complaint say, "It's solved." Figure 4.3 summarizes the structure and process of our student court.

Three Ways to Differentiate

Differentiation can be thought of in several ways—teacher managed, student initiated, and product driven. A teacher who attempts to be the sole manager of differentiated instruction can go a little crazy with the micromanaging of content and strategies. On the other hand, a teacher who attempts to turn over all responsibility for learning to the students may encounter a chaotic mess of a classroom. There needs to be a system for collaboration. I advocate a blend of three ways to differentiate.

▲ *Teacher-managed differentiation:* Ultimately, the teacher is responsible for instruction. The teacher decides what is taught and to whom, what strategies are applied and for whom. However, successful management of differentiation requires collaboration with the students.

▲ *Student-initiated differentiation:* Fostering self-direction is a way to develop natural differentiation of instruction. When a teacher manages the classroom to foster self-direction, the students can choose from an array of appropriate instructional activities matched to language levels. Ideally this takes place in a response-oriented context in which students have a voice in how they will create a response to reading, for example.

▲ *Product-driven differentiation:* When differentiation is driven by student products, it clarifies and simplifies how to accommodate instruction. A teacher can use the same content standards in a diverse group but make

FIGURE 4.3 Student Court

Materials
▲ Poster stating how to write a compliment or complaint
▲ Basket for paper and pencils
▲ Ample supply of half sheets of paper
▲ Plenty of sharpened pencils
▲ A two-pocket folder for holding compliments and complaints

Personnel
Four student judges, gender balanced (2 girls/2 boys)

Judges' Roles
▲ Collection and reading of compliments and/or complaints (1 judge)
▲ Decide whose turn to speak in court (1 judge)
▲ Ask clarifying questions (2 judges)
▲ Render a decision (all judges)

Teacher's Role
▲ Validate the process
▲ Ensure a weekly time to convene
▲ Maintain access to writing materials
▲ Assist in court proceedings
▲ Help carry out court decisions
▲ Call monthly elections for student judges

Procedure
▲ Students elect four judges.
▲ Judges decide what roles each will take on.
▲ As situations arise that call for the court's attention, students write down their compliments or complaints and submit them to the designated student judge.
▲ At a specified time each week, the student court, convenes, allowing 20–30 minutes.
▲ The court begins by reading compliments (judges may assign class rewards).
▲ Complaints are read next.
▲ One judge decides whose turn it is to speak; two judges ask questions.
▲ Teacher asks whether the judges need more information. If yes, the process continues. If no, the teacher calls for a decision.
▲ Four judges convene and make a decision.

Court Rules
▲ Compliments and complaints must be in writing.
▲ No one may use the court to shame another person.
▲ Students can complain about anyone or anything, including the teacher and administration.
▲ Students may speak only when it is their turn.
▲ Everyone must listen when someone else has the floor.
▲ A judge may not rule on a decision if he or she is a subject of the complaint.
▲ Judges that are irresponsible and/or misuse the court process will be impeached.

accommodations for what students will do to demonstrate their understanding. Rubric assessment facilitates product-driven differentiation. For example, a diverse group can conduct a character study, and each student can produce a written product according to his or her language level. Students at Beginning and Early Intermediate stages may compose a paragraph collaboratively on a chart, students at an Intermediate stage can write a paragraph with the aide of a graphic organizer, and students at Early Advanced and Advanced stages can write a multiparagraph study with the help of a graphic organizer. With three different rubrics that are matched to levels of English language proficiency, all students can participate in a character study while they produce appropriately leveled products.

Materials for Literature Circles

Just as the teacher must be equipped with a full set of language and literacy development options and sources, the classroom must be equipped with the materials and tools necessary for active learning. These materials and tools must be readily available so that students can follow their creative impulses. A teacher who has to go through an elaborate ritual of preparation cannot be very responsive to students.

Language and Literacy Sources

In a student-centered classroom, the teacher looks beyond the literary reader for sources of language and literacy development. Those sources can be drawn from written texts, as well as from visual performing arts media. As Table 4.6 indicates, the student-centered teacher has access to a tremendous number of possibilities.

Tools

Acquiring classroom materials used to be one of the more problematic issues I faced as a teacher until I began to look at the students as one of my greatest resources. Early on, I would scrounge or spend my own money to get what the students needed. But when I began to put the responsibility back on the students, the acquiring of materials became an opportunity for developing literacy and self-direction.

As an example, when a group of students wanted to put on a puppet show for the class and I did not have a puppet theater in the classroom, we sat down together and tried to figure out what to do. We talked about how the teacher across the hall had a beautiful puppet theater but was unwilling to lend it to another classroom. One student suggested building a puppet theater, but I suggested that we didn't have enough time before the performance date. Then Ernesto, one student in the group, suggested that the principal might be able to help out. So I recommended that the group draft a letter to the principal, requesting his help in obtaining a puppet theater.

The principal sent a memo back to the students, saying he would be delighted to help. He knew of another teacher with a puppet theater who was willing to let us borrow it. He would ask the custodian to move it, but he needed

TABLE 4.6 Language Arts for English Learners

Language and Literacy Sources	Supports	Possible Student Products
Songs	Story ladders	Anecdotes
Guest speakers	Story maps	Questionnaires
Video/films/laser disks	Venn diagrams, T-graphs	Labels, advertisements
Drama	Brainstorming	Rules/directions
Concerts	Sorting/listing	Greeting cards
Spoken recordings	Categorizing	Personal letters
Experiments	Outlining	Personal experiences
Photographs	Clustering	Cartoon captions
Posters	Charting	Poems
Bumper stickers	Word webbing	Reports
Drawings	Summarizing	Recipes
Literature	Journals, diaries, logs	Family histories
Newspapers	Notes	
Magazines		
Comics		
Articles		
Plays		
Essays		
Diaries		

Draft copy from the *Language Arts Framework for California*, February 1995.

more information as to when and where the performance would take place. The students responded to the principal by writing another letter with the date, time, and location of the show.

The show time drew close, and no puppet theater appeared. The students, a bit dismayed, came to me for help. My only advice was to send off a quick note to the principal, asking him to follow through on his promise to provide the theater. Needless to say, I was concerned at this point. The principal, however, immediately came to the room and began apologizing to me. I said that he needed to talk with the students as a group, and not to me. Then he gathered the group together and explained the oversight, apologized, and promised to provide the theater as soon as possible.

Within 5 minutes, the custodian arrived carrying a magnificent puppet theater on a dolly. But before the students began their production, we took a moment to reflect on the strategic use of correspondence to the right person and the effectiveness of holding that person, even the principal, accountable for his or her promises. We obtained a puppet theater, but the students also learned the power of written communication and how it can work for them to meet their needs.

Acquiring materials is not always that elaborate. Nevertheless, students are capable of obtaining what they need. Even if we needed a ream of writing paper, a school-supplied item, I asked the students to write letters of request to the office. If we needed cloth or some non-school-supplied item, I asked the students to think about where to get it and from whom to request it. It may have meant writing to parents, businesses, or community agencies, but what it really meant was that the students were learning how literacy worked for them and how to get what they needed.

The following is a list of materials and tools to keep on hand for ready student access:

1. *Writing materials:* Pencils, erasers, scratch paper, red pencils (for peer editing), lined newsprint for initial draft writing, white lined paper for final drafts, ballpoint pens, chart paper (for collaborative writing)

2. *Word processing and authoring tools software:* Inspiration, Kidspiration KidPix, PrintShop Deluxe, Storybook Weaver

3. *Drawing materials:* Colored pencils, pens, felt-tip markers, crayons, drawing paper, construction paper, chalk pastels

4. *Painting materials:* Tempera, acrylic, and watercolor paints; class sets of large-, medium-, and fine-tipped brushes; watercolor paper; easel paper; butcher paper for murals; sponges; drop cloths

5. *Clay and pottery materials:* Modeling clay, water trays, waxed paper, cellophane, rolling pins, objects for texturing and scrolling designs

6. *Papier-mâché materials:* Wheat paste, large mixing bucket, instant papier-mâché, water trays, masking tape, wire mesh, toilet paper rolls

7. *Mask-, hat-, and puppet-making materials:* Scissors, glue, hole punch, paper plates, ribbon, yarn, construction paper, felt cloth, socks, buttons, sewing needles, thread, tongue depressors

Reading Journals

A reading journal, a small composition notebook for note taking and reflecting, provides each students with a space for written reflection after reading a section or chapter in his or her book. Many teachers have students divide the page into two columns, one side for taking notes of events and characters, the other side for more reflective comments and insights into the reading. The note-taking side of the page can be seen, in reader-response terms, as the more efferent, or informational, reading of a text. The other side of the page is much more personal and reflective, evidence of a more aesthetic reading of the text. I also ask that students bring their reading journals to literature conferences for note taking during group discussion.

Involving family members in an English learner's education poses unique challenges. Not only does a difference in language pose a challenge, but immigrant families, especially from poor rural areas, may not be literate even in their own language. This is where journaling can help. I recommend that students take their journals home and read them to their parents on a weekly basis. Parents are informed that their role is to listen to their children read and then respond to the journal either in writing or orally. Parental response, minimally, is to ask two or three questions. Ideally, parents write a response in the journal that includes some questions; but even if the parents are not literate, they can listen and ask some questions. Parents are encouraged to share insights and tell their own stories. This

FIGURE 4.4 Directions for Making a Literature Folder

1. Begin with two 12 x 18-inch sheets of construction paper.

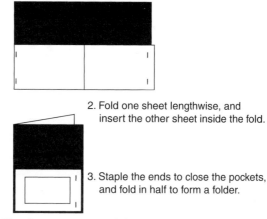

2. Fold one sheet lengthwise, and insert the other sheet inside the fold.

3. Staple the ends to close the pockets, and fold in half to form a folder.

4. Glue the progress record sheet to the front of the folder.

simple technique taps into the English learner's home. It informs the classroom teacher about the student's sociocultural knowledge and informs parents about literacy development at school. More importantly, it fosters a dialogue between home and school. I once had a parent stop me after school to ask me what we were doing in class because the previous night they had stayed up late telling each other family ghost stories in response to the student's journal writing that had mentioned a ghost in her reading.

Literature Folders and Home Reading Logs

In addition to a copy of the book or story for reading, students were given a literature folder to hold their written work and a reading journal. The folder was simply made of two sheets of 12 × 18-inch construction paper. One sheet was folded lengthwise, the other was placed inside the fold, the ends were stapled, and the whole thing was folded in half to form a folder with pockets inside and outside to hold the student's written work (see Figure 4.4).

Glued to the front of the folder was a half sheet of paper that I called a Progress Record Sheet. It contained a list of the expected written and creative projects each member was required to complete, a box for the date of completion, and a box for the grade (see Figure 4.5). The Progress Record Sheet keeps both the teacher and the student informed at a glance as to the progress of the group and of the individual student so that all parties are clear about what has to be accomplished. In this way, students are able to pursue their work on their own with minimal consultation.

The Home Reading Log is another simple form, one that helps parents monitor their child's reading habits and also provides a record for teachers of how much home reading is occurring. The form is illustrated a little later in the chapter.

FIGURE 4.5 Cover Sheet for Literature Folder

Progress Record Sheet

Name _____

Literature Studies Book Title _____

By _____

A. Writing

Title		Done	Grade
1.			
2.			
3.			
4.			

B. Poetry/music

1.			
2.			

C. Creative Ideas

1.			
2.			

D. Presentation
Describe Responsibilities

1.			

Conferencing with Small Groups

Conferencing is simply meeting with a small group and discussing a piece of litera-ture. The focus of the discussion is the students' responses to the literature, rather than their answers to predetermined questions about the story. All have an equal voice in the discussion, making it a safe arena to try out new ideas and tentative thoughts to see how they fly.

Grouping Strategies

There is no hard and fast rule about forming small groups. Rather than forming groups by an arbitrary decision, such as balancing ability levels, I preferred to ask students to form their own groups around books they wanted to read to-gether. I did ask that each group reflect the ratio of boys to girls that was in the classroom. For example, if 18 boys and 12 girls made up a class of 30 students, the ratio of boys to girls would be 3 to 2. Allowing for a range of groups, I would then ask that a group of 5 or 6 students have a minimum of 3 boys and 2 girls. Although groups could range in size from 4 to 8 students, in some cases I en-couraged highly motivated individuals to work by themselves. If 10 to 12 stu-dents were interested in the same book, I asked them to split to form two groups. Aside from that constraint, the students were free to form their groups around a captivating story.

The process of choosing literature and forming groups usually took a class period, or about 1 hour of sometimes serious negotiating. During that hour, the students had access to every book in the classroom. I explained that they were to look for a book with multiple copies so that each member had one to read. As students browsed through the books, I moved through the classroom and made suggestions, gave advice, and answered questions about the books.

Group Process

Once a group took form, its members decided on one member to be a group liaison, who voiced problems and concerns from the group to the teacher and from the teacher back to the group. The liaison also assisted the teacher with handing out materials and took a lead role in disseminating messages back to the group.

With the book selected and the liaison decided on, the students began to read. They may have read as a whole group taking turns or in pairs. If the pair was comprised of two skilled readers, they took turns leap-frogging through the text. If, however, one student struggled more with reading, he or she was to read with a more proficient reader; but instead of leap-frogging through the story, the more proficient reader read a sentence or two and the less proficient reader followed by reading the same sentence or two that had just been read. I asked any paraprofessionals or parent volunteers in the classroom to sit with a group or with an individual student needing special attention and to read the story aloud with dramatic emphasis. Then the students followed by rereading the story in pairs. Each student was also asked to read the story at home with an adult and was given a form to have signed as proof of having read for homework (see Figure 4.6).

FIGURE 4.6 Home Reading Log

Home Reading Log				
Name _____			Classroom _____	
Day	Date	Title of book and pages read	# of minutes read	Signature of adult
Mon				
Tue				
Wed				
Thu				
Fri				
Sat				
Sun				

The First Literature Conference

There were three goals for the first literature conference: (a) to reread the story or a portion of the story, (b) to connect with the group liaison, and (c) to engage the story in such a way as to provide direction for the first writing project. Once those tasks were completed, the group was on its own for the next day to work on writing. An initial conference lasted about 20 to 30 minutes. It was my goal to meet with half of the groups within the first 90 minutes of the Literature Circle time.

It was my experience that students at earlier stages of language proficiency might avoid writing unless nudged to start with collaborative writing, which encompasses listening, speaking, reading, and writing in a single activity. As a rule of thumb, I insisted that we begin with a collaborative writing assignment so that the fundamentals of language and literacy were addressed from the outset.

Subsequent conferences tended to be more open to the direction of the group's interest and less structured by time constraints. A group might choose to compose a poem or a song, generate another writing assignment, or come up with an idea for a creative project.

Ongoing Literature Conferences

Several aspects of reader response were at the forefront of my mind when I was in a conference with a group of students. First, I used open-ended questions to allow students to share their experiences, thoughts, and feelings related to a work of literature. Second, I listened for students to express metaphors, which function as windows into the aesthetic workings of their minds. Third, I guided collaborative writing by clustering students' words on chart paper and by organizing their thoughts with a color and number system that I call "color mapping."

OPEN-ENDED QUESTIONS.   A teacher's questions can either function as an open invitation to dialogue or act as a kind of check for correct answers. Open-ended questions invite students to share their thoughts. Closed questions have a predetermined answer in mind. Closed questions are useful for students at the early stages of language development to express themselves in single words and short phrases in their second language. With beginning English learners, open-ended questions are much more fruitful in the primary language, but this does not preclude their use. Reader response looks for the reader to share his or her insights, as tentative as they may be. Promoting self-expression is a valuable use of instructional time.

On occasion, my questions were very closed, and at times embarrassingly silly. One student, Daniela, taught me a vital lesson about my questions and their hidden assumptions. I had never considered Daniela to be one of my brightest students, but she taught me that an appropriate open-ended question can make a world of difference in affirming the unique intelligence of each student.

One day in February, I tried to initiate a discussion for an English language development lesson about George Washington. I asked, "Who was Martha Washington's husband?"—a poorly thought-out question, at best. Why that silly question occurred to me, I'll never know. Even more perplexing, what did I expect to accomplish by asking such a question? Was I hoping to trick the students? Was I looking to display my own knowledge? Was I looking to expose what I considered to be their lack of knowledge?

Daniela immediately raised her hand and blurted out, "Martin Luther King!"

Her answer to my question made me think that she was not going to catch on, yet it made me begin observing her more closely to figure out what was going on in her mind. I noticed that, during classroom discussions, she would often look up at the ceiling, her head would bob from side to side, and her mouth would move as if she were whispering a song to herself. I thought she was daydreaming and not paying attention to the lesson, but then I wondered whether something else was going on inside her head.

Finally, the day came when I asked a much more intelligent question. We were studying whales (*ballenas*, in Spanish). In their reading, the students found that whales communicated with each other through song and body movement. The whales slap their fins and their tails on the surface of the water to announce danger; they raise their heads out of the water and move them back and forth when in distress. In the middle of the discussion, I looked at Daniela; sure enough, she was looking at the ceiling, wagging her head, and mouthing some words to herself. I asked her a very simple and open-ended question. "Daniela, what are you thinking?"

This time, she spouted, *"¡Baila la ballena* (Dance the whale)!"

Another student suggested that it sounded like "La Bamba," the famous Mexican dance song. Before I knew it, the group had reproduced the lesson about whales as a song to the tune of "La Bamba."

La Ballena

Baila la ballena, baila la ballena, baila la ballena …
Para bailar la ballena, para bailar la ballena
se necesita una ballena grande,
una ballena grande y otra chiquita.
Ay arriba, ay arriba iré …
Yo no soy marinero, yo no soy marinero,
Soy capitán, soy capitán.
Por ti seré por ti seré

Para comunicar un mensaje
a las ballenitas
hay que mover la cabecita
y mover la colita.

Bamba, bamba . . .

The Whale

Dance the whale, dance the whale, dance the whale . . .
To dance the whale, to dance the whale
you first need a great big whale,
a great big whale and a small one, too.
Kick it up, kick it up I'll go . . .
I'm not just a sailor, I'm not just a sailor,

I'm your captain, I'm your captain.
For you I'll be, for you I'll be.

In order to send a message
to the dear whales,
you must move your head
and move your tails.

Bamba, bamba . . .

I realized that day that Daniela had a gift. She was very talented at putting words together in creative, poetic ways. Thinking back to when I had asked my closed question about Martha Washington, I realized that she was responding to the question on a more aesthetic level. She was playing with the words. As she looked up at the ceiling and wagged her head, she mouthed the words back and forth: Martin/Martha. In a word, Daniela was a poet. She was an unrecognized poet however, because I had not recognized her gift. I could not see it until I began to listen openly for her aesthetic response.

Louise Rosenblatt's (1986) theory of reader response speaks to this very situation. Reader-response theory recognizes that all readers bring something to their reading, that each person reads a text or situation through the lens of his or her own experience. It is the teacher's responsibility to find that "live wire" in each student and to connect instruction to it via the student's knowledge and experience.

In terms of Daniela, her live wire was tapped when I, as the teacher, became open to her way of thinking. When she took an active role in the lesson about whales, her learning increased, and the entire class benefited from her creative contribution. In other words, a transaction took place as she participated in mutually defining the lesson on whales. It took the simple act of asking an open-ended question and then listening for and responding to her wordplay and metaphor.

The way teachers use questions is an issue of thinking, knowledge, and empowerment. The extent to which students are heard and responded to indicates how thinking, knowledge, and power are shared in the classroom. It is an issue of thinking because it concerns inquiry into the ideas of all students; an issue of knowledge—that is, *whose* knowledge is invited into the classroom setting and *whose* knowledge is silenced at school; and an issue of power—that is, *who* has the power to affect the instruction in the classroom. Designing questions to look for preprogrammed responses, on the one hand, assumes that only the instructor has the insight and power to establish the parameters of knowledge. Asking and responding to open-ended questions, on the other hand, creates an ambience of openness to the collective wisdom of the students through shared thinking, knowledge, and power.

I often used the simple phrase "Talk to me" to initiate a discussion about the story we were reading. Occasionally, a brief open-ended question, such as "What do you think about this character?" was all that was needed for a group of students to open their minds and imaginations. Once the students opened up, I started to listen for metaphors. Metaphors unify thinking and express deep insights. When a student displayed metaphorical thinking, I knew he or she had connected with the text through a live wire.

METAPHORS.   Ingmar Bergman (1960) described filmmaking in much the same way that transactional learning takes place in the classroom:

> A film for me begins with something very vague—a chance remark or a bit of conversation, a hazy but agreeable event unrelated to any particular situation . . . These are split-second impressions that disappear as quickly as they come, yet leave behind a mood—like pleasant dreams. It is a mental state, not an actual story, but one abounding in fertile associations and images. Most of all, it is a *brightly colored thread sticking out of the dark sack of the unconscious.* If I begin to wind up this thread, and do it carefully, a complete film will emerge. (p. 11)

Rich metaphors like "brightly colored thread" lead to the workings of the mind and heart. Tugging at that brightly colored thread—my students' metaphorical thinking—made teaching an enlightening experience. In a diverse classroom, even though students were quite fluent in English, the use of Spanish was not discouraged, especially when it helped provide the students and the teacher with multiple ways to tug at rich cultural metaphors. Metaphors emerged in English or in Spanish spontaneously and popped out unexpectedly. When those brightly colored threads popped out, they signaled an opportunity to tug at something deep in the minds and hearts of students.

The spontaneous nature of metaphors is illustrated by an interaction I had with a student. Before school one day, I was conducting my supervising duties on the playground. The night before, a storm had poured buckets of water on the city of Long Beach, leaving it washed clean. The morning was brilliant as the sun broke through the clouds. And like a flash flood, without warning metaphors spilled out and filled our conversations.

A Salvadoran boy named Santos, standing near me, squinted as he looked up at the sky and said, "*El sol está enojado hoydía* (The sun is angry today)."

Surprised at this statement, I asked, "*¿Por qué dices que está enojado el sol* (Why do you say that the sun is angry)?"

"*Porque,*" responded the boy, "*me está pegando como un gigante* (Because it is pounding me like a giant)."

This brief conversation gave me pause. As I looked up at the bright sky, I, too, was pelted in the eyes by the sun's intense fury. Santos, in a rather matter-of-fact way, described the morning with the vivid imagery of a poet. I thought of all the time I had unsuccessfully tried to teach lessons on personification, similes, and metaphors. And here, in a seemingly mundane conversation, a child was deftly applying personification to an angry sun and adding a simile "like a giant" pounding his club down on earth. I wondered whether my students talked like this very often. I discovered that I was not tuned in to their use of metaphor even though metaphorical thinking was present in their daily conversations.

Sharon L. Pugh (1992) affirmed that metaphorical thinking is not only a higher order thought process but also pervasive, powerful, and generally ignored:

> Through metaphorical thinking, divergent meanings become unified into the underlying patterns that constitute our conceptual understanding of reality. Indeed, metaphor is so much a part of our thinking and learning processes that we usually do not think about the essential role it plays. (p. 3)

Metaphorical thinking provides an open window into the way one sees the world. Tuning in to what students say metaphorically gives insight into their understanding and background knowledge. Scant education takes place with decontextualized instruction or learning situations that are foreign; building on students' prior knowledge is essential to effective differentiated instruction with English learners. Building instruction around the metaphorical thinking of English learners is a way of "tugging at" the cultural and personal understanding a bilingual student brings to schooling.

Another example of metaphorical thinking took place during a discussion of Lynne Cherry's (1990) fabulous book on the Brazilian rain forests, *The Great Kapok Tree.* I was conducting a conference in Spanish with a small group of students. In the book, a tree sloth tries to persuade a man not to cut down the kapok tree. In our previous conference, I had asked the group to find out what they could about tree sloths. Now they were sharing what they had researched: that the sloth sleeps 18 hours a day, that a newborn clings to its mother with its claws for the first 6 months of its life and that it then goes to live by itself in the canopy of the rain forest. Then, out of the blue, Adrianna looked at the illustration of the tree sloth and said, "*Tiene la cabeza de coco* (It has the head of a coconut)."

Delighted with this entrée into her way of seeing, I asked, "*¿Qué más tiene* (What else does it have)?"

She immediately responded with *"Tiene la nariz de chocolate"* and provided her own English translation: "It has a nose like a chocolate bar."

I continued to encourage this line of thinking: "*¿Y algo más* (And anything else)?"

At this point, the entire group jumped in with all kinds of similes about the tree sloth, comparing its eyes to coffee beans, its smile to a banana, its body to a melon. This led the group to compose an original song about the newly created fruit sloth:

La Perezosa de Fruta

La perezosa de fruta, la perezosa de fruta.
Tiene la cabeza de coco
Que nunca se puede abrir.

La perezosa de fruta, la perezosa de fruta
tiene el cuerpo de sandia
igual que un melón.

La perezosa de fruta, la perezosa de fruta
tiene la nariz de chocolate
que me gustaria comer.

(Coro)

La perezosa de fruta
tiene el cuerpo de fruta
todo el cuerpo de fruta
de la selva tropical.
Cha, cha, cha.

The fruit Sloth

The fruit sloth, the fruit sloth.
It has the head of a coconut
that can never, ever be opened.

The fruit sloth, the fruit sloth
has the body of a watermelon
just like a ripe melon.

The fruit sloth, the fruit sloth
has a chocolate nose
that I would love to eat.

(Chorus)

The fruit sloth
has a body of fruit
the entire body of fruit
from the tropical rain forest.
Cha, cha, cha.

The group did not stop there, however. They continued composing, in English, a song about the life and habitat of the tree sloth:

The Sloth

The sloth moves very slow
slowly moves the sloth.
The little baby sloth
holds its mother with its claws.

The sloth moves very slow,
slowly moves the sloth.
When it is 6 months old,
it finds a way to live alone.

The sloth moves very slow,
slowly moves the sloth.
High in the canopy
it moves from tree to tree.

(Chorus)

The sloth moves very slow,
slowly moves the sloth,
as slow as it can be,
as slow as it can go.

The students did not even stop at writing songs about the sloth in Spanish and English. The following day each one brought in a kind of fruit or edible item to cre-ate an actual fruit sloth. It had a coconut head, coffee bean eyes, a chocolate candy bar nose, a banana for a mouth, a large papaya body, cucumber arms, and green chili peppers for claws. That afternoon the entire class sang their praises of the sloth, and then we all shared in eating our metaphorical sloth and celebrating the students' ingenuity.

The centerpiece of the whole event was a work of art, a children's literature selection. The students experienced a delightful mix of reading, responding, researching, writing, sharing, creating, and making music. Their imaginations completed the circuit of Rosenblatt's live wire between a reader and a text. The meeting of their minds around an engaging story made for a juicier curriculum. It was an organic experience of teaching and learning, a two-way path to interpretation.

COLOR MAPPING FOR COLLABORATIVE WRITING. Metaphors, ideas, feelings, and thoughts tumble out of students' mouths randomly; they do not think in outline form. Even for native English speakers, the task of getting ordered thoughts on paper can at times be daunting, and for English learners, even more so. One of the most important jobs for a teacher is to model strategies for getting this jumble of language organized on paper.

In talking with professional writers, I have learned that many conceive of writing in two phases: (a) getting ideas on paper and (b) organizing the ideas into a publishable form. Getting ideas on paper is paramount. Without the substance of ideas, the stuff of meaning, there is nothing to organize into a publishable form. Temporarily setting aside a concern for writing conventions, form, and sentence order for even a few minutes helps ideas flow without obstruction. Once the ideas are on paper, it is an easy task to organize a well-ordered piece of writing. To accomplish this, I used what I called "color mapping" for collaborative writing. A *color map* is essentially a common clustering technique coupled with a color/number coding system to help organize the form and structure of dictated sentences.

During a conference with a group of students, I began by asking open-ended questions, I listened for metaphors, and when I sensed that the group was onto a big idea, I wrote down their words on the back of the Literature Plan chart paper. As was mentioned, their ideas appeared randomly, so I wrote them down in the order they appeared, around an empty circle. Once the group indicated that enough ideas had been written down, we thought of a word or phrase to use as a title for our cluster of ideas. I wrote that title in the middle circle.

The next step was to identify similar ideas as related themes. I simply circled similar ideas with a colored felt-tip marker. Generally, two to four themes emerged running through a discussion, so two to four colors would be used to circle the phrases and sentences. This was also a time to scratch out written comments that might have been interesting at the time but that were not pertinent to the themes of the discussion.

The next step in the color-mapping process was to decide the order of the sentences within a given color code. The sequence of the sentences was indicated by numbering them in order with a black pen. The final step was to decide the order of the color-coded themes. I indicated the first set in the center circle with a swatch of color next to the numeral 1; below that, the second color and the numeral 2; and so forth (see Figure 4.7).

The students then had a set of organized ideas to work with; each color group represented a paragraph. The students could work right from the chart to write their

FIGURE 4.7 Steps in Color Mapping for Collaborative Writing

1. Draw an empty cluster map: a circle with lines drawn outward from the edge of the circle.
2. Listen to the student's discussion for a unifying theme. When the theme begins to appear, write down their words in sentence from in random order on the cluster.
3. Once the ideas are written down, ask the students to title the cluster. Write the title in the circle at the center of the cluster.
4. Color-code related themes and ideas by circling them with the same color marking pen.
5. Number the sentences in a logical order within in each color group.
6. Decide the order of the themes swatches and indicate their order in the center circle with color and their corresponding numbers.

responses to the book they were reading. In time, the students became so familiar with organizing their ideas as a group that doing the same task in pairs or individually was relatively easy. Usually, the entire process took about 30 minutes, but occasionally, the group was so engaged in discussing a story that time was taken to follow the students' lead. This kind of flexibility with time could happen because the other groups were generally engrossed in writing, reading, and creative projects.

The Ripple Effect

The transformation of my classroom for Literature Circles grew out of a change in my thinking about a metaphor of classroom instruction. Rather than treating the classroom as if it were an assembly line for dumping ideas into empty receptacles, I preferred the metaphor of the *ripple effect,* a term Carole coined in her textbook on teaching language arts (Cox, 2008). It illustrates how responding to literature leads from one instructional activity to another, but there is more to it than that. The ripple effect is actually the goal of a conference in Literature Circles. When someone reads a wonderful story, it is like the action of a pebble thrown into the reflective pond of the mind and heart. The story creates waves of lived-through experiences, ideas, and sensations that circle out and connect with other experiences, thoughts, and feelings.

On another level, the ripple effect can be a tool for sociocultural practice in the classroom. Apart from visits to the home, the ripple effect is the primary means of bringing cultural funds of knowledge to classroom instruction. Readers tell their own stories as they respond to a text; each one brings his or her own cultural lens and sensibilities to the reading. It is then in dialogue with the English learner that the teacher gains cultural insights that can be incorporated into literacy development.

Each one of us, students and teacher alike, comes to the classroom with a deep well of experiences, ideas, and feelings from a unique cultural perspective. While sitting quietly and appearing to be listening, a student may be mentally pursuing a whole new idea, remembering a related feeling, or reliving a tangential experience. These are all ways of making associations between one's own life and a text. The expectation in a response-centered classroom is that each participant has thoughts and feelings that can contribute to a deeper reading of a story. The teacher's primary role is to invite students to share their idiosyncratic musings and to find ways to express them creatively, while also learning the conventions of reading and writing. Both students and teacher share roles in the process.

Thus, in Literature Circles, no one is empty-handed; both teacher and students bring something to the table. The teacher's expertise in language and literature and the students' responses to the literature combine to produce writing, creative ideas, poetry and music, and imaginative presentations. The teacher brings a knowledge of available resources for literacy development, strategies of working with students to maximize their understanding of the text, questions for stimulating dialogue and thinking, preparation to respond to the direction a group of students decides to pursue, and the ability to form connections with other groups working on similar themes. The teacher facilitates the process of the Literature Circle by skillfully accessing the content of the literature and the readers' responses to the story. The students bring substance to the discussion with their unique contributions of lived-through experiences, insights, ideas, feelings, and imaginations. The conference is the pot in which the knowledge of both teacher and students cooks up the raw stuff of aesthetic responses to make a presentation of writing, creative ideas, poetry, and/or song (see Figure 4.8).

Transforming the classroom for Literature Circles means reorganizing grouping to maximize listening and responding. The groups function more as forums for creative expression. The development of language and literacy in Literature Circles is a creative time of sharing reading, writing, and imaging.

Differentiation

Differentiation impacts small-group conferencing when groups are first formed and as the teacher continues to interact with students. Forming small groups is done in consultation with the teacher, who is much more directive in the beginning.

FIGURE 4.8 The Ripple Effect in a Literature Conference

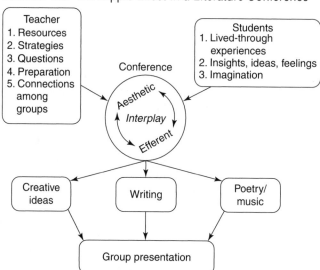

Given that groups are formed around book selections, the teacher initially narrows the selection of books in an effort to match books to students' levels and interests.

Consider the children in Carole's case studies. Whereas Anne would freely select a book to study with a small group from the start, Juan and Eduardo might need more direction. Over time, however, there would be less need for direction because the selection process would become progressively more open. And even in the beginning, if a student, or a group of students, expresses an interest in a particular book title, the teacher can certainly accommodate their wishes.

Differentiation also takes place in small-group interactions. A significant benefit of small-group conferences is that the teacher can modify questions according to language levels quite easily. Teacher–student interactions would differ markedly with different levels of proficiency.

However, the questions at all stages would be aesthetic and response-oriented in order to gain access to the individual student's perspective. Table 4.7 identifies types of questions at all five stages of proficiency, as well as actual examples.

The Literature Circle Plan

Literature Circles require a clear blueprint that teachers can use for planning and that students can readily follow. For students to authentically respond to their reading, they need a plan that is flexible and allows for creativity, yet one that provides

TABLE 4.7 Differentiated Questions for Small-Group Discussions

	Types of Questions	*Examples of Questions*
Level 1: Beginning	Yes/no questions, either/or questions	Is this your favorite part of the story? Which is your favorite part—the one about the pig and the spider or the one about the girl talking with her friend?
Level 2: Early Intermediate	Simple open-ended questions, fill-in-the-blank, closed-response questions	Tell me about your favorite part of the story. Your favorite story part was _____ ?
Level 3: Intermediate	Open-ended questions, asking for more details (what, where, when, how, why questions)	Tell me more about your favorite part—why did you like it so much? What was happening in the story?
Level 4: Early Advanced	All of the above plus synthesis questions, compare/contrast, inferential questions	How can we summarize what was said about our favorite part of the story? What have you noticed about what everyone is saying about this part of the story?
Level 5: Advanced	All of the above, calling for more elaboration	Put yourself in the story. How does it change from your perspective as a character?

an underlying structure to guide the process. Initially, I was very directive in the kinds of writing students were assigned to complete—assignments tended to be heavily weighted toward literary analysis. However, I began to see questions of identifying the setting, characters, sequence, and problem/solution as fairly superficial ways of exploring literature. The more interesting questions were how students related the story to their lives. In fact, students who authentically responded to their reading demonstrated a deeper understanding of typical story analysis. This did not mean that my students could not write a character analysis or examine the structure of a story; I conceived a simple plan that could encompass both response and analysis. If I needed to assign a particular form of writing, so be it; but if a student solicited an idea that had never occurred to me, the plan could include the new thinking.

Structure of the Plan

The Literature Circle plan is a form of scaffolding to structure the various literacy development activities the students are engaged in; it provides a structure but allows for creativity to flourish. Specifically, there are five basic elements to the plan: (a) written expression, (b) music and poetry, (c) creative ideas, (d) resources, and (e) presentation.

Written expression is purposefully an ambiguous category because I wanted to have the freedom to include any type of writing in response to literature. Keeping the term wide open allowed me to suggest, and when necessary to require, a specific genre of writing.

Music and poetry can be written expressions as well, but I separated them out as a special category for several reasons. First of all, I love songwriting and poetry. But I also understood that English learners can much more easily write a complete piece with metaphorical thinking using song or poetry. Songs and poems are not so rigid in their conventions as, say, expository writing. With some poems, grammar and punctuation are not issues, thereby facilitating the writing of whole ideas in a much more accessible format.

Creative ideas are meant to establish an avenue to unbounded creativity. I simply required that students think creatively about their literary responses and develop a project that expressed those responses. This opened up a way to integrate the arts with literature. The last two elements of the plan provide places to record and organize. The resources section is a place for students to list the various books, media, and human resources used in the plan. And presentation is a planning space to organize roles and responsibilities for the final sharing of their work.

For each group, I hung large back-to-back sheets of chart paper from the ceiling of the classroom, using fishing line and alligator clips. The hanging chart paper was easy for students to view from either side, and the clips made it easy for them to take the paper down to add more information or ideas. The front sheet was labeled with the title and author of the book or story the group had selected. Below the title and the author was a schematic that mapped out what the group would work on as they engaged the story (see Figure 4.9). Each small group was expected to produce a minimum of three process-writing pieces of various genres,

FIGURE 4.9 A Schematic of a Literature Circle Plan

Title _____   Author _____

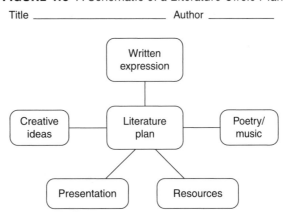

compose songs and/or poetry, and produce a creative project or two. On the back of the Literature Plan, students mapped out collaborative writing. At beginning levels, however, students were not involved in collaborative writing as such. Their work centered on producing language experience charts, which they dictated to the teacher and practiced reading as a group or as individuals. In their group work time, they illustrated the chart story or cut out the sentences to glue in a Big Book format with illustrations.

WRITTEN EXPRESSION.   Over the course of 3 or 4 weeks, a rhythm was established of small-group response times with the teacher, alternating with self-directed work based on those conferences. Approximately every other day, a small group could expect to meet with the teacher unless they requested more time to work on a given project. The goal of subsequent conferences was threefold: (a) to edit first drafts of student writing, (b) to grade and record finished work, and (c) to delve into the more creative ideas that sprang from a given piece of children's literature through music, poetry, or imaginative projects.

Editing.   There are many elaborate ways to work through editing a draft of writing. Peer editing is popular but requires that training and accountability be built into the process. Simple is better with editing, so I used a simplified system of editorial marks (see Figure 4.10).

To teach students to become peer editors, I used a student's draft as a model for whole-group instruction. I sorted the class into pairs, each of which received a copy of the student's writing. I also made an overhead transparency of the draft and projected it on a screen for modeling purposes. In addition, each student was given a red pencil for marking corrections. Sentence by sentence, we read through the draft as a group, and I asked the students to tell me where the writing needed to be changed. We marked up the draft, using the simplified system of editorial markings, and we discussed how to improve the writing.

FIGURE 4.10 Simplified Editorial Markings

1. Circle any suspect words.

2. Mark paragraph indentation.

3. Use a caret (arrow) to locate inserts.

4. Delete unwanted words.

~~Unwanted~~

5. Write in missing punctuation.

. , ; : ? ! "

When students peer edited on their own, a degree of accountability had to be built in. The peer editor was instructed to write his or her name at the bottom of the draft. Then, when I sat with the student author to review the work, I asked the editor to sit in so that both were involved in the review process. And when the peer editor had missed a problem, both could participate in the learning experience. The conventions of language were taught directly in context during the editing phase of the writing process. With published work, 100 percent correct spelling was required, and the same went for grammar and punctuation. Students need to learn conventional English, and they learn it best by crafting their own writing to meet the rigors of conventional writing.

Ongoing Evaluation of Writing.   Because students write at different paces, some may finish writing multiple drafts while others struggle to craft initial sentences. Although this can pose a problem in a traditional classroom, in the model presented here, writing and ongoing assessment are continuous. As some students finish writing final drafts, their work can be evaluated during conference time while slower writers get back to work. Or if slower writers need special attention, faster writers can initiate a new project and have their writing reviewed at a later time. This flexibility facilitates differentiated instruction.

After a two-part editing phase and rewriting, it is generally an easy task to assign a grade. At this point, major revisions or serious problems with a piece had already been discussed, so I focused on the degree to which the student had followed the editorial markings on the previous drafts. I assigned a grade of E(xcellent), S(atisfactory), or N(eeds improvement) accordingly. The final draft was stapled to the previous drafts to form a concrete documentation of the process the student had engaged in.

During the final evaluation phase of the group presentations, I asked the students to give me one or more of their written pieces to put into their student folders. The students kept their completed work in their folders, and the date of completion and the grade were written on the front on the Progress Record Sheet (see again Figure 4.5). I also recorded in my grade book the E, S, or N grade to maintain a quick reference to the completed work.

Music and Poetry

It has been my experience as a classroom teacher and teacher educator that teachers often forget, when presenting children's literature, that they are dealing with a work of art, rather than a chapter in a textbook. Students respond aesthetically to this artwork. They experience the emotions of exhilaration, fear, and surprise as they empathize with the characters in the story or identify with a poet's expressiveness. In the words of Rosenblatt (1986),

> The student should be helped to pay attention to the interfusion of sensuous, cognitive, and affective elements that can enter into the process of selective awareness and synthesis. No matter how limited or immature, this can provide the basis for growth. Aesthetic education should be rooted in the individual aesthetic transaction. The student thus can be helped to bring increasing sensitivity and sophistication to the evocation of "works of art," and can learn to bring to bear ever wider contexts for their interplay and study. (p. 127)

The teacher determines whether or not students will spend time exploring their aesthetic responses. Valuable instructional time is rarely taken for aesthetic inquiry. For an unexplained reason, teachers believe they are doing more teaching if students spend the bulk of their time analyzing story structure or copying vocabulary words. Time spent helping students increase their "sensitivity and sophistication to the evocation of 'works of art'" can only make the students better readers and interpreters of their own world. For this reason, I spent considerable time looking to students for their aesthetic responses and discovering how to represent those responses in music, poetry, and creative ideas.

In looking at her own students' languages of learning, Karen Gallas (1994) asked a second-grade student to explain why she thought she needed to compose a poem to express her thinking. This is what the student said:

> A poem is a little short, and it tells you some things in a funny way. But a science book, it tells you things like on the news. . . . But in a poem, it's more . . . the poem teaches you, but not just with words. (p. 136)

There is something deeper here. Art, literature, music, drama, and poetry dig deeper than the surface structure of language and its conventions. Taking time to explore the deep connections that students make by using the media of art, literature, music, drama, and poetry is quality time.

Poetry and songwriting can be done in a myriad of ways. I had a musical background and loved to write songs, so it was natural and fairly easy for me to help children put their words into poetry or song. However, colleagues would point out that it was not so simple for a person who could not carry a tune. So I began to observe what I did when I wrote a song. I noted that I played with familiar tunes initially by changing their lyrics but maintaining the melody. One other thing that I consistently did was attend very carefully to syllable counts for each line of a song. This led me to employ two techniques that help children write poetry and songs: (a) a word bank based on syllable counts and (b) a poetry or song frame that shows where to plug in the words selected from the word bank. (I discuss this in detail in my book *Differentiated Early Literacy for English Language Learners,* Boyd-Batstone, 2006.)

An example for poetry is haiku, a Japanese poetry form with several unique features, including syllable counts. In Japanese it is a 17-character poetry form; in English it is a 17-syllable form. The syllables generally are arranged in three lines with 5, 7, and 5 syllable counts, respectively. The theme is usually about nature but can also deal with other areas. Haiku often finishes with a comical or ironic ending.

For haiku the word bank is a simple T-table: One column is for recording words and/or phrases of 5 syllables; the other column is for words and/or phrases of 7 syllables. Of course, the words or phrases would be the students' expressions in response to a story or an event in their lives. The word bank simply arranges appropriate words and phrases that can be plugged into a poetry frame.

Haiku Word Bank

5 Syllables	*7 Syllables*

A haiku poetry frame is a guide to the structure of the poem. The student selects words or phrases from the left column of the word bank to insert in the first line of the frame; then words or phrases from the right column for the second line; and finally words or phrases again from the first column for the third line of the frame.

Haiku Poetry Frame

_____
(5 syllables)

_____
(7 syllables)

_____
(5 syllables)

For Beginning and Early Intermediate stage English learners, this can be done collaboratively on a sheet of chart paper. For Intermediate level and above, the process can be demonstrated on chart paper, and then students can develop their own word banks to write individual poems.

Songwriting can work in much the same way, using a word bank and a song frame. With a familiar tune such as "Are You Sleeping?" the structure would have lines of 4 syllables, 3 syllables, and 6 syllables. The accompanying word bank would look like this:

"Are You Sleeping?" Word Bank

4 Syllables*	3 Syllables	6 Syllables

Note that the word bank begins with 4 syllables to align with the first line of the song frame. If the word bank begins with 3 syllables, students will tend to misplace words on the wrong line of the song.

The accompanying song frame for the melody "Are You Sleeping?" follows. The process works the same as it did with haiku: After eliciting words and phrases with syllable counts of 4, 3, and 6, students can select and insert the appropriate words or phrases into the frame. Something fun about song writing is that students can also use nonsense words such as "cha-cha-cha" or "shoo-bee-doo." This is particularly helpful if the English learner has a limited range of vocabulary.

Song Frame for "Are You Sleeping?"

_____
(Title)

_____
(4 syllables)

_____
(4 syllables)

_____
(3 syllables)

_____
(3 syllables)

_____
(6 syllables)

_____
(6 syllables)

_____
(3 syllables)

_____
(3 syllables)

Creative Ideas

I included Creative Ideas as a section of the Literature Circle plan to have a way to encourage my students to think for themselves. It was my hope that students would develop a habit of risking to try their own ideas. I find it disconcerting to see children drawing blanks when faced with conceiving an idea of their own. An imaginative classroom environment is fostered by inviting creative thinking on the part of children. I also know that the more ownership they take of the work, the more engaged they become.

In my classroom, many of the art projects were generated from the Creative Ideas section, such as puppetry and mask making or costumes and props for dramatic representations of stories or scripts. It was common to see students writing, painting, and working with clay at the same table.

Although art was a common product of the Creative Ideas section, it was not limited to that subject area. One day I was showing a group of students an illustration of the various kinds of whales found in our oceans. I was doing this because one of the students had had a question about orcas in a story they were reading. The illustration was a graphic display of whales drawn to scale and ordered according to size. Compared to the blue whale, the orca appeared to be rather small at only 6 to 8 meters in length. Javier said under his breath, "That whale's tiny." I overheard his comment and said, "Really, how long do you think 8 meters really is?" He shrugged his shoulders and said, "I don't know." I followed with "Let's find out." Just as Eduardo had measured a boa constrictor, we began to measure the actual size of an orca.

I asked a student to bring me a ball of yarn and a meter stick. I tied a loop knot at one end of the yarn and gave it to Javier to hold. We measured 1 meter and tied a square knot to mark the length. Javier stepped back 1 meter. We measured a second meter and marked it with a knot. Javier stepped back another meter. We continued until we reached 8 meters knotted, and Javier was standing outside the classroom in the hall holding the end of the yarn. This small activity helped the students realize the actual size of a whale. You may be asking, "So what does this have to do with creative ideas on the part of the students?" After seeing the size of an orca measured out with yarn, some of the students got the idea to create a life-sized orca. I balked at the idea at first but suggested we draw one on butcher paper according to measurements and then paint it and mount it in the hallway outside the classroom. Hanging it up was the most difficult part, but we succeeded. We had to mount it on an angle as if it were breaching out of the water. Just for fun, on another sheet of butcher paper we drew Javier as if he were holding a fish out to give to the orca. The students traced his body, painted the paper, and mounted the picture of Javier in front of the breaching orca. There was no doubt about where to find my classroom after seeing a life-size orca being fed by Javier mounted on the wall.

In this example creative ideas allowed for thinking outside the box and outside the classroom. The orca activity involved measurement of the length, width, and scale of an orca. The students needed to find out about the size of the fins and tail. They struggled with design and logistics. And I asked them to write about orcas after their study of the animal.

Resources

As we worked to develop a Literature Circle plan, we drew on a number of resources. We began by noting the title and author of the storybook we were reading. As we continued to develop the plan, we recorded the various resources employed, whether printed material or other media. For example, the students recorded the citation of the illustration of the various whales they used and the other research they utilized related to the size and characteristics of orcas.

Recording resources on the chart paper provided a model for students as to how to cite their work. It served to instill a habit of attributing source material. It was also an authentic way to teach how to write references for their writing. I was able to naturally demonstrate the various components of a complete citation, which remained displayed on the Literature Circle plan for the duration of the project.

Presentation

Once the writing, music/poetry, creative ideas, and the various resources had been explored and developed, the group met to develop a presentation. A group presentation had three phases: (a) individual writing presentation in a small-group rotation, (b) whole-group presentation, and (c) evaluation. A group presentation was an opportunity to practice public speaking, and it provided the students with the opportunity to showcase their work not only to the rest of the class but also to parents. Built into the group presentation was an evaluation component in which students evaluated their own work and that of their peers. The process served as a culminating activity of an entire study of a book.

Everyone remembers those difficult times as a student, standing up in front of the entire class, with one shot to get a presentation right. That forum is intimidating and sets up students for ridicule. There is a much less imposing way to conduct group presentations. Thinking in terms of individual and group work, I conceived a presentation in two phases: In Phase 1, students shared their individual writing in a small-group rotation format. In Phase 2 a whole-group format, students shared collaborative projects and songs and answered questions from the audience.

PHASE 1: INDIVIDUAL WRITING PRESENTATION.   Phase 1 began with setting up the room for small-group interaction. I set up the room in three stations (see Figure 4.11). A station was no more than a table surrounded by chairs. I asked the students who were scheduled to present to sort themselves into three groups and to decide which group would be at each station. With a small group of six to eight students, no more than two or three students were at each station. Once the students positioned themselves in designated areas of the classroom, the rest of the class and visiting parents were sorted into corresponding groups.

My job as teacher was to manage a rotation sequence. I explained that each group had approximately 10 minutes to present its writing and to answer questions. I kept track of the time and reminded students when it was time to allow for questions about their writing. The rotation gave each student multiple chances in a small-group setting to practice presenting his or her work. It was not a one-shot experience; the students got three run-throughs as the audience rotated from station to

FIGURE 4.11 Classroom Layout for Group Presentations

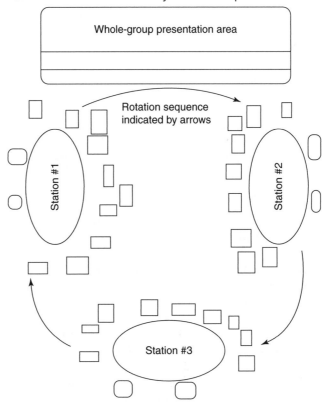

station. Other benefits were that the roundtable format lent itself to exchange of ideas and the smaller group was less intimidating.

PHASE 2: WHOLE-GROUP PRESENTATION.   Once we had gone through an entire rotation in which everyone had heard the individual presentations at each station, all nonpresenters pulled up their chairs to face the front of the room, where the small group met to present creative ideas, read poetry, and/or sing songs that had been generated from the Literature Plan. This presentation may have taken the form of a puppet show or a multimedia re-creation of the story. At the end of the group presentation, 5 to 10 minutes was set aside again for questions and answers.

PHASE 3: GROUP AND SELF-ASSESSMENT.   Finally, the students evaluated the presentation. However, before we sat down to write out an evaluation, I asked the entire group to talk with each other about what the presenters had done well, what had been learned, and how the nonpresenters would have done the same projects differently. We talked in pairs first and then shared with the whole group orally. This technique gave everyone a sense of what to write in the evaluation and gave me as the teacher a chance to emphasize the positive, rather than turn evaluation into a free-for-all of negative criticism.

FIGURE 4.12a Presenter's Self-Assessment Form

Name _____ Date _____

Presenter's Self-Assessment

Directions: For your group, answer the following questions.

Title/Author _____

_____

1. What did you do in the literature group?

2. What was the best project you worked on?

3. How can your group improve?

(front)

Once the class had discussed the merits of the presentation, all students filled out an evaluation form (see Figure 4.12). The presenters filled out the front side of the form, describing what they had done, what their favorite project had been, and how the group could improve in the future. Space was provided for a brief one- or two-sentence response to each question. It was a time of reflection, so quiet conversation was permitted as students filled out the form together.

The students who were the audience filled out a portion of the back of the form, describing what they had learned and what they would have done differently if it had been their project. The value of this time was that students could think about the presenters' creativity and get ideas for future projects or see what to avoid doing if the idea had not been successful.

It took 2 or 3 days to work through all the group presentations. Once the presentations were done and the students had completed all their work, they turned in their evaluation forms with their folders. I asked each student to flag one of his or her pieces of writing with a sticky note to indicate which one to show case in their portfolio. If I saw additional work to place in a portfolio, I asked the student's permission to put it in the file. I compared the scores of the work with the records in my grade book and returned the balance of the work to the student.

Product-Driven Differentiation and Assessment

The theoretical basis for differentiation and assessment has been discussed earlier in this book and this chapter. This section deals with general guidelines and applications

FIGURE 4.12b Observer's Evaluation Form

Observer's Group Evaluations

Directions: For each of the other groups, write in the book title/author, and answer two questions:

A. What did you learn?

B. What would you have done differently?

1. _____	4. _____
_____	_____
A.	A.
B.	B.
2. _____	5. _____
_____	_____
A.	A.
B.	B.
3. _____	6. _____
_____	_____
A.	A.
B.	B.

(*back*)

for differentiation and assessment. The focus here is on what students do and what written products they produce from a differentiated perspective.

I found that if I let student projects drive the differentiation, instruction and assessment were much easier to align according to differentiated levels. In other words, planning for differentiated instruction began with what the students were going to do. Once that was established, the level of instruction and the type of assessment would be clarified. Product-driven differentiation and assessment took away a lot of the confusion about how to teach to different stages of language development. The content of the instruction could be presented to all students, while the various products and assessment would be adapted to meet individual needs.

Differentiating Levels of Instruction

As stated earlier, there are essentially five stages of language development (California Department of Education, 1999). It always helped me, however, to think in terms of three major stages—Beginning, Intermediate, and Advanced—and on an as-needed basis to add the more nuanced levels of Early Intermediate and Early Advanced. Generally, using the three broad categories met the needs of English learners.

I utilized a set of general guidelines for teaching writing across stages of language development. What made my life easier was that I could begin instruction at or near the Beginning stage and as I saw that more advanced students were clear about the concept, I could send them off to work. Skills and concepts that were uniquely specific to a particular stage were dealt with in small-group instruction. Here are my suggested guidelines for differentiated writing instruction:

> *Beginning:* Use chart stories, with the teacher acting as scribe and students contributing orally; use picture/word cards extensively to identify vocabulary and to order words in sentences.
>
> *Early Intermediate:* Model writing and use collaborative writing that is closely tied to modeled writing on chart paper; use sentence strips extensively to order single paragraph writing.
>
> *Intermediate:* Use group-generated word banks and charted stories; use writing frames extensively; color-code sentences to form multiple paragraphs.
>
> *Early Advanced:* Demonstrate prewriting with individual semantic maps and writing frames, with assistance as needed; introduce outlining skills.
>
> *Advanced:* Use unassisted student-generated semantic maps and frames for prewriting; encourage students to explore more complex forms of writing involving editing and designing group projects such as newsletters.

More specifically, I have included here a number of ways to respond to a story in writing, which are differentiated for Beginning, Intermediate, and Advanced stages of English learners.

1.   Rewrite the story in your own words.

Beginning	Intermediate	Advanced
▲ Have students draw pictures about the story, changing it somehow (characters, setting, or problem). ▲ Discuss the changes using the pictures. ▲ Use a finger puppet to place the character in other settings and juxtapositions to other characters. ▲ Write the new version as a collaborative chart story.	▲ Outline ideas for alternative stories on chart paper. ▲ Ask, "How would I act if I were the main character?" ▲ Ask what-if questions about changes in characters, setting, or problem. ▲ Make up alternative endings. ▲ Have students write a paraphrased version of the story in one to three paragraphs.	▲ Have students explore how their presence in the story would change it. ▲ Have them imagine walking into a scene alone or with a friend. ▲ Have students write a full narrative with beginning, middle, and end.

2. Write a review of the story.

Beginning	Intermediate	Advanced
▲ Use a two-column graphic organizer to discuss and record the merits or pros of the story and the weaknesses or cons of the story. ▲ Evaluate the quality of the story based on pros and cons. ▲ Ask students to divide into opinion groups (pros in one group, cons in another) and consider justifications for each group's opinion. ▲ On chart paper, model how to write a letter to an author. ▲ Ask students to copy the letter format but add one additional sentence.	▲ Conduct the same initial steps as the Beginning level in discussing and recording ideas and forming opinion groups. ▲ Have students write a letter to the author about the story, citing specific reasons that it is so well written and/or suggestions for improvement. ▲ Mail author letters to the publisher.	▲ Chart the pros and cons of the story. ▲ Consider alternate endings. ▲ Have students write notes that justify a particular opinion from the chart and the story. ▲ Have them write a letter to the author that includes the critique with suggested improvements. ▲ Mail the author letters to the publisher.

3. Write a reflective piece.

Beginning	Intermediate	Advanced
▲ Use book illustrations of a specific character to initiate discussion. ▲ Record descriptive details about the character, using a cluster map as a graphic organizer. ▲ Ask either-or questions about impressions of the story (e.g., "Did you think the character chose wisely or unwisely here?"). ▲ Model how to convert the graphic organizer into a short paragraph of three or more sentences.	▲ Begin with a simple open-ended question (e.g., "What were you thinking about the character's choice?"). ▲ Record all comments in random order on large chart paper. ▲ Color-code like ideas. ▲ Decide the order of the ideas within each color-coded group—number them in order. ▲ Provide an opening sentence (e.g., "I was thinking about the character's choices . . ."). ▲ Have students write one or more paragraphs—each paragraph corresponding to a color-coded group of sentences.	▲ Initiate discussion about a character's actions with a simple opener, like "Let's talk about. . . ." ▲ Pose what-if hypothetical questions. ▲ Ask students to justify their responses based on the story details. ▲ Encourage students to individually cluster their ideas, color-code like ideas, and number color-coded ideas. ▲ Have students write a multiparagraph reflection.

4. Make a script for a drama or media production.

Beginning	Intermediate	Advanced
▲ Have students make simple masks for each character. ▲ Establish a beginning scene with a sketch on chart paper, or use an illustration from the storybook. ▲ Improvise dialogue and actions. ▲ Highlight key words and/or phrases that are unique to specific characters or that are repeated by specific characters	▲ Guide the script writing with a large sheet of chart paper divided into two columns (left column for dialogue, right column for actions and set directions). ▲ Elicit and record dialogue and actions from the students. ▲ Have students type up the finished script on a word processing program. ▲ Make copies that are highlighted for each character, and perform a readers' theatre production.	▲ Introduce a two-column script frame on single sheets of writing paper. ▲ Coordinate a script writing as a group project. ▲ Assign an executive editor, narrative writer, stage directions writer, and props designer.

5. Compare the story with another.

Beginning	Intermediate	Advanced
▲ Begin with a picture walk through two stories of the same genre (e.g., fairy tales). ▲ Ask how they are the same and how they are different. ▲ Chart responses on a graphic organizer, such as a Venn diagram or an extended T-graph. ▲ Write the comparisons in paragraph form on a chart. ▲ Have students illustrate the chart.	▲ Discuss the similarities and differences of two stories. ▲ Share responsibilities of writing ideas on a graphic organizer, such as a Venn diagram or an extended T-graph. ▲ Guide students in writing a three-paragraph comparison—the first paragraph discussing how the stories are similar, the following two paragraphs detailing the differences in the stories.	▲ Have students pair up to discuss and record the similarities and differences between tow or more stories. ▲ Have students go into greater detail and draw conclusions about why there are such differences.

6. Report an event of the story as if it were in a newspaper.

Beginning	Intermediate	Advanced
▲ Ask and call for who, what, when, and where questions. ▲ Note the facts on chart paper for a small group in order to model listening, speaking, reading, and writing. ▲ Compose the story as a small-group collaborative project on chart paper. ▲ Have students illustrate the story.	▲ Call for "wh-" questions to identify specific details. ▲ Note the facts on chart paper in bulleted format. ▲ Outline a story on chart paper. ▲ Assign students to write the story in pairs or individually.	▲ Discuss the details of the story. ▲ Consider an "angle" for the story (e.g., the perspective of a particular character or a specific aspect of the story to highlight). ▲ Encourage students to each take a different perspective of the story.

7. Compose a poem.

Beginning	Intermediate	Advanced
▲ Use a simple poetry frame that does not require conventions of grammar or syntax, such as a triante poem. ▲ Write students' words and phrases on word cards so that they can manipulate their position on a poetry frame. (See "Music and Poetry" earlier in the chapter.)	▲ Assist students in creating a word bank for a kind of poem (e.g., cinquain, haiku, biopoem, free verse). ▲ Provide students with individual writing frames to structure the composition. (See word banks and frames earlier in the chapter.)	▲ Have students design their own word banks and poetry frames to facilitate their composing. ▲ Conduct a poetry slam, in which students spontaneously create poems in a friendly competitive setting. Haiku poems are ideal for this.

8. Compose a song.

Beginning	Intermediate	Advanced
▲ Write a song on chart paper with a small group. ▲ Note syllable counts of each line of a familiar tune. ▲ Orally generate words and phrases that match the syllable counts in a tune. (See "Music and Poetry" earlier in the chapter.)	▲ Help students create a word bank that corresponds to a familiar tune. ▲ Provide students with individual song frames to scaffold the writing. (See word banks and song frames earlier in the chapter.)	▲ Have students create their own word banks and song frames based on a familiar tune or an original tune.

Assessing Student Work with Differentiated Rubrics

In order to assess differentiated student products such as writing, a rubric is required that is aligned with content and required language conventions. Often when English learners are writing about the same topics, the content of the writing is essentially the same, but the required conventions may vary significantly. The assessment rubric should align with the consistent content but be differentiated for language conventions.

Separating content from language conventions is very helpful for a number of reasons. First of all, the teacher can teach the same content to all students while making accommodations for language conventions in the final product—for example, the length of the writing, specific grammatical constructions, use of punctuation, and so forth.

Another reason to separate content from conventions in assessment is that the separation helps identify the strengths of the writing as well as its needs. For example, English learners tend to make frequent word choice and grammatical errors, but their ideas may be very insightful. Separation allows the teacher to highlight the quality of the ideas while also addressing the various conventional errors.

On the other hand, English learners may fall into the rut of using the same high-frequency words and simple sentence patterns over and over. As a result, their writing may be grammatically correct without punctuation errors, but it may lack content. If the assessment addresses only conventions, the teacher may be faced with a collection of correctly formed sentences that have little or no content.

Another reason for separating writing content and language conventions in assessment is that ideas come first, whereas accurate conventions are taught and crafted later on in the writing process. This is important to ongoing assessment. A teacher can suspend evaluating language conventions as students are developing their ideas, especially when students are responding to their reading. They can feel free to express their thinking without worrying about conventions. This approach does not devalue the use of conventions; it is just a matter of addressing what comes first—content. In fact, one of the most enjoyable parts of teaching writing is seeing ideas sprout from the students and helping them cultivate those seed thoughts into well-stated writing. That is the essence of mediated development.

A note about spelling conventions: Writing fluency is greatly enhanced when students concentrate first on getting their ideas on paper and then correct for spelling in the final draft. When teaching process writing that involves editing, the spelling requirement can remain 100% accuracy for all students. Alternatively, a teacher might require that key words be spelled correctly and allow for invented spelling of other words. It makes sense to correct spelling errors in the editing phase of process writing and require complete accuracy in the final draft. However, demanding spelling accuracy at all times may frustrate English learners.

Table 4.8 gives suggested rubric criteria for narrative writing about a personal experience. You will notice the adaptations according to the stages of language development. Note that the writing content remains relatively consistent across stages

TABLE 4.8 Differentiated Rubrics for Narrative Writing

	*Beginning	*Early Intermediate †Intermediate	*Early Advanced †Advanced
Writing content	▲ Describes a personal experience ▲ Identifies a time and place ▲ Selects important events	▲ Describes a personal experience ▲ Writes in first person ▲ †Describes setting as time and place ▲ †Shows, rather than tells, events ▲ †Articulates the significance of the experience	▲ Describes a personal experience ▲ Establishes a point of view ▲ Describes setting with rich details ▲ Shows, rather than tells, events ▲ †Articulates the significance of the experience ▲ †Articulates a lesson learned moral
Language conventions	▲ Dictates and copies one or more paragraphs ▲ Follows logical sequence of events ▲ Uses a graphic organizer ▲ Spells all key words correctly ▲ Uses accurate ending punctuation	▲ Has one or more paragraphs ▲ Follows logical sequence of events ▲ †Uses appropriate formats for action and dialogue ▲ †Spells all words correctly ▲ †Uses accurate ending punctuation	▲ Has multiple paragraphs ▲ Follows chronological or thematic sequence of events ▲ Uses appropriate formats for action and dialogue ▲ †Spells all words correctly ▲ †Uses accurate internal and ending punctuation

in terms of theme, setting, and events. Where it varies is in the style and focus of the writing. As for language conventions, the criteria become more demanding with each stage of language development.

One final note about differentiating rubric assessment is this: When students begin to incorporate elements in their writing that reflect higher stages of language development, they are indicating that they are ready to be assessed at a higher level. For example, if a student begins to reflect on the significance of an experience, whereas prior writing was merely descriptive, then the teacher would begin to assess the student at a higher level. The same goes for conventions: If the student consistently uses ending punctuation or expands descriptive vocabulary, it indicates to the teacher that it is time to assess the student at that level.

A Thought from Carole

During many recess and lunch periods, Paul and I discussed what had happened in Literature Circles; several ideas emerged as a result of Paul's teaching and my observing his teaching. First of all, time and good books are keys to reader-centered instruction with English learners. It is also very labor intensive. One good discussion lasted an hour and a half. Equally important, the rest of the class pursued their literature group projects without coming to Paul for help, perhaps respecting the sanctity of a really rich literature discussion in progress. Students had learned how to use their time and had learned to help each other rather than constantly coming to the teacher for help.

This was rather unusual, not the kind of teacher-centered and text-driven instruction I have seen frequently during many hours spent observing in elementary classrooms.

It was the kind of teaching teachers may have felt comfortable trying only with the "top group," rather than with those who were struggling or learning English as a second language. Paul generally asked only a few open questions, most often beginning with the prompt "Talk to me." Then he waited, and often waited some more, until they did. As a result, his students maintained interest in stories and each other's comments without extensive teacher questioning.

The student-centered teaching in Paul's class included several components with the potential to generate rich literature discussions supporting second language development:

Good books
Aesthetic questions plus lots of wait-time for student responses
Listening on the part of the teacher
An open agenda
Longer blocks of time with group rotation, not daily meetings

I am not proposing a set schedule that includes these components in some sort of formulaic procedure. These are the components of what happened with good results for Paul. Keep in mind that each literature discussion is unique, a journey not taken before.

EXPLORING IDEAS

1. Teachers teach to their strengths. What are your artistic and creative strengths? How could you use these as a resource in a reader-centered classroom?

2. Look back through the chapter. In what ways did Paul foster self-direction with his students?

3. How was accountability built into the management of Paul's classroom?

4. "Whiz kid," "scaredy cat," and "office shark" are three metaphors that organize thinking about people. Consider what metaphors are common to the students you are or will be teaching.

5. Read a short story and write down questions that would invite discussion. Trade the questions with a partner. Ask your partner to select the open-ended questions and to comment on which questions would maximize aesthetic responses to the story.

6. To what extent do prior experience, knowledge, and culture influence the reading of a story?

7. In a small group, share with each other which children's books were favorites as you were growing up. What was it about these books that touched your lives?

8. In a small group, plan out a Literature Circle for a favorite children's book. Plan the kinds of writing you would do—poetry, music, drama. What creative ideas emerge from the story? Present your plan to the rest of the class.

9. Practice using the color-mapping strategy to collaboratively write a story with a small group of three or four other students. Remember to take down ideas randomly and to organize them later by marking similar ideas with the same color and numbering the ideas in sequence.

10. Pick a favorite song. Count the syllables in each line. Rewrite the song with different words that match the number of syllables per line. Sing your new composition.

REFERENCES

August, D., & Shanahan, T. (Eds.). (2006). *Developing literacy in second-language learners: Report of the National Literacy Panel on Language-Minority Children and Youth.* Mahwah, NJ: Erlbaum.

Bergman, I. (1960). *Introduction to four screenplays of Ingmar Bergman* (L. Malmstrom & D. Kushner, Trans.). New York: Simon & Schuster.

Boyd-Batstone, P. (2006). *Differentiated early literacy for English language learners: Practical strategies.* Boston: Allyn & Bacon.

California Department of Education. (1999). *English-language development standards for California public schools.* Sacramento, CA: Author.

Chamot, A. U., Barnhardt, S., El-Dinary, P. B., & Robbins, J. (1999). *The learning strategies handbook.* White Plains, NY: Longman.

Cherry, L. (1990). *The great kapok tree.* New York: Harcourt Brace.

Cox, C. (2008). *Teaching language arts: A student-centered classroom* (6th ed.). Boston: Allyn & Bacon.

Gallas, K. (1994). *The language of learning: How children talk, write, dance, draw, and sing their understanding of the world.* New York: Teachers College Press.

Gu, Y., Hu, G., & Zhang, L. J. (2003). *Eliciting learning strategies from lower primary school students in Singapore.* Paper presented at the Educational Research Association of Singapore (ERAS) Conference, Singapore.

Pugh, S. L. (1992). *Bridging: A teacher's guide to metaphorical thinking.* Urbana, IL: National Council of Teachers of English.

Rosenblatt, L. (1986). The aesthetic transaction. *Journal of Aesthetic Education, 20*(4), 122–128.

CHAPTER FIVE

Engaging English Learners with Literature Circles in the Classroom

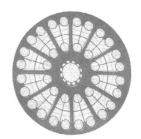

*E*xploring literature leads to literacy development that is naturally differentiated. When a response approach to exploring literature is coupled with literacy development, it signals a particular understanding of words themselves.

> The word in language is half someone else's. It becomes "one's own" only when the speaker populates it with his own intention, his own accent, when he appropriates the word, adapting it to his own semantic and expressive intention. Prior to this moment of appropriation, the word does not exist in a neutral and impersonal language. . .; but rather it exists in people's mouths, in other people's contexts, serving other people's intentions: it is from there that one must take the word, and make it one's own. (Bakhtin, 1981, pp. 293–294)

In a student-centered environment, literacy development takes on the form of dialogue. The teacher listens for the students' leads in order to match instruction appropriately to student strengths and needs. Direct instruction takes place, but it may not be the first instructional act. When the teacher invites students to connect the story to their own lives, they begin a journey on their own paths to interpretation.

What paths do readers follow as they read? Readers trek to faraway lands or unfamiliar islands. Sometimes they explore ancestral homes in their reading. As they read, they hoe their own rows and create stories in their minds. The experience is primarily aesthetic (Rosenblatt, 1986). Readers create images, feel sensations, share their own stories, and express their interpretations of the stories verbally and nonverbally through conversation, writing, music, and visual and performing arts.

In the classroom, the teacher initially establishes the environment for reader response. If the teacher's stance is predominantly efferent, the students will follow by reading for informational purposes so that they can give correct answers on a test or some other form of assessment. But if the teacher is predominantly interested in connecting the text to the students' lives, aesthetic reading comes to the forefront. In reader response, the students' aesthetic experience is the ground of prior knowledge, which connects the multiple worlds of children to their reading. Exploring aesthetic readings of children's literature is an inclusive process that invites diverse understandings and divergent thinking. Reader response calls individuals from all cultures to share their experiences and to join in the journey. As children read, they find their own stories.

Jackie: *I love my picture.* (She holds up a watercolor painting of a lone *vaquero* standing in the shade of a huge saguaro cactus.)

Paul: *What do you love about it?*

J: *The fields . . . the man standing all alone.*

P: *Do you want to write a poem about it?*

J: (Nods head yes.)

P: *When you create a poem, you paint a picture with words.*

Jackie's painting was a response to a number of books she had read and shared in a small group. She followed her own path to interpretation: reading, composing metaphors, painting images with watercolor, and painting pictures with words. Her path began with a story from Puerto Rico. It took her to a book about an island off the coast of Maine, to another book about the saguaro cactus of the deserts of Arizona, and to a painting of a huge saguaro in Oaxaca, Mexico.

One late spring morning, I found myself caught up with Jackie's small group in a single sitting for more than an hour and a half. Later, I was astonished to realize that it had taken place in a classroom of 30 students with curious minds and busy hands but without pandemonium breaking out. The other students saw my engagement with one group as an hour and a half of uninterrupted work time for their own literature-based projects.

What kind of instruction captures the imaginations of a group of young students and their teacher for such a long period of time? In this chapter, I follow Jackie (See photo, Paul and Jackie conference about her writing) through a morning in my classroom to paint a picture of what captured both our imaginations. The experience was recorded in the form of Carole's field notes; she sat on the outskirts of the group

Carole Cox

Paul and Jackie conference about her writing

and took copious notes of our conversations and her observations. I later pored over her field notes and added my comments about what I had experienced at the time. We also got together and discussed what had occurred, comparing our experience with the various theories circulating in schools. The students appeared to be the most actively engaged in language development when the story of their lives was touched by literature and the expressions of their interpretations resonated aesthetically.

My own emergent understanding of reader-response theory contributed significantly to my understanding of what was happening in my classroom. It began to change the way I listened to my students' side comments, digressions, and personal narratives as we discussed a story. In those meanderings, paths to interpretation began to open. In the following pages, I retrace the steps that led the students and me from island hopping to desert trekking. I discuss how the day was structured for reader response and self-direction; look at classroom setup, organization, and management for whole and small-group instruction; and discuss issues of planning for the next day, responding to needs and solving problems. I detail here a literary path to create a response-centered classroom.

A MORNING IN PAUL'S CLASSROOM

Even though my students came from low-income families, parents generally held high expectations for their child's academic success. Jackie's father, for example, like all my students' parents, spoke Spanish at home and knew some English at a functional level. He summed up his dreams for Jackie this way:

> I did not get to go to school past the second grade. I had to work hard in the fields and suffer a lot without much to show for it. I don't want Jackie to have to suffer the way I have. She must do well in school to get a job that pays well so that she can have a better life. (Spoken at a parent–teacher conference)

Whether a reciprocal relationship exists between schooling and obtaining a good job is not the issue here. Jackie understood that going to school was her job, and she attended to it seriously and conscientiously. School was not a burden for her. She enjoyed her friends, journaling, reading, and other subject areas. But she was the kind of student who, on first observation, was easy to overlook. Her quiet demeanor belied the vibrant imagination she brought to school. When given the opportunity to follow her own paths to interpretation in a small group, Jackie expressed her ideas about her reading in the form of art and poetry. She explored a wide range of literature, and as a product of her exploration, she developed language and literacy.

On this spring morning. Jackie and a number of her classmates greeted me at 7:45 as I entered the school's main entrance, and they followed me into the classroom. Some of the students dropped off their backpacks and went outside to play until the bell rang; many stayed in the room to socialize or get some extra time on one of the class computers. With only two computers for 30 students, time at the keyboard was at a premium. Next to each computer was a calendar of who would have first priority to use the computer. If the students listed on the calendars did not need to use the computer, they could trade days with other students. The primary software was word processing for the production of books, newsletters, and poetry. Before I set my books down, the computers were already booted up, and the students were settling in to the new day.

On a dry-erase white board at the front of the classroom, I outlined the day's activities, which included a meeting with me and Jackie's small group, *La Isla*. I also used the marker board as a reminder to students to hand in their permission slips for a walking field trip to the public library the next day. I listed the students who had yet to hand in their permission slips, with the intention of erasing their names as they returned them. In a wooden box below the message board, the students deposited their homework folders with work from the previous night. My aide's first task of the morning was to check the homework and to mark the monthly homework chart for those who had done their work.

On the other side of the room, several students organized the behavior chart for the day. It consisted of poster board with 31 small library pockets (one for each of my 30 students and one for me to monitor classroom behavior). Each library pocket contained three 3 × 5-inch colored paper rectangles: one green, one yellow, and one red. A green paper showing in a pocket meant good classroom behavior, a yellow paper meant marginal classroom behavior, and a red paper meant inappropriate classroom behavior. Below the behavior chart was a grid with each student's name and mine as well. Two students put a stamp next to the name of each student who had "maintained green" the previous day. They noted students who had gained 10 stamps and gave their names to my aide. She prepared certificates with a gift pencil as a reward for 10 stamps on the chart. Earlier in the year, the students had voted to include me on the behavior chart so that the behavior monitoring could be a shared experience.

Jackie and her friend Daisy prepared the individual math folders for the class to work on during roll call. These were simply short, self-correcting math exercises to prepare students for an upcoming standardized test format. Each student had a folder with an exercise sheet according to the level he or she was working on. The girls placed the appropriate sheet in each folder and set it on the student's desk so that as the students sat down, each knew immediately what to do.

The classroom setup routine freed up my time to respond to parents or special needs that arose first thing in the morning. My students were a tremendous resource and help in organizing the room for instruction, and I used that help extensively. However, not all students in the room were busy working; many were just socializing. I liked the fact that they felt the classroom was a comfortable place to be.

Whole-Group Instruction

At 8:30 the day officially began with the entire class. I personally found it easiest to begin with the whole group. This approach allowed me to deal with classroom business such as announcements, roll call, previewing the day, reading aloud, journals, and class interviews. While I took the roll, the students worked on their individual math folders. After they completed their work, they switched folders with a partner to check their work. Once the work was corrected, Jackie and Daisy collected the folders, which they would prepare for the next day.

Reading Aloud

At 8:45 I sat down in a chair at the front of the room with the Spanish version of *James and the Giant Peach* by Roald Dahl (1982). As the class moved over to listen to the story, Abel and David wanted to show off some of their work based on the book *Island of the Blue Dolphins* by Scott O'Dell (1960). They were interested in the marine life in the story, especially the references to whales and dolphins. Abel held up a mobile of the various whales he had read about. I recommended that he use those whale designs to create illustrations for a book about the whales he was researching. David called out, "Mr. B.-B., did you know that sperm whales can stay under water for almost an hour?" I said, "That's probably why they've got such big noses. Let's listen to the chapter about James with all his creature friends inside the giant peach being attacked by sharks as they float in the ocean."

We did not have enough copies of *James and the Giant Peach* for a class set, but several students had checked the book out from the library to read along and to read ahead of the class. As I read, I tried to explain that the sharks could not bite off large chunks of the peach because of the shape of their snouts. David stood up, went to the chalkboard, grabbed a piece of chalk, and began to draw. He said, "Mr. B.-B., this is how you draw a shark. Its nose sticks out this way, and his mouth is back here. The peach is so big it can't bite a hole in it."

Collaborative Interview

At 9:30, as a follow-up to the reading, we had a guest student visit our room—Gordon, a fourth grader who had recently visited the local marine life museum. The class conducted a collaborative interview. Collaborative interviews are used in my classroom as a whole-group language development activity. They follow a 7-step process:

1. Students one by one ask questions of the interviewee.
2. The teacher transcribes the answer on chart paper but with a twist: The student who formed the question tells the teacher what to write. (The reason for this is twofold: When students tell the teacher what to write, it engages them in active listening and also makes them responsible for accurately paraphrasing the answer in third person, thus eliminating confusion in the transcription.)
3. Students take notes as the interview is conducted.
4. At the end of the interview, the responses are organized by using the color mapping technique explained in Chapter 4. Similar answers are marked with the same color, sentences are numbered in order within each color group, and color groups are numbered in order.
5. The students color-map their notes as modeled by the teacher.
6. For homework the students write up their color-mapped interview notes in paragraph form.
7. The chart is also rewritten by the teacher and illustrated by student drawings.

For this interview, Gordon chose who would ask him questions, with one rule: If you start with a girl, then you follow with a boy, then a girl, then a boy, and so

FIGURE 5.1 Science Tied to Literature

Science content
▲ Anatomy of marine animals
▲ Sperm whale's ability to dive for over an hour
▲ Shark's snout
▲ Marine museum

Instructional note
▲ Spontaneous moment
▲ David free to demonstrate newfound knowledge
▲ Gordon student guest expert (sharing marine life experience)
▲ Interview to uncover knowledge using dialogue

on. The students asked Gordon about his favorite marine animals. Gordon had several books that his family had purchased, and he also shared a homemade book about whales. The students had lots of questions about the museum, the whales, and how he made his book. Figure 5.1 gives an outline of how science was tied to literature in this lesson; Figure 5.2 lists strategies for the monolingual teacher in this type of interview.

Individual and Small-Group Instruction

I liked to give the students time to reflect and write on an individual basis after a whole-group experience. It not only changed the pace of the instruction but also provided space to think. Interactive journal writing was ideal for creating such a space. Students also needed time to read for pleasure on their own. I found that the two activities complemented each other when scheduled side by side.

Interactive Journal Writing

Following the interview, at 9:45 I asked the students to return to their desks and to write in their journals. Writing in journals interactively in my classroom meant that a written dialogue went on daily between the students and the teacher and among

FIGURE 5.2 Interview Strategies for the Monolingual Teacher

▲ Model writing with the transcription on chart paper.
▲ Faithfully transcribe the student's words.
▲ Think aloud with students about how to phrase sentences.
▲ Check for understanding by asking the interviewer to paraphrase the answer.
▲ Check with the interviewee to ensure fidelity to what was originally stated.
▲ Make special note of key words that convey essential meaning of the topic.
▲ Ask students to tell you how to spell key words.
▲ Draw a picture to illustrate a word whenever necessary to increase understanding.

FIGURE 5.3 Interactive Journaling Strategies for Monolingual Teachers

> ▲ Use a billngual aide to dialogue with and respond to non-English speakers.
> ▲ Write authentic responses, commenting on the story behind the drawing.
> ▲ Share your own similar experiences.
> ▲ Read the entry with the student.
> ▲ Label pictures in the drawing for the student.
> ▲ Feel free to ask students to write about another topic if entries appear redundant.

the students as well. Both students and teacher wrote a personal reflective piece in the journals. Once a written piece was completed, it was taken to a respondent, who read the journal entry with its author and then wrote a reflective response in dialogue form. I say "dialogue form" to emphasize that the respondent was not there to correct or edit someone else's journal entry. The written response was simply a conversation in print that modeled standard conventions of writing. Figure 5.3 identifies interactive journaling strategies for monolingual teachers.

I found it difficult to adequately respond to each journal every day by myself, so I organized the class to assist in journal writing. With 30 students in the room, I divided the class into five groups with six students in each group. On Mondays, Group 1 helped respond to other students' journals; on Tuesdays, Group 2 responded, and so forth. In this way, I was no longer alone as the sole respondent to the class. With my aide, the six students, and me, the eight of us could respond to the rest of the 24 students. In other words, by changing the management of the journals, I moved from a 30:1 ratio to a 3:1 ratio of writers to respondents. This freed me to spend quality time reading the journal entries of a few students at a time, talking with them about what they had written, and writing an authentic response without feeling the rush to quickly dash off something in all 30 journals. Occasionally, students used the journaling time to write about their pleasure reading (see Figure 5.4 for a sample of Jackie's journal writing).

Reading for Pleasure

As students finished their writing, they knew it was time to read for pleasure. The students selected books from the in-class library, their own books from home, or books borrowed from the school and public libraries (see Figure 5.5 about stocking the classroom library). The purpose of this activity was to cultivate a personal love for reading, which required that students have the power to select their own books and to pursue their own interests. The interactive journal writing and pleasure reading took us to recess time. After recess we were ready to begin small-group work.

Conferencing with the Teacher

The first segment of the morning had concentrated on whole-group instruction and then on creating individual space; the students had been involved in listening, speaking, writing, and reading activities. After recess, during the Literature Circle

FIGURE 5.4 Copy of Jackie's Journal

FIGURE 5.5 Stocking the Classroom Library

Literacy begins with a juicy story. Consider the following when stocking your classroom library:

▲ Select quality stories with vivid illustrations.
▲ Avoid purchasing sets of readers controlled for vocabulary and predictability.
▲ Buy literature books in groups of 6 to 10 copies so that they can be shared.
▲ Buy several class sets of captivating chapter books to read aloud with the class.
▲ Conduct a class Book Shower so that families and members of the community can purchase books for the school.
▲ Coordinate book purchases with other teachers at your grade level to increase the selection available for the students.

FIGURE 5.6 Integrating Content Area Instruction

▲ In a response-centered learning environment, content area emerges according to each story.
▲ History and science may emerge at the same time among the various small groups.
▲ The process is not linear, with every student studying the same concept at the same time.
▲ Regular, direct instruction in content areas continues at different times during the day.
▲ Integration of content area instruction is the application of previously learned concepts of mathematics, social studies, science, or the arts to a new context.
▲ Reference materials (encyclopedias, field guides, maps, and dictionaries) need to be available for easy access.
▲ Textbooks can be used in two ways: (a) as a traditional text for instruction and (b) as a source of reference for emergent integration of content.

time, I met with Jackie's small group to discuss their reading. This was the most exciting time of the day, when students engaged their imaginations and the literature functioned like that pebble thrown into the pond, creating a ripple effect of wave after wave of ideas and creative endeavors. (Figure 5.6 focuses on the integration of content area instruction.)

At 10:25 the students reentered the room, ready to work in small groups, which were formed around literary works the students had selected. The current Literature Circle format had five groups, each taking its name from the primary book the group was reading: *Encounter* (Yolen, 1992) about Christopher Columbus's arrival and takeover of what is now Puerto Rico, from the perspective of a Taino Indian; *Columbus* (d'Aulaire & d'Aulaire, 1955), a book with a much more conventional reading of the "discovery" of the New World; *Los Delfines,* from a Spanish version of the book *Island of the Blue Dolphins* (O'Dell, 1960); the *Doll House* group, reading *The Doll House Murders* (Wright, 1983); and *La Isla,* taken from a story written about the island of Puerto Rico, "La Gaviota Roja" (Belpé, 1987).

Each small group was developing a Literature Plan, which involved in-depth reading of the literature, research, extended reading, student-generated writing projects, poetry or music composition, creative ideas and projects, and a class presentation. During the Literature Circle time, the groups met with me or my aide to discuss the reading and to chart their Literature Plans.

As was described earlier, the charts were hung by alligator clips tied to fishing line that was attached to the ceiling. This arrangement made the charts visible and easily moved or stored. The students looked to the charts for directions as to what they needed to work on. If it was a writing project, the initial cluster of ideas was written out on the chart. If it was an art project, the materials needed and procedural steps were listed on the chart as well. Writing on the charts was a shared responsibility of the teacher and the students. Pens were readily available for students to note their ideas and directions on the chart.

At the start of the work session, each member of a small group already knew what he or she had to do from the previous day's projects. The students working together on reading, writing, and creative projects gave evidence of wave after wave of ripple effects splashing around the classroom. The *Encounter* group was developing a play about the encounter between the Taino Indians and Christopher Columbus. Several of the students were reworking a draft of the script while others were creating props and costumes. The *Columbus* group was interested in the various flags of the period, noting that Christopher Columbus had planted a flag as a symbolic claiming of new territory. These students were busy researching the flags that various European countries had designed in the 15th century. Some members of the *Los Delfines* group were pursuing their marine life interest with Gordon, our classroom guest, who was demonstrating to them how he had made his own whale book. Others were rereading the story to each other or making whale and dolphin mobiles with wire hangers, string, and stuffed paper whales. The *Doll House* group was struggling with a longer novel in English. They had to work harder at their book, so they sat in pairs, reading a chapter to each other with the help of my aide. Two of the group members were seated at a computer, writing spooky poems based on the book. And the *La Isla* group took seats next to me to discuss their story in a conference.

Jackie's group, *La Isla,* had been reading "La Gaviota Roja" by Pura Belpré (1987), a story about a boy from the island of Puerto Rico who finds a rare, red seagull with an injured wing and seeks to nurse it back to health. In addition to Jackie, the members of the group were Baudelio, Carmen, Jeanette, and Vicente. We began the conference by tacking the Literature Plan chart to the chalkboard behind me. The group sat in a small circle so that all members were facing each other for dialogue. I began by asking the students what they were currently writing about. They showed me drafts of their writing about seagulls. Their papers already had red editorial marks from peer editing. I reviewed each draft and made my own comments and suggestions in pen. I then showed the work to the author, the editor, and the group to highlight common errors or things to look for when editing someone else's work. One of their collaborative writing projects was a song about Puerto Rico and a bird. The group had practically written the song before coming to the group that day, but they were having trouble with the chorus section. We worked on it some with little success until Adrianna, from the *Doll House* group, overhearing our struggle, stepped up and provided a countermelody with words that fit for an appropriate chorus (see Figures 5.7 and 5.8).

FIGURE 5.7 Suggestions for Composing Poetry and Song with English Learners

▲ Remember that all students are composers.
▲ Count the syllables per line in a familiar song and substitute phrases with the same number of syllables.
▲ Rhyming is fun but not essential for poetry or song.
▲ Use phrases that paint a picture: metaphors and similes.
▲ Play with the language.

FIGURE 5.8 Lyrics to "En Puerto Rico," in Spanish with an English Translation

1. En Puerto Rico hay muchos ricos igual que tú y yo.	1. In Puerto Rico are many rich people just like you and me.
En Puerto Rico hay muchos pericos que me gustarían mirar.	In Puerto Rico are many parakeets that I like to see.
Aunque me piquen en mi pobre nariz, todavía los puedo amar.	Even though they peck me on my poor nose, I still love them so.
2. En Puerto Rico hay muchos ricos igual que tú y yo.	2. In Puerto Rico are many rich people just like you and me.
En Puerto Rico hay una cotorra que no decía "Cataño." La cotorra regresó y Yuba la amaba.	In Puerto Rico is a parrot that refused to say "Cataño."* The parrot returned home and Yuba still loved it.
3. En Puerto Rico hay muchos ricos igual que tú y yo.	3. In Puerto Rico are many rich people just like you and me.
Si tú me quieras todavía igual que los pericos, no te hagas tontita y vente aquí conmigo.	If you still love me like the parakeets, don't be foolish and come along with me.
A San Juan de Puerto Rico.	To San Juan of Puerto Rico.

*Cataño is the name of a town near the city of San Juan.

A JOURNEY OF DISCOVERY, EXPRESSION, AND LITERACY

With the writing reviewed, we set out on a long literary journey in an open-ended way. I started our travels by saying in our conference: "Tell me about the story. . . . Talk to me . . . ." Instead of starting at the beginning of the story, Jackie and Baudelio talked about the point in "La Gaviota Roja" when the boy, with the injured bird in a box on his lap, took a taxi ride around the island of Puerto Rico from Ponce in the south to the capital city. San Juan, in the north. I pulled down a map of Puerto Rico, and we retraced the route the taxi followed. Vicente wanted the group to make its own map of the island, so we grabbed a large sheet of butcher paper and a pencil for drawing a 4-foot map of the island. While the group talked about how to make the map, Jackie's friend Daisy walked up to our group, carrying a book in her hands as if she were holding a golden ring on a pillow. The book that Daisy gave to Jackie was *Island Boy* (Cooney, 1988). Even though the book was in English, Daisy knew she had contributed something special to the group, so she stayed on the outskirts of the circle to see what we would do with the book.

Island Boy followed a family living on an island off the coast of Maine through several generations. None of the students had ever been to Maine or lived on a island; however, the story of this family, particularly the "Island Boy," connected with many of their experiences. As I read the book aloud, many small, seemingly insignificant parts of the story caught our attention. The group first noticed that Tibbetts Island was much smaller than Puerto Rico and that it was inhabited by only one family. They were fascinated with how a family of six boys and six girls worked out sleeping arrangements in a small home. They also noticed the wide variety of sea birds mentioned in the book. No one in the group knew what a cormorant was, so I asked Jeanette to bring over a copy of a field guide to bird watching in the United States. We compared the varieties of gulls, terns, cormorants, eiders, and sea pigeons, noting their colors and sizes. The students were surprised to see how much Little Mattias, the youngest member of the family, changed as he aged. It took a moment to realize what had happened to Old Mattias, the grandfather, who was lost at sea at the end of the book.

An In-Depth Discussion of a Story

The following is an excerpt of the conversation conducted in Jackie's small group with the book *Island Boy* (Cooney, 1988). I selected this portion of the conversation, not because it is a flawless example of student—teacher interaction, but because of the richness and variety of the dialogue. As I read over the transcript, I saw occasions where I missed opportunities to follow the students' paths to interpretation; I also saw significant connections. Interspersed with the dialogue are my reflections and commentary about what I was thinking during the discussion. The comments are at times instructional and at others times, reflections of my own self-critique. The purpose of this section is to listen over my shoulder and to think aloud with me as a group of students respond to the reading of a wonderful story.

Teacher: *What happened to [Old Mattias]? Talk with your neighbor.*

(Asking students to talk with their neighbors is a safe way to start discussion. Students can try out their ideas on a friend before risking sharing in front of the group. For English learners, it also provides a run-through of what to say so that they can make sure they have the words to describe what is on their minds.)

Vicente: *He went away in a small boat.*
Jackie: *He died* (pointing to a picture of the funeral).

(Baudelio was wide-eyed. Jeanette and Carmen were surprised and learned forward to see the book.)

Vicente: *He got lost in the storm.*
Teacher: *Do you know what a funeral is?*
Students: (Nodding their heads yes)

(In asking, "Do you know what a funeral is?" I was checking for their understanding of the word *funeral*. I was confident that they knew what a funeral was in Spanish, but I wanted to know that the students did not miss it in English. I was interested in pursuing the issues of life and death and rituals brought up in the story; but as you will see, the students had other ideas.)

Baudelio: (Taking the book in his hand to show the page of the funeral, he pointed to the boat docked in the foreground of the picture.) *They found his boat.*

(Long pause)

Teacher: *What did you think about the story?*

(The discussion appeared to stall, so I used an open-ended question to get it going again. The question put the direction of the discussion back into the students' court. Leaving the direction of the discussion with the students shifted my role from transmitter of information to responder to the text.)

Carmen: *Why wouldn't they let Little Mattias work?*
Teacher: *Do you have big brothers and sisters?*
Carmen: *Not me.*
Vicente: *I have a little brother. He follows me everywhere.*
Teacher: *Is he always interested in what you do?*
Vicente: *Yeah.*
Jackie: *My little sister is Norma.*
Teacher: *Do you call her Little Norma, Normalita?*
Jackie: *Gorda* (Spanish for "chubby").
Baudelio: *I've seen her. She's fat.*
Jeanette: *When I was a baby, they called me Gordita.*

(Looking back at my response to Carmen's question, "Why wouldn't they let Little Mattias work?" I think it would have been better for me to repeat her question for the entire group to answer, saying, "That is a good question. Why wouldn't they let Mattias work?" As is evident by Carmen's response, my question took the discussion away from her thinking. My response to Carmen was meant to put her in touch with her own "lived-through experience" (Rosenblatt, 1986) as she tried to figure out the story. She was inquiring about Little Mattias as a toddler. My question was intended to bring the entire group into answering her question; however, it led to a digression. Not to worry, as they say. Dialogue rarely follows a systematic path from a to b, particularly with young children. Rather than pull the group through a single line of thinking about the story, I poke and prod from many angles until the group latches on to an idea of substance. If one line of thinking appears to lead nowhere, I or, ideally, one of the students simply changes the direction of the conversation.)

Teacher: *Where were you children born?*
Jackie: *Here.*
Vicente: *In a park . . . Drake Park* [the local neighborhood park].

(Everyone laughs.)

Vicente: *No, here.*
Baudelio: *Harbor City Hospital.*

(Carmen pulls down a map of Mexico from the map set on the chalkboard and points to where she was born.)

Carmen: *My house was here, Guerrero. A little girl was playing with a plastic bag there, and she died.*
Teacher: *Your cousin?*
Carmen: *My friend.*
Teacher: *Did she live in your home?*
Carmen: *She was my neighbor. My dad told me that he can never get lost at home because everybody knows him. Like in the story. Everybody knew Mattias.*

(The above segment is a digression that I initiated to get the students more in touch with their own lives as they engaged the story of Mattias, the island boy. I found it fascinating that even with my question seemingly out from left field, the students brought it back to engage the book. I was not sure where the discussion was leading at this point. I continued to listen for the group to latch on to a thought. After Carmen's comment came a lull in the conversation. Many teachers begin to panic when confronted with silence but I see silence as a time to breathe and think.)

Baudelio: (Takes the book and shows the final page, with all the people coming to the funeral and a final picture of Little Mattias standing under the red astrakhan tree where Old Mattias was buried.)

(Long pause)

(One technique of guiding group discussion is to use wait-time to let the group reflect on an idea or an image. During the discussion, the book was passed around from student to student. Here, Baudelio selected a point of interest, but Jackie jumped in to touch base with her favorite part. Notice how Baudelio got to answer my question later in the discussion by nonverbally hanging onto the book, open to his favorite page. Asking about a favorite part of the story is a simple, open-ended question that allows readers to share where they connected most powerfully with a story. Notice how the book and the students' lives intertwined as they talked about their favorite parts.)

Teacher: *Baudelio, do you have a favorite part?*
Jackie: (Breaking in) *The pillow fight. One time, my sister and I were having a pillow fight, and my little brother came in and threw his bottle at me, and the milk spilled all over the bed.*
Teacher: *I have two older brothers. We'd get into pillow fights from our bunk beds. One time, I fell off and almost broke my arm.*
Baudelio: *I did that to my brother.*
Vicente: *I liked the part when they slid down the hill in the snow.*
Carmen: *Once I went to the snow with my family. We slid down the hill and hit a tree and it fell over. Then we made . . .* (points to the snowballs in the book).

Baudelio: *Snowballs!*

Carmen: *We had a big snow fight, I was all wet. And my mother said, "Why are you all wet?" My dad said, "Because you kids were throwing snow." Then I sat in my bed and got it all wet with snowballs.*

Teacher: *Yuck!*

(Baudelio held onto the book tenaciously and continued to look at the picture of Little Mattias under the tree. During the earlier discussion, I kept asking myself, "What is Baudelio trying to tell the group?" In thinking about the book, the image of the tree growing up through the seasons, cycling from blossoms to bearing fruit to losing its foliage to budding again, seemed to parallel life on Tibbetts Island. In fact, at that moment I realized that Barbara Cooney used the tree as a metaphor for the family as it cycled through several generations. Old Mattias is even buried at the foot of the tree. The theme of trees jumped out at me. I recalled my favorite trees as a child and as an adult. As I thought about Little Mattias standing under his tree, I wondered whether anyone in the group had a strong attachment to a special tree.)

(Baudelio continued to show the picture of Little Mattias standing below the tree.)

Teacher: *Baudelio, do you have a favorite tree?*

Baudelio: *Apple tree.*

Vicente: *A little orange tree about a block from here.*

Carmen: *Fruit tree.*

Baudelio: *I took a little wood and made a tree house to climb in.*

Teacher: *I loved climbing trees; I was the world's greatest tree climber when I was a boy living in Hawaii.*

Jackie: *At Ocean Park, by my house, I was climbing a big tree and got sticky sap all over me.*

Teacher: *What did you do about it?*

Baudelio: *Make glue?*

(Laughter)

Jackie: *I like the big cactus because it reminds me of home.*

Teacher: *It sounds like this group needs to make trees.*

Baudelio: *Make a tree house . . .*

Personal Expression in Response to a Story

Trees indeed became a unifying metaphor for this group; it gave the group a way to understand the seasons of the family in Barbara Cooney's book *Island Boy*. Just as Old Mattias and his grandson Little Mattias sat under a special tree, we all had a favorite tree. As we discussed how to make a tree, I was caught up by my own lived-through experience of being an island boy living in Hawaii as a child. As we worked on our projects, I chatted away about when I was a boy and how much I had loved climbing trees. I had lived near a row of palm trees that were bowed by the wind at such an angle that I could run halfway up a tree without even having to hold on with my hands. We talked at length about our favorite trees: where they

FIGURE 5.9 The Effect of Icons on Language Arts and Content Area Instruction

▲ In responding to literature, students adopt *icons:* unique characters, plants, animals, or inanimate objects that serve as meaningful connections between the story and their own lives.

▲ Like signposts, icons hold a reference point around which much of a student's learning may be directed.

▲ An icon is a personal choice embedded in an individual's cultural background and experience.

▲ Jackie's icon was the saguaro cactus because of its tie to her family's home in Sonora.

▲ The saguaro cactus icon opened ways to aesthetically develop language arts, social studies concepts, and science.
  ▲ Language arts: reading or writing poetry and prose about the cactus
  ▲ Social studies: studying Mexico's art and plants
  ▲ Science: exploring the life cycle of the saguaro cactus

were planted, what they looked like, making tree houses, climbing the branches, sitting in their shade, eating their fruit. We experienced the effect of ideas rippling out of the group's discussion.

Jackie loved the saguaro cactus, which is common to northern Mexico and the Southwest United States. The saguaro cactus reminded her of her family's home in Sonora. She went to the class library and found the book *Cactus Hotel* by Brenda Z. Guiberson (1991), illustrated by Megan Lloyd. This beautifully illustrated book traces the life cycle of a saguaro cactus as it pops up in the shade of a paloverde tree in the Arizona desert. Jackie began to develop her own personal Literature Plan, which included making a papier-mâché cactus, creating a book about the life of a cactus plant, cataloging the various animals that live in the community of the tree, writing poetry, and re-creating a famous painting with watercolor. Figure 5.9 summarizes how an icon from reader response can affect language arts and content area instruction.

Jackie looked through the book *Mexico: Splendors of Thirty Centuries* (O'Neill, 1990), published by the Metropolitan Museum of Art, and found the painting *The Candelabrum of Oaxaca* (p. 535) by José María Velasco: a lone *vaquero* (Mexican cowboy) standing in the shade of a magnificent cactus.

Later that week, Jackie reproduced that painting in watercolors for herself. Her watercolor painting reflected the magnitude of the saguaro, and her poetry sang of the companionship the saguaro provided and also included the paloverde from the book *Cactus Hotel*. She went on to write about the gila woodpecker, which lives on the saguaro's seeds and fruit and makes its home in the cactus (see Figure 5.10). (The following year, in the fourth grade and under a different teacher, Jackie continued her personal investigation of the saguaros. When I visited her room, she showed me another book she had created about the various saguaro cacti and the other animals living in the *Cactus Hotel*.)

FIGURE 5.10 A Poem and an Essay About the Saguaro Cactus by Jackie Hemandez, in Spanish with an English Translation

El Saguaro y el Paloverde

El saguaro está grande,
más grande que los otros.
Tiene las ramas grandes,
más grande que las del
paloverde.

El hombre mediano recoje
las hojas del paloverde
con el rastrillo,
porque no le gusta que
estén las hojas junto al saguaro.

El Pájaro Carpintero

Los animals van al
saguaro para tomar el neclar
de las flores. Un ratón viejo
se come la fruta que cae
del saguaro. La fruta tiene
dos mil semillas.
  El pájaro carpintero tiene
el pico grande. Tiene
la frente roja como
la flor del saguaro. Come
las semillas del las flores de saguaro.
El pájaro carpintero hace su nido
en el saguaro para protegerse
de sus enemigos. Las espinas
del saguaro no le pican
al pájaro carpintero.

The Saguaro and the Paloverde

The saguaro is big,
bigger than the other cactus.
Its branches are big,
bigger than those of
paloverde.

The medium-size man rakes
the leaves of the paloverde
with a rake
because he does not want
its leaves to touch the saguaro.

The Gila Woodpecker

The animals go to the
saguaro to drink the neclar
of its flowers. An old rat eats
the fruit that falls from
the saguaro. The fruit has
two thousand seeds.
  The gila woodpecker has
a large beak. It has
a red forehead just like
the flower of the saguaro. It eats
the seeds of saguaro flowers.
The woodpecker makes a nest
in the saguaro for protection
from its enemies. The needles
of the saguaro do not pierce
the gila woodpecker.

11:55. Before I knew it, lunchtime had arrived, and it was time to clean up. Throughout the discussion of *Island Boy,* I had kept my eye on the rest of the class, who kept actively engaged in their own projects. It would be impossible to have this kind of open-ended, creative experience in a traditional classroom setting. Spending more than an hour with one small group is possible only if the rest of the students are clear about their tasks and are very much self-directed. Fostering self-direction demands that the teacher trust the creative insights of the students to develop a plan of action that will hold their interest and challenge them intellectually. Of course, having a teacher's aide who knows to look for groups that need special assistance is a tremendous help. My aide was tuned in to the needs of the groups so that she could provide an idea or a push in a creative direction. *Island Boy* was a special experience, and we as a group got carried away by Barbara Cooney's literature.

FIGURE 5.11 Engaging the Teacher's Imagination

▲ Teachers respond creatively to their own reading.
▲ When a story touches a lived-through experience, every reader is imaginatively engaged in reader response.
▲ Sharing the connection between the reader and the text is a pleasurable experience for the teacher and the students.
▲ Time files when you're having fun!

But the whole class was accustomed to occasionally getting carried away by a good story, so they knew to just keep working on their projects. When lunchtime came around, many of the other small groups had also gotten carried away by the stories they were reading and responding to and did not want to stop working. Figure 5.11 highlights how student-centered teaching engages the teacher's imagination, too.

Before sending the class out to lunch, I took 5 minutes to meet with the group liaisons. They briefly reported to me about their groups' progress and shared their need for materials for producing their presentations. As was mentioned in Chapter 4, I did not see the teacher as the sole provider for the classroom. When questions of needed materials arose, my first response was to put the responsibility back on the group, asking, "What are you going to do about it? How can you get what you need?" If it was an item the school readily provided, such as colored paper or paints, I asked the liaison to write me a note as a reminder to get the item from the storeroom. If the item required special effort, however, we spent a moment thinking of the resources available to us, such as asking another teacher, writing a request to the principal, or asking parents via letters to provide the needed items. Putting the responsibility back on the students brought them into the planning process.

Often the small-group liaisons reported on problems the groups were experiencing. The problems were as diverse as not liking the book they selected and wanting to switch and having personal difficulties with one or more members of the group. In the case of the story selection problem, I requested that we have a conference together the next day to articulate what was wrong with the book. If the complaints were valid, I encouraged the students to write to the publisher, expressing their views and suggestions for improving the story. Then they were free to switch books. With interpersonal problems, I asked the offended party to write down his or her complaint on a piece of paper and give it to a classroom judge. The judge read the complaint to the entire class after lunchtime, during student court (see Chapter 4), so that the class could discuss the problem and devise their own solutions.

Retracing Jackie's Path to Interpretation

The path that Jackie took with her reading was not lockstep. She did not follow a preplanned route mapped out by a teacher's guide far removed from Jackie's life and thought. To chart her reading on a map, you would conclude that she had an open plane ticket, rather than a set itinerary. She began by reading a story about a boy on the island of Puerto Rico who saved the life of a rare red seagull. The next stop was Tibbetts Island, off the coast of Maine, where a family's life cycle paralleled that of a red astrakhan tree. Jackie's interest in trees took her back to her family's original home in Sonora, Mexico, and to the desert plains of Arizona to read about a saguaro cactus that was a hotel for a myriad of insects and other animals. Jackie did not go off flying by herself, however; she was accompanied by a small circle of friends who shared her interests. As teacher, I established the learning environment that trusted her to pursue her interests.

The key to captivating students' and teachers' imaginations is bringing quality literature into a conference that provides for rich transactional learning. What I continued to discover as a teacher was that responding to student transactions could be just as captivating for me as it was for my students. Even though no one in the classroom, including the teacher, had ever been to an island off the coast of Maine, Barbara Cooney's story touched the lives of each of us. Both the students and the teacher were engaged in sharing their lived-through experiences as they heard the story. In a culturally diverse classroom setting, a conference affirms what each student brings to the table. Each of us is a resource of rich experience and personal knowledge of our own world. The process of exploring literature is a shared experience. Figure 5.12 summarizes the keys to following Jackie's path to interpretation in a small group.

Bringing your own life to the text shifts your teacher–student relationship. Paulo Freire (1970) identified this shift in relationship as *dialogical,* one of students–teacher and teacher–students. As teacher, I listened to learn from my students about how they read a text; as students, together they shared with me each other's lives and insights. And I also had room to muse and share my understandings of the reading or how the book touched my life. I was still knowledgeable as the teacher and educational leader of the classroom, but I did not presume to know what my students were thinking until they told me what was on their minds. This strategy makes

FIGURE 5.12 Keys to Following Jackie's Path to Interpretation

▲ Have quality literature on hand, in abundance, in the classroom.

▲ Look for ways that a story touches lived-through experiences.

▲ Affirm the rich experience and personal knowledge that each person brings to the classroom.

▲ Shift the teacher–student relation from lecture to dialogue.

▲ Use open-ended questions to open dialogue: "What was your favorite part of the story?"

▲ Pay attention to the aesthetic reading of a text: "How do you feel about . . .? What do you imagine when . . .? What does this story remind you of?"

▲ Listen for cultural metaphors in response to reading.

▲ Take time to wait for a response (deeper responses come more slowly than superficial ones).

▲ Tie responses to language development and content area learning.

teaching a shared process of exploring the paths to interpretation that the students generate. And once the teacher and students begin to discover their paths to interpretation, they can begin to respond to the text in meaningful ways that work to develop the students' language and literacy.

For Jackie, that morning in my classroom was filled with opportunities for developing language arts. She was actively engaged in listening, speaking, reading, and writing. The product of the Literature Circle was a wide range of language arts activities generated by her own interests. As she pursued her path, she produced oral and written language and nonverbal expressions of art. She composed prose, poetry, and song, authoring her own language and literacy development.

Jackie as Author, Artist, and Explorer

Louise Rosenblatt (1986) posited the idea of following students' "paths to interpretation" of literature, looking for their aesthetic responses to literature as an art form. Following Jackie's path was an experience in interpreting literature, writing prose and poetry, painting, and bookmaking. She made excellent decisions about the direction of her study and ways to express her ideas. She engaged her mind in the books and acquired essential skills for literacy development. Following her path to interpretation, then, was not a mindless act of pushing her out of the nest to fly on her own. She was guided to explore her interests within the context of literature conferences, process writing, and editing and was held accountable for her work with a final class presentation. The Literature Circle, beginning with a story and following class musings to culminate in a class presentation, did not limit her to reading a single story. The 6-week cycle was a way of framing an expedition to explore children's literature. The limitations were the parameters of the students' and teacher's imaginations.

All students bring ideas, imagination, and prior experiences to the table. Their minds are continuously active and curious. They are knowledgeable, but their knowledge is partial, just as the teacher's knowledge is partial. The coming together around a story in a literature conference connects that knowledge and is, as Howard Gardner (1991) quipped, "a time when my creative sluices [are] opened and the juices allowed to flow" (p. 56).

The paths of creativity are not straight. They wind around, double back, and sometimes take the reader beyond initial plans and itineraries. I did not set out to ask Jackie to explore the worlds of Maine's Tibbetts Island and Arizona's saguaro cactus. We started in Puerto Rico. Some students stayed in Puerto Rico, continuing to write and compose in response to the story of Ramon and the red seagull; others stayed on Tibbetts Island, mapping its story, but Jackie needed to move on. Whether in Puerto Rico, Tibbetts Island, or Arizona, the students engaged in significant experiences of reading and writing, of expressing themselves and giving voice to the wanderings of their minds.

Developing literacy with quality children's literature in a student-centered environment treats readers as authors. The students' ideas are substantive and authoritative in reader-centered instruction. Rosenblatt (1978, 1986) calls aesthetic responses to literature a "poem" in which the reader generates a unique and personal understanding of his or her own reading. Reading is an act of authorship, a creative experience of reliving the story, of re-creating the text anew. Jackie and her classmates came to realize that their reading was their open ticket to explore new and old territory. They grew to understand that following their own paths to interpretation was a task in becoming authors and artists and explorers to develop their emergent literacy.

A Thought from Carole

The small-group discussion of *Island Boy* by Barbara Cooney that Paul describes in this chapter was memorable for me, if for no other reason than it lasted an hour and a half—a long time for a group of third graders. During that time, Paul and the students in the group were totally absorbed in reading, and the rest of the students were equally engaged in working on self-directed small-group projects of their own. This one group's discussion focused primarily on the students' as well as Paul's more personal, aesthetic responses to the book, an excellent example of reader-response theory in action and Rosenblatt's notion of literature as a means of personal exploration. By drawing on their prior knowledge and links with their own life experiences, these students also used their second language of English in a natural, context-embedded, instructional framework advocated by second language theorists such as Cummins and Krashen.

Both Paul and I commented afterward that we regretted that we hadn't videotaped it. But because it began spontaneously when Daisy brought the book to Paul, we couldn't have known what would happen. I did take extensive field notes, however, which revealed several significant things to me as I was able to reflect on what had happened that day:

1. *The book was magic.* Although not particularly related to the backgrounds or cultures of Paul's students (it takes place on an island in Maine in the 19th century and is about people of obvious British ancestry), it is a great book, very literary and beautifully illustrated, and touched something in everyone, creating a magic spell that lasted an hour and a half. The book worked on many levels (e.g., death). Paul noted that several words needed explaining but that they were "good words."

2. *The discussion was like a "lap reading."* Several students frequently came up and touched the book; traced their fingers over illustrations, looking for something: counted something; or asked to look longer at an illustration. They talked with each other and with Paul. This is the kind of interaction that happens when a parent reads to one child or to more than one in a family bedtime situation.

3. *Lots of clues to understanding English were used.* Paul pointed frequently to the rich and detailed illustrations; Paul and the students frequently turned back to previous pages to check for understanding and to make links with what they'd already read; Paul gestured a lot and made faces to make the book understandable to his students (e.g., "Ma's fierce eye" he demonstrated by making a fierce eye himself, and he drew a barrel stove on the chalkboard and showed how it worked).

4. *The students were engaged.* They asked many questions, referred back to things they had already read, and made comments linking the story to their own lives.

Some sat spellbound a lot longer than I had ever seen them sit in one place before. Wide eyes were the rule. Carmen was by no means fluent in English: The only thing she had ever said to me was on the day I brought Easter eggs to the class; she came up to me shyly as I was leaving and said hesitantly, "Have a nice . . . on rabbit day." I noted that she was very engaged in this discussion, however, which was all in English. Paul concurred that it was an unusually sustained discourse in English for Carmen.

5. *Aesthetic questions led to linking the story to students' prior knowledge.* Paul asked questions about the students' birthplaces, their families, their favorite trees, and so on.

6. *Students were given time to respond.* Paul waited a long time each time for responses to emerge, rather than rushing for a quick answer to a question.

7. *The teacher shared his own experiences.* Paul was a co-discussant, modeling for the students as well as just wanting to share his experiences of climbing trees as a child and his own family stories.

8. *The mood was that of a fireside chat.* All students seemed relaxed responding in English, and all responded. They sat on the floor and in chairs around Paul. It was intimate, warm, and cozy. Baudelio, often a very tentative student who receives special resource help, was very relaxed and the most "checked in" I had ever seem him. He sat close to Paul, smiled, and responded to other students as well, not the usual pattern for him.

These observations are offered, not as a recipe guaranteed to succeed every time, but as a description of the parts of one really great meal that could happen again, if not in exactly the same way.

EXPLORING IDEAS

1. Look back at the transcript of Paul's discussion with students about the book *Island Boy.* What questions would you have asked?

2. If you were Jackie, where would the book *Island Boy* take you? Would you imagine a saguaro cactus in the desert of the Southwest? Or is your favorite tree in another part of the world?

3. Think about integrating language arts with content area instruction. When would language arts dictate mathematics, science, or social studies instruction?

4. Create a mathematics, science, or social studies unit that draws on children's literature.

5. Think about the issue of trust in teaching. In what ways did Paul demonstrate trust toward his students?

6. Practice conducting a collaborative story interview with another member of the class. Use chart paper to record responses. Color-map the responses on the chart paper by marking similar ideas with the same color, and then number the order of the responses within each color group. Finish by writing up the interview in ordered form.

7. Maintain an interactive journal with your classmates. Between lectures and discussions, take 5 minutes to write down thoughts and ideas. Exchange journals with another student or the instructor to write a response.

8. Conduct a literature conference in a small group in your class. Read a book such as *Island Boy* to the entire group. Ask one member of the group to role-play the teacher and to practice using open-ended questions, listening for metaphors, and noting how the story touches actual lived-through experiences of the group members.

9. Share a favorite children's book with the class. After reading it, brainstorm creative ways to express responses to the story.

CHILDREN'S BOOKS

Belpré, P. (1987). La gaviota roja. In *Campnitas de oro* (pp. 121–135). New York: Macmillan.

Cooney, B. (1988). *Island boy.* New York: Viking Kestrel.

Dahl, R. (1982). *James y el melocotón gigante.* Madrid, Spain: Alfaguara.

d'Aulaire, I., & d'Aulaire, E. P. (1955). *Columbus.* Garden City, NY: Doubleday.

Guiberson, B. Z. (1991). *Cactus hotel.* New York: Henry Holt.

O'Dell, S. (1960). *Island of the blue dolphins.* Boston: Houghton Mifflin.

Wright, B. R. (1983). *The doll house murders.* New York: Holiday House.

Yolen, J. (1992). *Encounter.* New York: Harcourt Brace.

REFERENCES

Bakhtin, M. M. (1981). *The dialogical imagination.* Austin: University of Texas Press.

Freire, P. (1970). *The pedagogy of the oppressed.* New York: Continum.

Gardner, H. (1991). *To open minds.* New York: Basic Books.

O'Neill, J. P. (Ed.). (1990). *Mexico: Splendors of thirty centuries.* Boston: Bullfinch Press.

Rosenblatt, L. (1978). *The reader, the text, and the poem: The transactional theory of the literary work.* Carbondale: Southern Illinois University Press.

Rosenblatt, L. (1986). The aesthetic transaction. *Journal of Aesthetic Education, 20*(4), 122–128.

Compendium of Case Studies

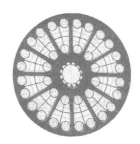

JUAN: The Beginning English Learner

ANNE: The Native English Speaker

EDUARDO: The Intermediate/Advanced English Learner

INTRODUCTION

The case studies of Juan, Anne, and Eduardo describe each child's background and home influences, language development, characteristics as a student, and response styles to literature. These children were participants in a 6-year longitudinal study of children's stance towards literature that I, Carole, conducted (Cox, 1997, 1998; see Chapter 3 references). I read and discussed books in one-on-one read-aloud sessions with these three and other children in their classes from kindergarten, beginning with 57 students, through fifth grade. With regard to English proficiency, Juan is a beginning English learner, Anne is a native English speaker, and Eduardo is an intermediate/advanced English learner.

Chapters 2, 3, and 4 have directed you to read selected parts of these case studies and to think about points of connection to the chapter content and the theories, research, and practices described there. You should also think about the case studies in terms of your own teaching—what might be learned by taking a closer look at a particular child and how you might apply this knowledge in your own classroom.

It is critical for teachers to know as much as possible about each of the students in their classrooms in order to meaningfully engage each one in exploring literature, developing literacy, and differentiating instruction. Theory and research from the fields of reader response, learning English as a second language, social constructivism, and sociocultural perspectives suggest that listening to children tell their ideas, interests, and life experiences is the first act of instruction.

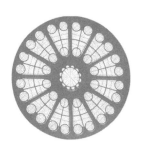

Case Study of Juan:
The Beginning English Learner

MEET JUAN

Juan spoke little English when he entered school in kindergarten and told me, "I don't know that much because I speak Spanish." He made remark-able progress in English through first grade. He was not in a bilingual pro-gram, nor did he have any primary language support in the classroom, and he has struggled in school. He loves soccer and riding horses when he visits his grandfather's ranch in Mexico. He greatly admires his father, who is dedicated to helping Juan succeed.

Background and Home Influences

Family ties strong, including extended family in Mexico
Parents with limited education, less than high school in Mexico
Importance placed on learning English and succeeding in school

Language Development: English as a Second Language(ESL)

Spanish spoken at home
Placed in English-as-a-second-language (ESL) pull-out class
Learned English quickly by end of first grade

Juan as a Student

Intellectual potential greater than school performance
Repeated first grade; special education pull-out class
Still receiving special services through fifth grade

Juan's Response Style: Makes Personal Connections

Links literature to his own experience
Most fluent when telling family stories
Enjoys, understands, and appreciates literature

Connections to Principles and Practices

Juan's father is dedicated to Juan's success but opposes bilingual education
even though Spanish is spoken primarily at home and Juan has had limited
literacy experiences at home in either language—an example of a gap between home and school language and culture.

Juan learned to speak English easily but struggles in English-only classrooms—
an example of limited bilingualism lacking primary language support, other
factors notwithstanding.

Juan responds fluently in read-aloud sessions with me, is interested in reading,
and takes time in one-to-one sessions; he is less responsive in classes in
which emphasis is on grammar versus communication.

Juan makes personal connections in response to literature—an example of the
importance of linking reading to life in reader-response approaches and second language approaches that emphasize prior experience.

BACKGROUND AND HOME INFLUENCES

Juan is a first-generation Mexican American. His mother is an at-home mom, and
Juan has three siblings: an older sister and two younger brothers. Spanish is the
home language. Juan's father speaks English but slips into Spanish when he can't
think of a word he wants or becomes philosophical.

Both parents attended school in the same Mexican village of about 5,000 people.
Juan's father went to school for 6 years, and his mother for 7, although she repeated
grades and didn't go every day. Juan's mother said she doesn't remember anything
from her school days, doesn't enjoy reading, and doesn't have time with four children. The father said he loved school and "read most books I have in my hand." The
only books in their childhood homes were the ones they were given at school.

Juan's parents said he does not like to read enough to initiate reading events.
The father tries to read to Juan every night but sometimes works late. They average
reading three times a week. They read stories and the children's page in the newspaper on Wednesday. He said, "The reading Juan likes the best are comic books,
sometimes history, like George Washington or somebody. Sometimes I read to him.
I don't know if he picks it up or not."

Sometimes Juan's older sister reads to him. She is his best English-language role
model but loses patience when Juan reads to her and does not know all the words.

Juan's father and sister apparently do not discuss Juan's ideas about a story or the meaning of the text. They focus instead on reading the words correctly and pronunciation.

Juan's father wanted to continue in school because his father wanted him to become a "big person—a doctor or a priest, a professional," but they didn't have money. He left school at age 13. Like many other Mexican Americans with ambition but without money, Juan's father emigrated to the United States at age 15. The family lives in a non-Latino area because the father's employer bought a house for the family to live in so that the children could go to a "good school." Juan's father said, "He [Juan] have to be somebody . . . a doctor . . . a lawyer. . . ." To this Juan said, "No—a mechanic so I can fix your truck. [His father laughs heartily.] I really want to be a policeman."

Juan's father has been unhappy with the bilingual program his daughter is in. He also wasn't happy when he found out she signed up for typing as an elective in middle school instead of Spanish. He said she will take Spanish in the future.

The extended family is an important influence in Juan's home. His father expressed dismay at the differences in the importance his non-Latino associates place on the extended family. Juan's family members from Mexico come to visit frequently, and Juan and his family return to Mexico frequently. They also exchange letters regularly, and relatives who live locally take an active role in caring for the children in Juan's family.

LANGUAGE DEVELOPMENT: ENGLISH AS A SECOND LANGUAGE

The school Juan attends has a 14.7 percent English learner population, and Juan is the only Latino student in his class. The opportunity to speak Spanish does not often arise at school. None of the teachers at his school speak Spanish. He participates in a pull-out English-as-a-second-language (ESL) class held in the foyer of the auditorium.

Juan made remarkable progress in learning to speak English from kindergarten through first grade. The first time I read to him in kindergarten, he was very shy. The book was *The Snowy Day* (Keats, 1963). All he said was "I don't know that much because I speak Spanish," which is a lot to say if you supposedly don't speak English. A year later, at the end of first grade, he gave 14 separate spoken responses to a book and was one of only four students out of 38 to offer to read aloud to me.

At the end of first grade, a test of oral English placed him at the intermediate fluency level. His placement in ESL class, however, continued through fourth grade, even though 2 years earlier he had reached the M (mastery) level on the IDEA Proficiency Test (IPT), which is used in the district to evaluate oral proficiency in English for identification and redesignation of limited-English-proficient (LEP) students. The scores on this test range from A to F—the best score—until a student reaches the M level. This test is one of three components for redesignation as a fluent English speaker: IPT score, achievement test scores, and teacher recommendation.

On the basis of his IPT score of M, Juan should have been redesignated as fluent English proficient (FEP) 2 years earlier, but he was not. Evidently, low achievement test scores and a lack of teacher recommendation were prevailing factors. Interestingly, at the end of fourth grade, Juan also took the California Assessment System (CAS) 2 standardized test while most other students in the district took the Metropolitan Achievement Test (MAT) 6 to assess students' mastery of basic skills in reading, language, and mathematics.

Paul told me of two interesting consequences of Juan's lack of redesignation as FEP. One was that Juan's standardized test scores could not be used in school or district averages because most other students took a different test. The second was that Juan was not eligible for obtaining other services unrelated to language because he was still classified as LEP. The question arises as to whether Juan's educational interests were best served or whether he was not reclassified in order to keep his anticipated lower test scores from the school average.

In fourth grade, Juan told me with some pride that he had a cousin who was bilingual Spanish/English, had learned French, and was on a scholarship at UCLA. I told him I had lived in France, and we talked about how a person learns to speak a language by using it with other people. Later in this same discussion, he told me about a cousin who had been killed in a random drive-by shooting because the cousin was Latino—not a gang member, but a good student, baseball player, and prom king. Juan said his dad was concerned about things such as dress and being mistaken for a gang member and especially wanted Juan to stay in school. Juan said, "When I grow up, I want to give him a Corvette and a house in Mexico. If you're bilingual, you can get a job helping doctors and they pay you a lot of money. Or I could go to college and play soccer and get a lot of money."

JUAN AS A STUDENT

Juan's kindergarten teacher had a very student-centered approach. She mentioned self-esteem first when asked how she teaches. She wanted children to love to be at school, enjoy it, use their own ideas and think, and work independently. It was important to her that children discover things on their own through play and experimenting.

With literature, she liked children to think about what is happening in a story or what could happen—not just retelling an event or the name of a person, but relating it to their own experiences. She suggested these kinds of aesthetic prompts to them: "If I tried to do that . . .," That story reminded me of . . ., "Maybe I could handle it that way," and so on. She liked lots of discussion during and after reading, for students to create their own story.

At the end of the school year, this teacher thought Juan would have a hard time in school, not just because of language but because it was hard to get answers out of him. She suggested it might be immaturity and language but that it might also be some kind of learning problem. She said it was difficult to talk with him about a book, for example, because he didn't seem to know what was going on. At the end of kindergarten, Juan scored at the 1 percent level in language (English) on the Test of Basic Experience (TOBE) 2.

Juan's first-grade teacher did lots of literature-based activities. During one week, all the students designed and made puppets of the characters from *Katy*

No-Pocket (Rey, 1944) and shared them with the whole class. Afterward, the teacher reread *Katy No-Pocket,* and they discussed the book along the way. She asked the students, "What do you think Katy is thinking?" She called on Juan, but he didn't answer. Other students hypothesized: If she has more babies, she'll have more pockets; the baby's excited; maybe the mother will let him have friends. Juan's teacher said,

> Juan tried hard but frequently "shut down." He would not make eye contact when you talked to him. He was more comfortable after school. He would cry if pushed. He wants to be a leader. He was uncomfortable making choices. An effective approach with him is using consistent guidelines and positive reinforcement.

Juan tested at the average level for cognitive abilities. It was noted that there seemed to be a consistent discrepancy between his ability and his achievement in reading and writing. Juan was retained at the end of first grade, primarily because of his limited English and low reading scores.

Juan repeated first grade with another teacher. He was put into the "lowest" reading group. His teacher used a highly structured phonics reading program, the Spaulding method. Here is a Spaulding lesson on writing letters that she did one day with Juan's group. She called them "phonograms." She wrote the following letters on the chalkboard: *d g y x z e o s v*. Each child had a red pencil and copied the letters as they talked.

Juan: *I did it wrong.*
Teacher: *What do you do when you do it wrong?*
J: *Correct it.*
T: *Raise your hand if you left a space and wrote "qu."*

(Juan raises his hand, but another child, Mark, doesn't.)

T: *Mark, did you write it?*
M: *Yes.*
T: *You need to raise your hand so I know. Put your finger on the next phonogram. Read to me the next phonogram. Now write it down. You should have written this [J]. What does this letter remind you of Juan?*
J: *My name.*
T: *Move to the next phonogram [P]. What does it say?*
J: *P-P-P with mouth.*

This teacher remained in tight control of all classroom activities. Talking with other students was highly discouraged. She read aloud, and the students answered the questions she asked that directed them back to the text for answers.

Art or writing in response to literature occurred only once a week and was very teacher-directed. For example, after reading aloud a story to the whole class about scary things in a tree, she directed students to draw their own creatures in a tree. She told them to work without telling or showing their neighbor what they were doing: "I'll show you what everyone's done."

Despite this direction, Juan whispered to his neighbor that he would draw a two-headed snake. He couldn't seem to get started, however. He whispered to his neighbor, "My uncle has a snake, and he puts it around his neck. Sometimes he puts it around my neck and lets me touch it." Then he started to draw but continued to tell his neighbors about his extensive snake experience. He went to the teacher to show her, and she came to his desk to write his name. He said, "I can write my own name. I have another name. I have four names. My mom's name, too." The teacher said suspiciously, "Is that so? I don't know about that fourth name." She obviously did not know about use of the mother's maiden name among Latinos.

This teacher used the same commercial reader as the other first-grade teacher for reading lessons with the whole class. Because Juan was repeating first grade, he had already heard most of these stories. He seemed bored and frustrated by some of the repetition, and as a result he appeared uninterested in the work. His teacher thought it was a developmental problem or that he was "lazy." Juan's father said he knew Juan could work more in reading but that Juan was learning to speak English so well that they didn't want to "push" him in reading and "confuse him." His mother said, "When he doesn't know a word, he asks me what it says. This year, I only tell him one time and he remembers. Last year, I had to tell him many times. Many times, he confuses the *b* and *d*." They thought his repeating first grade had been successful because "he seemed to be learning a little more every day." Unfortunately, the teacher did not share this view of his progress.

In second grade, Juan's teacher did lots of cooperative group work, in which students interact with each other. She encouraged discussion when she talked with the whole class and language exchange among students in groups. She incorporated many activities across modalities. By this point, Juan had repeated first grade and was receiving special education help in a pull-out class. He also took ESL classes. His second-grade teacher commented:

> He's hard to describe. You have to look. He is a sensitive and deep person. He wants to be a perfectionist. He loves sports. That's all he wants to talk about. He says he wants to move back to Mexico like his Uncle and have a ranch. That's his goal. He is very intimidated to speak in front of the class. He doesn't readily participate in whole-class discussions but is a leader in small groups. His writing is simple but to the point. When he tells his story aloud, he will embellish it greatly. He is more confident with his writing skills now. He will write some and then tell us aloud the way he wants it. I have met his father three times. He is very loving and wants the best for Juan. He is not able to spend enough time with him to make a difference. A lot of his upbringing has been by his older sister. He puts her on a pedestal. He doesn't talk much about his mom. She has no English, really. I think maybe Juan may be embarrassed about that. He goes to ESL and RSP [special education]. His spoken and written language don't match. I think there may be perceptual problems. He took a big step in February. He started to go to the library when it stayed open after school to pick out a book he knew he could read. He picked sports books, and he would tell stories aloud based on his reading. He did a biography report on Bob Griese, former quarterback for the Miami Dolphins. There is still a big gap between Juan's potential and his performance. He speaks well, and he does choose to read, especially about sports. He never chooses to write. They worked on that in RSP.

At the end of second grade, all students in Juan's school took the MAT 6 test. He tested at 4 percent in reading, 19 percent in language, and 54 percent in mathematics. It was noted at this time that Juan did not read or write Spanish.

Juan's third-grade teacher said he seemed frustrated, and the RSP teachers said, "Something is missing; you can only teach him strategies." He was still in an ESL pull-out class.

When I asked him about school, he said that it was fun and that he was doing fine. About reading, he told me his dad was going to take him to the public library after school—if his dad came home early and could still take him to soccer practice. I asked him about books he liked to read. He said:

> Sometimes I pick out sport books, sometimes make believe books, sometimes truth books. My favorite book was a sport book about Péle. . . . At home, I read by myself, but if I don't know a word, I ask my sister and she tells me. She's fifteen. My dad reads with me, too. Actually, I read to him—soccer books, regular books, all kinds. I read to my little brother. He's in kindergarten. I read to him, and then my dad signs his home reading chart. Once I read to him, then my dad signs mine, too, and then he signs my little brother's. I read "Cinderella," easy books.

Juan talked about his motivation for doing well in school:

> My dad says if I study I can go to Mexico for a whole summer by myself. I would stay with my grandpa, grandma, and other grandpa. On the ranch, a baby horse got born. But it died. He was running and there were like little things on the bars so no one could go in there and there's only one way by a gate and you could have to walk a half a mile and he got in there.

When Juan was in fourth grade, an English language development (ELD) teacher came to Juan's class and worked with him. His fourth-grade teacher said he gained a lot of confidence and was more mature.

JUAN'S RESPONSE STYLE: MAKES PERSONAL CONNECTIONS

Juan responded little in kindergarten. Even though the situation was very informal— we sat on the floor in the hall outside the classroom—Juan was nervous and ill at ease, even frightened, compared with the other 56 students. He seemed inhibited because of his limited English although he spoke well enough to say to me, "I don't know that much because I speak Spanish," when I read to him the first time. The only other thing he said was "He's sleeping" about the little boy in the book. Juan said little the rest of the year—one comment about the size of the ducks in *Make Way for Ducklings* (McCloskey, 1941) and once to tell me he got *Miss Rumphius* (Cooney, 1982), one of the stories I read, out of the library.

What a difference a year made. Juan's development in English through first grade was remarkable, and he showed a marked change in his behavior during our reading sessions. From saying little or nothing in kindergarten, he had a lot to say and seemed to enjoy talking with me about books.

He sat close, smiled, touched the book, and turned the pages back and forth to look again at parts of the story I had already read. He responded primarily aesthetically. He seemed most engaged with the text when he could associate it with his own experience. After I read *Umbrella* (Yashima, 1958), he talked about a friend:

> Like my friend Jonas, he got an umbrella when it was a cold day and it went over a car. [He got an umbrella?] On the car. He was holding it like that. It was cold and it was kind of rainy. The wind blowed it all the way to the car right there. It was kind of funny and we was laughing. [Oh, really? It blew away from him?] Yeah, and he was saying, "It's not funny. It's not funny." [It wasn't to him?] It wasn't funny to him. No.

This was the longest sustained speech on a single topic that had occurred so far in our reading-aloud sessions. Notice that he didn't talk about the book; rather, the book triggered the talk about his friend.

At the end of first grade, when I read the single, long simple sentence that is the text for the picture book *Rosie's Walk* (Hutchins, 1968), Juan commented about what was happening throughout the reading and asked a few questions. Afterward, he said very forcefully, "I want to read." It was as though he had waited during the reading, made a few comments he thought I wanted to hear, but primarily wanted to show me his new reading ability. He seemed to be remembering more than actually reading the words, focusing on the meaning of the story. He said "chicken" for *hen* and "gate" for *fence*. What's interesting is that while reading, he asked pointed questions and developed plausible hypotheses and explanations as a result and did not wait for me to ask him about the book, as he had done before. He was more actively involved in the reading. This was not surprising because he was doing the reading and seemed to feel in charge of the situation. We were codiscussants, rather than teacher and student. He seemed pleased with himself when we finished. He asked me when I'd be coming again. He asked whether he could read to me again then.

Juan was one of only four of 38 students who asked to read to me at the end of first grade. He got many words wrong, but he tried hard and obviously understood the story by substituting words that made sense for ones he didn't know and seemed to enjoy himself—quite a change from the child who had told me, "I don't know that much because I speak Spanish" only a year before.

Three important things occurred during our read-aloud sessions in first grade. The first time I read, he demonstrated his ability and confidence in speaking English, which had developed significantly over a year's time. He responded much like the majority of the other students, taking a predominantly aesthetic stance. The second time I read, he really opened up by making associations with the story and his personal life. His speech in English was fluent and extended. He had a lot to say. The third time he asked to read aloud to me. During the reading, instead of asking me questions about things that puzzled him, he asked the questions but developed his own hypotheses and explanations. He was more confident about not only his English and reading but also his ideas. This was *meaning construction* in the best sense of the term, integrally tied in with language development, literacy, and personal response to literature.

During his second year in first grade, Juan's response was predictable and similar to that of many students. *Caps for Sale* (Slobodkina, 1947) is a predictable pattern book. Juan answered the question posed in the text: "What do you think he saw?" Juan had little else to say in response to the book. This was typical of many of the other students who responded to this book.

Juan's richest—certainly most fluent—response was to the second book I read in second grade, *The Nicest Gift* (Politi, 1973). We talked and read for close to an hour. He acted out the story through facial expressions, pantomiming, and voice characterizations. He was highly engaged in the story. I believe two things triggered the explosion of association-type responses Juan made. First, the book has words in Spanish, and second, he could correct my Spanish pronunciation:

Juan: *Where is this?*
Carole: *L.A. Downtown.*
J: *This?* (Pointing to hills around the city)
C: *Hillsides. East L.A. His house is pink* (reading) . . . *caballito.*
J: Caballito. (He corrects my pronunciation.)
C: *Thank you. What does it mean?*
J: *Little horse.*

His interest was piqued here. Juan's first language was suddenly important, and he knew more about it than I did. After this, he made one personal association after another with his own life and the lives of the Latino characters in the book.

J: *Tamales? My mom makes 'em. My grandma at Mexico and she has a rancho and she has my horse and when my dad went to Mexico and took 'em and when there was a fiesta we were in 'em—me, my dad, my grandpa.*
C: *You ride?*
J: *Yeah.* (Pretends the chair is a horse and shows me how to get on and ride on it.)

After that, he never got out of the saddle but galloped through this book, telling me one story after another about his life. Sometimes one part of a picture or even one word—especially when he could correct my pronunciation—would set him off on an extended anecdote. He was having fun. I was amazed to see how much he had to say. I read. He talked. I listened. He talked some more. This was different from going from saying very little in kindergarten to talking and reading in English. That could be expected from his three years' experience in English-only classroom in second grade. What was notable was how much more he had to say when he was interested, engaged, and could draw on his own life experiences as a basis for talking and responding. He also knew he was impressing me. And I was, indeed, impressed. He told me many things, especially about his family. For example,

> [I read". . . calls out *como* . . ."] That means "How are you?" My dad were gonna go to Christmas down there. [Mexico?] Yeah. But no fair. They're going and I'm not. [Not going to take you?] No. Plus, my uncle's getting married and my uncle wants me to give those little things that men put on, right here . . . [Boutonnieres?] Yeah. Mom said, "No, 'cause you'll miss school." But I said, "He wants me." She goes, "No. Stay here. With aunt or grandma." I'd rather stay with my grandma. My aunt just likes to go to the beach with my other uncle and get wet and I say that's boring, even cold. He shouldn't go to the beach when it's cold. My cousin is nice, though.

Juan most's characteristic response type is association. He most frequently shared family stories and stopped to talk about a part of the story when he could make an association with his own experience. He asked questions for information and suggested explanations for things in the story through dialogue with me. He searched for explanations and for understanding of the story while he did so. The story *The Nicest Gift* (Politi, 1973) was about a lost dog and a boy's search for him. Juan wove questions and hypotheses and explanations for the whereabouts of the dog throughout his family stories. At the end he told me he liked the whole thing, especially the way the story went up and down and around, just like the pictures of the hillsides and city streets of Los Angeles—a rather sophisticated analogy, comparing the structure of the story to the style of the illustrations.

During another read-aloud session with me in second grade, before we sat down, Juan asked whether he could read to me. He told me his dad had said, "Please, could I?"—but not, Juan declared, with the tape recorder. As he read, he stopped and commented often. His reading became very halting at points. It seemed to me he had been "overphonicked." If he didn't know a word, he would say the first letter—and then look at me. Through my experience with Juan since kindergarten, it was obvious he understood and enjoyed stories but seemed to believe he should use other types of knowledge—such as letter names—when reading, even though this technique rarely worked for him.

For example, when he was repeating first grade, he substituted words in *Rosie's Walk* (Hutchins, 1968) that still made sense in the story and enabled him to keep reading. It seemed, however, that after a year in a class with a teacher using the Spaulding method and tightly controlling all classroom activities, he believed reading was a process of "sounding out," rather than of putting meaning and sounds together. He had also had RSP and ESL classes that had emphasized "the code" and that took a grammar-based rather than a communicative-based approach. He seemed much more tense talking about reading. He still enjoyed it when I read to him and interacted with me freely.

In another read-aloud session in second grade, after he read and stopped several times, I asked whether he wanted me to read to him first and then he could read to me if he wanted. He was happy with this. His responses to the book I read, *Ira Sleeps Over* (Waber, 1972), were similar to those of many of the other students. Most comments were aesthetic: He hypothesized about story events, noted a part he liked, asked questions, and made associations. His efferent responses were typical, too: about story content and an explanation. He did not provide the detailed family stories as he had done in response to *The Nicest Gift*.

In second grade I began asking students questions about reading: How do you feel about reading? What books do you read? What about reading at home? in school? Juan's answers were revealing:

I'm trying to get my Super Nintendo. Study, my dad says. I tried to pass a test today. [Which?] Spelling. [How do you feel about reading?] Good. [What are you reading?] About flowers and how to take care of them. Three stories. [How do you feel about reading in school?] Sometimes I'm embarrassed. [Why?] 'Cause I don't know some of the words. But I'm trying to practice them at home. [How?] My dad usually helps me. [What?] He reads with me, and sometimes my mom even helps me. She knows a little English. [Do you have your own books at home?] A lot. A whole bookshelf full. Sometimes my sister and I read. I read to her, and then I read to my mom, and she reads to me and Dad. [Is your sister older?] She's fourteen. She's a good reader. [You said earlier you wanted to read to me.] Yeah. But without the mike. Why do you want to read to me? [I'm interested in what children think about stories.] Mmmmm. [Did your dad ask if you could read?] Yeah. My dad asked if I could please read to you! [OK. Read to me!]

At the beginning of third grade, Juan was glad to see me. He said nothing while I read *A Chair for My Mother* (Williams, 1982) but responded at the end. He mentioned a few parts he liked and told how bad he "would feel if all his stuff would be gone." When I asked about school and reading, he told me a lot, especially about his family here and in Mexico and the ranch in Mexico.

It's important to note that Juan's pattern of making associations with his own life and telling family stories did not occur each time he read. He barely spoke at all in kindergarten. In first grade he spoke much more, and his responses were varied. The most frequent type was questions during *Alexander and the terrible, horrible, no good very bad day* and associations during *Umbrella* (Yashima, 1958). The most significant thing is that he asked to read to me at the end of first grade. In second grade he simply responded to the questions in the predictable pattern book *Caps for Sale* (Slobodkina, 1947) but exploded with responses to *The Nicest Gift* (Politi, 1973). The fact that the book had Spanish words—and Juan was in the driver's seat when he corrected my Spanish pronunciation—and that he could relate things the Latino family did in the book to his own Latino heritage seemed to be all he needed in order to talk for almost an hour in a rich and meaningful way about the story and his own experiences. Theory and research tell us over and over that this is exactly what children should be doing when they read: becoming actively engaged in the reading process and story, linking it to their own lives, and seeking meaning as they read.

I would not suggest that the key to helping English learners is to simply read them books about their own culture in English, with a few words in their native language sprinkled throughout. See, for example, in Chapter 5 what happened in Paul's class when he read the book *Island Boy* (Cooney, 1988), the story of a family in Maine of obvious British heritage. His Latino students related to it, but not because of language or culture. In Juan's case, however, an insightful teacher would do well to notice his interest in talking about this book and run—not walk—to the library to get him other books about Latino families by Leo Politi or other authors and any books with Spanish words, particularly about families.

Further, it would be a mistake to assume on the basis of Juan's response that all children who resemble him in terms of English language development and Latino culture will respond to this book in the same way. The case study of Eduardo is a good example of a child of Latino heritage whose response style is different from Juan's. They are two different children who share a common heritage.

In fourth grade, when I read *Song of the Swallows* (Politi, 1949), Juan was very confident and mature. We reminisced about my visits. He was attentive to the text and pictures. We talked about San Juan Capistrano Mission and ways California had changed. He was interested in where it was, what it was like there, and so on. This discussion led him to talk about his family's life in California, covering things like immigration, family in two countries, a cousin who was shot in a drive-by shooting, the importance of not being mistaken for a gang member, and staying in school and going to college. It was a seamless discussion, beginning with the book but going through his future. He obviously understands and appreciates literature and art. Midway in the discussion of everything from not wearing baggy pants to the advantages of being bilingual, he said, "What we're doing is ELD [English language development], isn't it?"

A Thought from Paul

Juan's case study calls to mind the image of a flawed performance with devastating consequences, like a novice violinist in front of an impatient audience. Even though Juan entered school without support in his primary language, he was expected to perform as a fully fluent native English speaker. When he failed, he was retained in first grade, pulled out for ESL instruction (even after attaining mastery level on the IPT of oral English proficiency), placed in special education, and given a heavy dose of phonics instruction. Juan appears to be the product of a system that refused to recognize and validate his background knowledge, experience, and culture.

With the exception of additional help in English, none of the above treatments apply to Juan's educational needs. The treatments may, in fact, have a reverse effect on his education. One has to wonder why the school retained him for lack of English fluency. Even more damning is the question of why special education was chosen as the remedy for his struggle to read aloud in English. By fourth grade he is in a dilemma: He has received no academic support or literacy development in his primary language, so the language he speaks at home, the language he thinks in, is negated at school; he continues to struggle with the mechanics of English, so he is therefore neither fully bilingual nor fully monolingual in English. Add to that the stigma of retention and special education placement, and you have a strong candidate for a future dropout. Failing to perform in English reading, he is fed phonics in the hope that he will pronounce words correctly in English.

The haunting words of Juan, "I don't know that much because I speak Spanish," give evidence of an environment in which his knowledge, culture, and language are devalued. The significance of reader response, particularly in a multicultural context, is the repositioning of knowledge from the text to the reader. Reader response looks to the reader to express his or her own insights in response to the text. Reader response treats Juan more as an author than as a performer. He is an authority on his own life, family, feelings, and ideas. As he reads and hears stories read by Carole, he creates his own story and thus constructs his own understanding.

Juan brings to reading a wealth of experience. He makes sense of his reading as he is given the opportunity to connect the words to his life. Connecting the text to life takes place in dialogue with others about the multilayered meanings of story, the public and personal understandings of the text. It is not a question of performance. It is a question of authorship, of connecting one's experience to a juicy story.

EXPLORING IDEAS

Think about Juan's experience as a non-English-speaking child entering kinder-garten and a developing English learner in terms of what current second language theory suggests is good second language education practice:

1. How would you evaluate the schooling of this English learner?

2. Compare the approaches of Juan's teachers in first grade, in first grade the second time, and in second grade. What models do they each reflect of learning English as a second language acquisition, and teaching with literature?

3. What would you do about Juan's English language and literacy development if Juan were a student in your class?

4. What are ways you and Juan's father might join forces in Juan's education?

5. Observe and participate in several types of classrooms/programs that serve English learners: English-only classroom, classroom with primary language support (e.g., bilingual aides, flexible scheduling, peer tutoring), ESL pull-out class, or dual-immersion classroom. Keep notes of what kind of language and literacy instruction is provided. Compare the classrooms/programs with each other and the theoretical models of teaching with literature and second language education described in Chapters 2 and 3.

6. Observe in two different classrooms of English learners in which different home languages are spoken (e.g., Spanish/English, Korean/English). What differences, if any, do you notice?

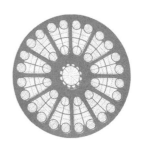

Case Study of Anne:
The Native English Speaker

MEET ANNE

Anne has been an excellent student, has been identified as gifted, and has been placed in a gifted pre-kindergarten program at a public school. She enjoys art, has played the violin since age 5, takes dance lessons, and has participated in drama programs and Girl Scouts. She is small, blonde, and outspoken. Someone watching her challenge an older child for breaking a school rule on the playground said, "She doesn't know how small she is, does she?"

Background and Home Influences

Literate family who are readers; books in the home
Many and regular reading experiences
Related story experiences: drama, music, song, dance, art

Language Development: Native English Speaker

English spoken at home
Adults, siblings, and friends who listen to and talk with her
Communicates well with others; has a strong "voice"

Anne as a Student

High grades and scores on standardized tests
Quiet in school, compared with outspoken at home
Frustrated with lack of time to read and assigned writing

Anne's Response Style: Challenges the Text

Questions what puzzles her; shreds the story
Hypothesizes possibilities, associating her own experience
Has intense drive to create personally meaningful interpretation

Connections to Principles and Practices

Anne learned by doing, both speaking and reading—an example of social constructivist, communication-based language learning at home (many opportunities to use language and engage in literacy experiences).

Anne is a successful student with a quiet "voice" inside school but a strong "voice" outside—an example of a transmission model of learning (teacher directs and may talk more than students).

Anne challenges the text—an example of a transactional model of reading (active role of reader in creating literary understanding; a primarily aesthetic stance toward literature).

Anne is angry about and frustrated by the lack of opportunities to read in school and to read for personal exploration—an example of dissonance between a child who loves and enjoys reading and teacher- and text-centered classrooms.

BACKGROUND AND HOME INFLUENCES

Anne comes from a white, middle-class home. Her mother is a teacher; her father owns his own business. She has two brothers. One was 13 when she was born; the other was 2 ½. Many children's books are in the home. Her mother takes her and the younger brother on weekly trips to the library.

Reading is a family affair. When Anne was a baby, her mother read to both young children every day, several times a day. She now encourages Anne's father and older brother to read to her. Her father most often reads to her at bedtime, choosing classics like *Goodnight Moon* (Brown, 1947) and *The Runaway Bunny* (Brown, 1942). He also likes the interactive book *Pat the Bunny* (Kunhardt, 1940) and small board books with action rhymes like "Teddy Bear, Teddy Bear, turn around." Anne's older brother reads to her, too, when he takes care of her when their mother is busy. He has learned that she is easier to handle when he is reading to her. He is an active teenager and likes to act out the books. He often chooses *The Three Billy Goats Gruff* illustrated by Marcia Brown (1957). He reads the book dramatically, using a different voice for each character. Anne's younger brother is usually involved in the reading sessions with their older brother, and they all like to act out the story, with the big brother as the troll. He also likes to read Anne's favorite, *The Tall Book of Mother Goose* (Rojankovsky, 1942). They all act these out, too. Anne plays Miss Muffet, and one of her brothers is the spider. Or Anne is the cat with the fiddle, and one of them is the cow that jumped over the moon and the little dog that laughed to see such sport. One of them is always the dish that runs away with Anne, who is always the spoon.

Anne has also had exposure to stories through CDs of children's books and songs. She has watched *Sesame Street* and other public television shows for children. Anne's family and home have supported her language and emerging literacy development by providing a print-rich environment, models of literacy, and many opportunities to experience literature and stories in an active, engaging way.

LANGUAGE DEVELOPMENT: NATIVE ENGLISH SPEAKER

Everyone in Anne's family is a native English speaker. She spoke early and well. She was always verbally assertive, not afraid to talk to others or speak her mind. Her family encouraged her to do this. Her babysitter came to the home when her mother worked. The sitter took Anne out into the neighborhood, where she played with other children and interacted with their families. The sitter took her shopping and on errands, so Anne was frequently involved with people in the community. She talked a lot, did not wait to be spoken to, and had no trouble expressing an opinion to children or adults or telling others what they should do. Her brothers describe her as having a "big mouth." Her father says, "There's no question about who's in charge here. It's Anne."

ANNE AS A STUDENT

Anne went to a private preschool half-days when she was 2 years old. She had many experiences with books, as well as finger plays, drama, and art. When she was 3 years old, Anne was tested for the public preschool gifted program and qualified. She said she liked books and enjoyed looking at pictures while the psychologist tested her. He wrote, "Anne is a 3-year-old girl who at present time is functioning, according to educational testing, 1 1/2 years above her chronological age in math and 2 1/2 years above in reading. She is a very friendly child who appears to enjoy educational tasks. She should profit greatly from being placed in a preschool class for the gifted."

She attended from 8:00 AM to noon each day. Her teacher read aloud frequently. In addition, students dramatized stories by dressing up like characters and acting out the stories, and they made their own book versions of *Brown Bear, Brown Bear, What Do You See?* by Bill Martin, Jr. (1967). They even performed a class musical about Australia, in which Anne sang a solo about kangaroos. She had many varied experiences with books, stories, and their extensions. Her teacher described her as a child with "excellent concentration, sense of order, inner discipline."

Anne went to kindergarten half-days in the afternoon. Her kindergarten teacher provided daily time for sharing, reading aloud, and self-selected reading. Because Anne was beginning to read independently, the morning kindergarten teacher spent time reading one-on-one with her.

Because Anne's kindergarten teacher liked to sing, she used poems that could be put to a tune, such as Dennis Lee's "Alligator Pie" (1975). The students sang the poem, used hand motions to go with it, read other books about animals, and did a "musical" about animals. They made masks and costumes and presented the musical to the parents. The teacher also provided many art, cooking, and hands-on experiences related to books.

Anne liked her morning teacher and the time she was given to read books, and she self-selected books on her own. Her teacher described her this way:

> Cute little thing. Bright but quiet in a large group, but will talk your ear off in one-on-one situation. Lots of good ideas about books. Read her a story and she can pick out that little idea between the lines. Wonderful little girl. A thinker. You know those little wheels are turning, you know she's thinking when you're talking or reading a book. She's thinking of something great to say, or a story.

At the end of kindergarten, Anne was tested for the elementary gifted program and qualified. The psychologist who tested her noted that "she was quick to answer questions but took time when necessary, was socially confident and at ease with adults, and had a delightful sense of humor."

Anne's first-grade teacher had great charisma, and Anne loved to go to school. The school district had just adopted "literary readers", which are commercial readers that contain excerpts from children's books. The teachers used the accompanying teacher's guides and the "pupil response" booklets with prompts for students to write after reading. Although Anne still loved books and reading, she did not like these readers.

During reading-aloud sessions with me, she asked questions and talked throughout the reading of the book. By the third session, at the end of the year, she asked to read to me herself. During a classroom observation made of a literary reader lesson on the story *Anna Banana and Me* (Blegvad & Blegvad, 1985) described in Chapter 3, however, she was uncharacteristically quiet. If you remember, Anne's teacher took a more text-centered approach, using questions from the teacher's guide, focusing on having students arrive at an agreed-upon meaning of the text, and guiding students to come to similar conclusions. Although Anne was very talkative in the one-on-one reading sessions with me, she did not readily answer the more efferent, text-based questions from the teacher's guide.

At the end of the year, Anne received an E (excellent progress) in reading on her report card. Her teacher wrote, "I am pleased with Anne's social and academic growth. She takes her job as a student very seriously and is held in high regard by her peers and her teacher."

Anne's second-grade teacher was very relaxed, and Anne was also relaxed in school that year. She had become an avid, independent reader. During a classroom observation I made, I saw the teacher read two versions of *The Three Billy Goats Gruff*. The teacher had a sheet of chart paper with two columns titled "Alike" and "Different." The students were directed to write lists for both columns, and the teacher explained that they must always have a specific reason for writing.

Anne's report card and standardized test scores at the end of this year showed that she was succeeding academically according to her teacher, school, and district criteria. She received an E in reading. Her teacher noted, "She writes well and is an excellent reader." She scored 99 percent in reading on the MAT 6 Test.

In third grade, Anne read and talked enthusiastically all the way through our reading-aloud sessions but rarely responded during group discussions in class. She complained about writing and other assigned activities after reading and about assigned reading and book reports. This year I began asking students what they were reading on their own and how they felt about reading. Anne said, "I like to read a lot. I'm reading *Scared Stiff* [Roberts, 1991] and *A Ghost in the Window* [Wright, 1987] from the library at home. I'm more than halfway through it, and it hasn't mentioned anything about a ghost. It's supposed to be a ghost story. There's a ghost on the cover."

I asked her about reading in school and reading at home. "I don't like reading at school very much because I don't have very much time. Like when I'm at home, I can read all I want. I can't at school." Anne again received a grade of E in reading.

Anne's fourth-grade teacher provided many content-rich activities. Anne thought her teacher was fun at the beginning of the year but soon began to struggle with the paper load. Book reports were assigned one after another. The teacher chose the books the students could read from each genre (e.g., mystery, biography), and she assigned very structured projects to go with each report. For each of the three biographies the students were required to read from a limited selection of titles, they did one of three projects: (a) dress as the character, (b) make a paper doll, or (c) make a soda-can doll. Anne generally enjoyed these things but did not enjoy the books she had to read.

Uncharacteristically, she rebelled against the structured written reports for all the assigned reading in the class. At the end of the year, the class read the paperback *The Big Wave* (Buck, 1986) from the commercial literary reader series, and the teacher gave them 10 pages of questions photocopied from the pupil response booklet. Anne stalled on these and barely finished before the year was over. At one point she asked me whether I thought she would graduate from fourth grade if she didn't do them. She told me she'd been kept after school and had had her name on the board frequently for not keeping up on this kind of work.

Her report card showed, however, that her teacher believed her to be an excellent student who understood the content taught and had exceptional reading skills. The school district switched to a new type of progress report that uses a 1 (low) to 6 (high) scale with a description of each level in all areas graded. On the Reading/ Literature Assessment Scale, her teacher gave her a 6 (exceptional) and an E (excellent effort). The scale defines 6 Exceptional Reader like this:

> An enthusiastic, independent, and reflective reader. Is capable of reading in all content areas and can read a wide range and variety of materials. Consistently produces work that demonstrates comprehension. Is able to make predictions and draw inferences without teacher support.

Despite her high evaluation, Anne was frustrated about reading and her experiences with literature and literature assignments in school. Here are some things she told me at the end of fourth grade about how she felt about reading at home, in school, and in general. On reading at home:

> I love to read at home. My favorite authors are Betsy Byars and Lois Lowry. I'm reading the *Anastasia* books. My favorite series books are *The Baby-Sitter's Club* and the *American Girl* series.

On reading at school:

> I hate reading in school because you have to read what they make you. Unless it's a good book, but even if it's a good book they read it to you or you have to read certain parts when you have to. The only time I like reading in school is when the teacher's reading aloud and we can read along, or when we can read for fun—which is never. We never have time to read.
>
> You have to write down the stupid thing. [She sounds very frustrated and is practically crying.] I hate that. You gotta write down everything you do. I don't get how that is reading. And one time I told the truth and she put it wrong. She said, "What was your favorite part?" and I didn't have a favorite part. I said I just liked the whole thing and she counted it off. So I have to make up something, which is real dumb. And they do the hardest things and they get mad at you when you get behind or something. Like, "If you could interview Abel [*Abel's Island* by William Steig, 1976], what questions would you ask him? [In an authoritarian voice.] You had to list twenty questions, and you couldn't ask yes-or-no questions or simple ones. Why not? Cause sometimes they're the important questions. Answering questions instead of reading is the dumbest thing in the whole entire world.

After her extended and even angry comments about what she didn't like about reading in school, I asked her what she would like to do in reading at school.

> Read it! [emphatically, followed by a long pause here] Think about it. You don't have to talk to anybody. I like thinking. After I read a book, I think for a million years and then go back and read my favorite pages again. Sometimes I read through a book really fast, and then I go back and read my favorite parts again.

Finally, because she had so much to say about how reading was taught and what she didn't like about it, I asked how she would approach reading if she were the teacher. She didn't hesitate:

> I'd just say, "Read this book. Go read whatever book you want, and if you want to come tell me about it, you can; or if you don't, just think or just go do something else like read it again or read another book." I'd make it so that you'd bring as many books as you want and just read, read, read, all day.

She had really warmed to the subject by this time and continued to tell me how she felt about reading in general—but more, I think, about her feeling of powerlessness in school, especially with regard to not having the kind of experiences with literature she would like and really wanted. On reading in general:

> I love to read. It's my favoritest thing in the whole world. If there was no such things as books, I'd die [spoken dramatically]. 'Cause it's not fair if nobody invented books. I'd be so mad. I'd invent a book. What if suddenly, that really mean guy . . . Adolf Hitler . . . what if someone like him came and took away all the books in the world? I'd be so mad that I'd say, "You're the stupidest, ugliest, meanest person in

the whole entire world." I'd punch him in the nose. Didn't you do that once when you were little, you told me, [in a previous session] when someone teased your little brother? [Yes.] Did you get in trouble? [Not exactly; I was little and blonde and a girl. Nobody thought I'd do anything like that.] *Blonde?* What does that have to do with it? Little? Girl? I'm blonde, little, and a girl. If somebody as mean as Hitler took over, I'd beat him up.

My question about reading obviously touched a nerve with Anne, and I sensed that a lot of feelings she had kept quiet were exploding now. She was ready to punch Hitler in the nose if he took books away. She was only partly joking, and I don't think she really meant Hitler. I sensed real anger here. Remember, this is not a child who has not succeeded in school, but one who has been extremely successful, from standardized test scores to teacher performance evaluations. Her comments about reading, as well as those of other students in this study, mirror her feelings that reading is something she wants but can't have in school. Real reading takes place in the library or at home. Think about how this could influence decisions that teachers make about teaching with literature and about language and literacy development for all children.

ANNE'S RESPONSE STYLE: CHALLENGES THE TEXT

Anne's most frequent type of response in reading-aloud sessions with me was to aggressively question something she found anomalous. To seek a resolution, she formed hypotheses, tested them against her own experience, and developed an explanation.

To understand Anne's response style, picture a courtroom with a trial in session. At any point during testimony, an attorney can question a witness to clarify details, to prevent simplification of a complex question, or to expand partial information. Anne was the attorney. The text was the witness. She was relentless whenever she saw even a possibility to chip away at what appeared to be generally accepted as the truth but might not be. Anne was most actively engaged with the text when she could challenge it through questions, uncover ambiguities, and probe for possible explanations.

Anne's response style was to challenge the text. She pounced on any part that struck her as odd. She wrestled it to the ground until she had developed some sort of satisfactory explanation for herself. She did not ask questions because she was confused and wanted the teacher to explain things to her; rather, she asked questions because she was confused and was trying to figure it out herself.

In kindergarten, for example, during my reading of *Make Way for Ducklings* (McCloskey, 1941), she stopped me toward the end of the story, when the mother duck, followed by her ducklings, waddles across the street and into the Boston Public Garden to make a home. Something was apparently bothering Anne.

Anne: *Why is it public?*
Carole: *Public? That means anybody can go there.*
A: *Oh. Like a public school.*
C: *Yes.*

A: *Anyone who wants to can go there?*

C: *Yes.*

A: *No. No. Not robbers. Not people who don't know this school.*

C: *Not robbers?*

A: *Not just robbers, but people who are bad at this school. Guess what happened once?*

C: *What?*

A: *Lauren—and I forgot, someone else—but they were by, you know, the corner of the kindergarten gate. They said there was this boy, he came into the school and he had this knife and he killed an old man there.*

C: *What?*

A: *They saw him, and then after, um . . . It's a true story!*

She was also one of the 3 students out of 57 in kindergarten who asked to read words. It is important to note that these were the words that were hand-drawn by Robert McCloskey to show quacking and sound effects: "Quack! Honk! Weebk!" These were the only words any of the three asked to read.

In first grade Anne talked throughout the reading of *Alexander and the Terrible, Horrible, No Good Very Bad Day* (Viorst, 1972). She questioned many things. Alexander said over and over that he was going to Australia because he was having a bad day. Anne obviously didn't think this was a good idea. She had strong feelings about this. She didn't hesitate to talk directly to Alexander and tell him exactly what she thought:

> But why are you going to Australia? Why are you going there? It's boring! There are too many kangaroos. There are too many ostriches. Too many . . . Oh, God.

She enjoyed *Rosie's Walk* (Hutchins, 1968) and took the book from me and read it aloud, one of only 4 students out of 30 to read independently to me in first grade.

In second grade Anne talked all the way through the reading of *Caps for Sale* (Slobodkina, 1947) and at the end said, "Can I read?" She pretended to put a cap on her head before she read. As she read, she flipped back and forth among the pages, comparing them. She slouched in the chair when I read but sat up energetically while she read, touching the book and acting out her ideas. In this response she again stopped the story to challenge a character's idea. The peddler in the story has not been able to sell any of his caps; he is tired and decides to sit under a tree. This scenario did not sit well with Anne. This time she put herself in the same situation. She began to read the story aloud and then stopped to challenge the peddlar's statement:

> "That's a nice place for a rest," thought he. *It is*? I would get ants on me. Because trees have ants on them. I wouldn't want to sit there. They hurt me. I would sit in the ocean. With my bathing suit on. I'd try to turn into a mermaid. I like lying in it with my life jacket on.

In third grade Anne talked all the way through *Ira Sleeps Over* (Waber, 1972) and read parts aloud herself. This part of her response to this book clearly showed that her characteristic response style is to shred the text. In one part of the story, Ira is spending the night at his friend Reggie's house. They are telling ghost stories. Ira has been afraid to go to Reggie's house even though they are best friends and live next door to each other, because he sleeps with a teddy bear and is afraid that Reggie will laugh at him. Anne dealt with this issue but first challenged the idea that ghost stories are necessarily scary. She didn't think so.

> What if it's a good ghost story? Ghosts don't have to be scary. I love ghost stories. [She makes ghost sounds and tells about a ghost book she's reading.] . . . Is he hard of hearing [when Ira asks him whether he sleeps with a teddy bear]? No. I don't think so. He just doesn't want to answer because he thinks they'll make fun of him. He's pretending to be asleep. I think I figured it out. He pretended to fall asleep because he didn't want to talk anymore about his teddy bear. And maybe he thought Ira wasn't going to get his teddy bear. I think that's dumb. What's wrong with a teddy bear? I like taking my teddy bear to my friend's house. You know what I think? He should do? I think he should—even though he's just saying that so his sitter won't make fun of him—he should every night practice sleeping without his teddy bear. So he'll get used to it.

In fourth grade Anne talked throughout the reading of *A Chair for My Mother* (Williams, 1982). She had heard the book before, but this did not seem to diminish her enthusiasm. She followed her usual pattern of asking questions when something intrigued or puzzled her, something she thought was amiss. She began immediately on page 1:

> How old is she? I think she's my age. No, I think she's seven or eight. When does this take place? Her pants look like the '70s or '80s. They have bell bottoms, well, not exactly bell bottoms but it looks like the '70s.

In fifth grade I was surprised that Anne almost tried to sit on my lap as I read to her. She seemed needy for the intimacy of a personal one-to-one reading session. I had wondered whether she would still feel this way. Contrasted with what she had said in fourth grade about never being able to read, it was not surprising that she wanted to slip back into an almost lap-reading mood. She asked questions all the way through my reading of *Song of the Swallows* (Politi, 1949) and frequently put herself into the story, comparing it with her own experiences and the ways they were alike and different.

Anne followed a pattern in her responses. She questioned, challenged, or noted something that puzzled or intrigued her, something she was uncomfortable with and wanted to "fix." She hypothesized or speculated on some possibilities, often associating her own experience to reinforce her concern or to support one of her hypotheses. Somewhere she explained why it could have occurred or what the outcome might have been.

Sometimes it was a quick response; at other times she launched into an extended monologue or occasionally drew me in for information or verification. Not much of what I said seemed to move her away from her drive to figure out whatever intrigued or bothered her to begin with. These were the times when she was most enjoying the reading and the story—when she made it her own. She demanded ownership of her reading. Her comments about reading in school, however, showed that she was rarely able to exercise her passion for reading and her strong voice in response to literature, nor did she even have time or opportunities to read in school. There was a dissonance between Anne's experiences with literature inside and outside school, and she was increasingly dissatisfied and frustrated with it. She wanted to read and believed she couldn't. She had strong feelings about her reading but believed she couldn't express them. Her metaphor for the teacher and reading in school was Hitler burning books.

A Thought from Paul

While reading this case study of Anne, I've had some thoughts about the implications of reader-response theory for all students, not just the English learners I have always taught. My original assumption was that marginalized children were the most silenced when it came to responding to anything that went on in school. I believed that affluent, white, English-speaking students like Anne are readily perceived as having knowledge and experience to contribute to the discussion of a literary text and are encouraged to give voice to their thoughts in response to literature, whereas low-income English learners tend to be taught with the notion that they have a deficit. And students who sense being perceived as deficient resist instruction. They know they are being devalued and respond accordingly. Most of the programs that I have seen designed for remedial instruction as well as for English learners control the words, the texts, and the thoughts that students have access to in school. Many of my students come from illiterate homes where few books are available. But after I read Carole's case study of Anne, it became obvious that, even in predominantly English-only classrooms, students are not given the opportunity to respond to literature from their own experience.

EXPLORING IDEAS

1. Compare Anne's reading experiences at home, in class, and with me. What are some of the similarities and differences? How do you think Anne sees her role as a reader? the role of the adult? How do you think Anne's teachers see her role as a reader? the role of the adult?

2. What ideas do you have about teaching with literature and about language and literacy development after reading this case study?

3. Keep a journal of children's responses to literature and their reading patterns. If you are teaching, do this with your own students. Keep a notebook with a page for each student, noting such things as books they read, reading behaviors, reading conferences with you, and responses during discussions.

4. Start a case study. Choose up to three students in your own or someone else's class. Observe them in the classroom, interview parents (and teachers if you are not the classroom teacher), and tape-record them reading and responding to literature in a one-to-one session or in small groups. Collect student writing related to experiences with literature.

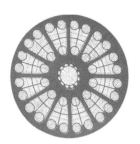

Case Study of Eduardo:
The Intermediate/Advanced English Learner

MEET EDUARDO

Eduardo is fluent and literate in both English and Spanish, a reflection of his early years in a bilingual and bicultural Mexican American–El Salvadoran American home. Although his teachers have recognized his creativity, he was deemed "immature," repeated second grade, and then began to do well academically. He is very imaginative, and his response to a book often begins with the speech tag "Know what?"—meaning he wants to tell you a new story of his own.

Background and Home Influences

El Salvadoran American mother with limited education and English
Encouragement from mother, some books for reading provided
Great expectations for Eduardo, wonder at his potential

Language Development: Fluent in English and Spanish

Most proficient English user in family, loves to talk
English his first language (native English-speaking Mexican American father)
Mother and stepfather native Spanish speakers

Eduardo as a Student

Deemed immature by teachers; repeated second grade
Began to succeed; creative ability valued
Notable storytelling ability, curiosity, and imagination

173

Eduardo's Response Style: Tells His Own Stories

Hypothesizes, uses text as springboard for own stories
Uses much metaphorical and symbolic language
Freely breaks through the boundaries of the text

Connections to Principles and Practice

Eduardo easily became a fluent speaker of the two languages spoken at home, English and Spanish—an example of communication-based language learning occurring naturally in the home.

Eduardo is highly verbal in his English-only classroom but immature–most successful in an interactive classroom—an example of a student-centered approach benefiting a highly creative but nonconforming child.

Eduardo has unfulfilled potential for literacy development—an example of a gap between school literacy expectations and limited literacy experiences at home.

Eduardo breaks through the boundaries of the text in responding to literature—an example of highly idiosyncratic personal transactions between reader and text.

BACKGROUND AND HOME INFLUENCES

Eduardo lives with his El Salvadoran mother and maternal grandmother and his Mexican American stepfather. All of them are native Spanish speakers and speak Spanish at home. From birth through the preschool years, Eduardo's native English-speaking Mexican American father lived in the home. Eduardo has one younger brother. Although it appears that Eduardo spoke English as his first language, his mother and grandmother have provided him with his first culture, which is El Salvadoran.

Eduardo's mother grew up on a ranch and completed 6 years in a rural school in El Salvador. She says she enjoyed school. She describes it as "academia de señoritas," where the students learned sewing and embroidering, as well as basic skills. Her own mother, who lives with her, learned to read when her daughter was 11 years old. Her own father—Eduardo's maternal grandfather—was illiterate. It was difficult to obtain books or magazines where they lived in El Salvador.

Although Eduardo's mother says she tried to speak English to him in his early years, she did not read to him. She does not read English easily. Now Eduardo initiates reading events with her, but he is the reader. Nonetheless, she says she guides him and helps him sound out words she does not know herself. Eduardo began reading independently at about the middle of first grade (about the same time he asked to read to me during our sessions at school).

Eduardo's mother works long hours cleaning homes and usually can spend time with him only on weekends. She says he does read by himself in his room and comes to her only when he needs help. When she does read to him, he corrects her English pronunciation. She says, "En inglés, he doesn't want any accent at all. So I say read it for me, and he does." She says he likes to read, and she buys him books when he asks for them at Kmart or the grocery store or the school book fair. She says he also likes to read in the library when it is open after school.

Eduardo's mother believes he is a special boy even though she is concerned that he doesn't listen to his teachers and often wants to do things his own way. I asked her to describe Eduardo to me:

> He like to work, he talks when he grow up he's going to work. A lot of people say he's so smart you know, we had a friend, she's from America and she says Eduardo has this, you know, like grow up, and I say I don't know I say, but then she say it's OK for him, he talk like grownup people, and I say, "Oh!" He say when he grow up he going to have money, he going to work so hard, and some-times he say he want it be a policeman and things like that, yeah, he thinks. I think he thinks too much, I don't know why. When he don't go to school, when I stayed home with him and we sat down with him, he talk too much. If you stay with him all day, all day, he talks you know. I don't know. I think he's . . . he thinks too much and I think I'm excited with him. I think he's a special boy, he tries hard. [She gets teary-eyed.]

LANGUAGE DEVELOPMENT: FLUENT IN ENGLISH AND SPANISH

Eduardo's Home Language Survey, filled out by his mother and returned to school in kindergarten, says that he is a native English speaker, that English is the language spoken most frequently at home, that the adults in the home speak English to him, and that English is the language spoken most often by adults at home. This may not be entirely the case, however. Eduardo's mother can communicate in English, but during interviews she requested that the questions be in Spanish. She states that she spoke English only when she was with her first husband—Eduardo's natural father. After 10 years in the United States, she is still more comfortable with and prefers to speak Spanish.

Eduardo's natural father was an English-speaking Mexican American born in the United States. He lived in the home until Eduardo was 4. During this time, Eduardo's mother attempted to speak in her limited English to her son, rather than in Spanish. Her current husband speaks Spanish. Eduardo now finds himself living in a Spanish-speaking household in which he is the most proficient speaker of English. He loves to talk and used metaphors and similes, even in kindergarten. He has a poet's voice, and he uses it. If you will listen, he will speak.

EDUARDO AS A STUDENT

Eduardo attended a full-time preschool day-care facility for several years because his mother worked out of the home all day.

In describing her approach, Eduardo's kindergarten teacher said she tries to meet the needs of children as much as possible. She takes a more text-centered ap-proach to teaching with literature. She asks the class what the book is about and then has students join in on repetitive phrases. She asks for lots of recall and predic-tion. She uses a commercial reading series to "teach skills of inferences, recall, word recognition, beginning and ending consonant sounds, decoding, context clues, and phonics." She said she wants to turn children on to reading. Here's how she described Eduardo:

> This little boy is something [laughing]. He is bright but very immature. He's allowed to do what he wants to do at home, so he doesn't "have time" to do what you're asking him to do. There's a lot going on in his brain, and sometimes he's right on top of it and he almost amazes you. And the next day, he'll sit in front of you and fall asleep.
>
> He's got it up there. It will all fall in place for him in a few years when he's older and can really focus in. Some English and Spanish is spoken at home, and Grandmother speaks Spanish most of the time. Eduardo is "Let me hurry and get this done and let me get on with other important things like play Legos." I've had to say, "How do you feel about this? Take your crayon like this and do better." He'll say, "OK." We've spent lots of time on learning to complete a task and getting it done. He works independently but not all the time. He tries. He's often tired in the mornings. Sometimes he comes in in the morning with the most beautiful eyes and says, "I need to tell you something," all determined. I have to listen, and I also have to stop.

Eduardo enjoyed stories in first grade. His teacher (the same one Juan had when he repeated first grade) took a very teacher- and text-centered view of literacy development. She used the Spaulding phonics method extensively, along with a commercial reading series and literature. When she used literature, the students did very teacher-directed art or writing activities.

Eduardo's teacher read *The Giving Tree* by Shel Silverstein (1992) one day. She wrote the title on the chalkboard and asked all the students to read the title and to show that they had by putting their thumbs up. She said, "Some didn't show me with your thumb that you read it. What does it say, Eduardo?" He read, "*The Giving Tree.*"

The teacher read the book; the students were on the floor around her. They were very attentive and quiet. Eduardo had his chin on his hand, intensely absorbed in the story. She asked, "Why do you think the page says the tree was happy after it gave away its trunk?" Eduardo said, "Do you think the tree was happy? No. 'Cause the boy cut off his trunk and branches. Why did he take so much?"

After the reading, she told the class, "Today you're going to write the story in your own words for the beginning, the middle, and the end. Fold a paper in three columns—1, 2, 3, just as we do in spelling: 1 for the first part, 2 for the second part, 3 for the end." She showed an example from last year and told the class she did this every year. She told them, "Many things happened in the middle, but only one thing at the beginning and the end. You can use more sentences in the middle. Use at least one sentence." On spelling, she said, "Do your best." She directed them to go to their seats and explained "base lines," or where to write on the page.

Eduardo was at his seat, already writing. The teacher knelt at his desk and reexplained the assignment to him. She carefully monitored him. Later, his hand went up, and he pounded the desk with a pencil. No one came. His paper flew off the desk. The teacher came over, and he handed the paper to her. She said, "Read it back." He did, and she said, "OK."

His teacher described him:

He's immature and wants things when he wants them. He says, "But I want to talk." He responds well to positive reinforcement for a short time. He is loving but also doesn't behave at home. Academically, there is definitely something there. He has progressed a lot. He came in here not knowing most of the sounds of the alphabet. It's a problem to keep him on-task. In this last month, I've seen lots of growth. He can sound out some words, but he's still at the place where he doesn't always know it's a word.

He is reading in a pre-primer. He is the highest in the lowest group and not aware that he's the highest. He hasn't understood that he has a place in the group. He helps other people when he's on-task. He's low in math. He sometimes forgets simple operations.

He doesn't participate in group discussions, but rather sits back and has to have something to play with. He can't zero in on things because of his immaturity. He's made inadequate progress this year. He is fluent in both English and Spanish. His mom can speak English but has a cleft palate and is hard to understand. His stepfather speaks limited English. I haven't seen them too much. He works well with the aide. My student teacher fell in love with him.

It's hard to tell about his understanding of literature. I concentrated on Spaulding with him this year. I put him in Scott, Foresman's [a publisher] *Taking Off!* In two weeks, his attitude was, "I'm reading." He doesn't read in a group, but with VIPS [Volunteers in Public Schools, parents who work with children on a regular basis]. He does great with them. He interacts constantly. He wants to tell you he's reading.

He must first understand something at the literal level. He has to picture it, and then he takes off. He talked about the tenth row of seats in our class. We don't have a tenth row. He said he pictured it in his mind and then got up and walked to where he pictured it. A story read ". . . only a merry-go-round horse." He read it ". . . only a chair-rest." All the students did self-portraits, and he showed himself doing karate. He showed his leg multiple times to show movement. He doesn't do things like anyone else in the room.

When Eduardo was in second grade, his teacher had a very student-centered approach with an emphasis on actively engaging students. She incorporated activities across modalities, used cooperative groups, and encouraged language exchange.

Eduardo demonstrated that he was a creative, divergent thinker in this class. During even fairly mundane lessons, he brought his own unique view to bear. The teacher showed cards with such phrases as "My room" and asked students to make it a complete sentence. One student said, "My room is dirty." Eduardo said, "My room has dirt and sometimes on my walls I have balloons. They pop. My hair is spiked, and I can pop a balloon with it." It takes very little to set Eduardo off telling a story.

When they were supposed to write their ideas down, however, he struggled. Whereas his ideas and oral expression were fluent and fluid compared with those of other students in his class, his writing skills were much less developed. It didn't seem to bother him, however, and he worked hard at writing.

Although Eduardo seemed to flourish in this class, he was retained to repeat second grade with this same teacher. His test scores on the MAT 6 were 42 percent in reading, 46 percent in language, and 54 percent in mathematics. His teacher indicated that he was retained primarily because of his immaturity, rather than his lack of writing ability or reading problems. He attended summer school at his home school.

When Eduardo was in second grade the second time, his teacher continued to recognize Eduardo's strengths and special qualities. She observed the following about him during his second year in her class:

> He's a smart cookie. He's very literate in both languages. He's serious. His writing has progressed. He writes great stories. He is a great storyteller and creator of narrative. He loves science. He tells stories about nature and the outdoors. He is a thoughtful participant in groups and listens to others. He's very aware and sensitive and watches the reactions of others when reading. When he sees things are not going well, he interjects humor.
>
> His mother speaks limited English and has hired a tutor for him. Eduardo brings the tutor lists of things he doesn't understand so that they can talk them over. His mother sees the spark in Eduardo and wants to nurture it. She gets him magazines and takes him places.
>
> It would be great if you could cap him in a bottle and open him up to the rest of the class. He's eager to do everything. He has gone from the bottom to the top in performance and has grown up a lot this year. He has almost outgrown his mother. She sees him slipping away, and she's sad. He's a peach.
>
> He likes to read. He loves *Zoobooks* and easy chapter books: *The Boxcar Children* series by Gertrude Chandler Warner and mysteries like *Nate the Great* (1986), Marjorie Sharmat stories. He will choose to read on his own, and he will really read. He lives in the library on days that it's open after school. He will sit in the rocking chair in the library and bring library books to me to read.

After repeating second grade, Eduardo's scores on the MAT 6 were 76 percent in reading, 88 percent in language, and 83 percent in mathematics—a tremendous leap from his scores the previous year.

Eduardo's third grade teacher took a fairly traditional approach. Students were less active in her class, and it was not unusual to see the teacher at her desk and students doing worksheets at their desks. They went to her if they had a question. Eduardo told me that school was fine, however, and that he enjoyed reading and writing. He volunteered information about books he was reading and his reading habits.

He said that, at home, he read the dictionary and liked books like "a legend story, a fake one, and it tells you about the sailors and something." He said he read to himself at home and drew—monsters, aliens, people. He read *The Stinky Cheese-man* (Scieszka, 1992) and got excited, asked me whether I'd read it to any children. He told me he read it to his little brother, along with other books like *Snoopy* and "little books, Disney books."

This year his test scores on the MAT 6 declined in three of the four areas. His score on the spelling section went from 88 percent to 93 percent, but his scores in reading went from 76 percent to 55 percent, language from 88 percent to 75 percent, and mathematics from 83 percent to 40 percent. These may not be a true reflection of his performance. He may have had a bad testing day.

In fourth grade Eduardo was more focused but still very creative and visionary. He told me about his reading—*The Adventures of Ratman* by Ellen Weiss (1990)— and said that he likes adventure books "where you go different places, see other things you've never seen before like dragons, magical things, and animals." He also talked about becoming a scientist and helping people and maybe discovering a new species of animal or becoming a doctor and going around the world looking for plants that could help people because "the horror of letting people die makes me feel real sad. Is there a cure for AIDS yet? . . . The more you help people, the more better the world is." He said he wanted to go to college and believed "there could be something spiritual looking over me." He could channel his ideas and articulate the stream-of-consciousness series of images he has always been able to generate.

EDUARDO'S RESPONSE STYLE: TELLS HIS OWN STORIES

Eduardo is a storyteller—a natural with a powerful imagination. Picture him in front of a fire, telling stories as the smoke drifts up, perhaps even making up a story about something he pictures in the smoke. A book or story or even a word or two is enough to set Eduardo's imagination to work. One thought or idea or image triggers another. On the surface, they may not seem related, at least according to an adult understanding of narrative. When listening to Eduardo, I found myself straining to follow and understand his type of narrative, not because of what he said but because of the way he said it—enthusiastically, authoritatively, as if it ought to be perfectly obvious that the story made sense, had a logical flow, and was completely understandable if only I was astute enough to follow it.

His most frequent response type is hypothesizing: speculating, predicting, retrospecting, anticipating, generating story options, and breaking through the boundaries of the text—although this was closely followed by associations, relating his hypotheses to his own experiences. Whereas Anne likes to shred a story and Juan uses it as a reason to tell about his family, Eduardo jumps on it like a trampoline to springboard to other images, tales, or worlds. He is the most creative of the three.

In kindergarten, for example, when the little boy in *The Snowy Day* (Keats, 1963) makes a snow angel, Eduardo keyed in on the idea of angels in general, rather than the snow angel in the story. This excerpt shows how his ideas bounce off one another and finally lead to a hypothesis about stars.

> Oh, angels. I like angels. Do you know what an angel is. [What?] It's an angel that got wings. And do they got this something on their head. Yeah. I know. You know what um I saw the one that um—once I went to Disneyland and I went under the water, then I saw a mermaid. Yeah, the one where all of the fish was not real. I saw a shark and they weren't real. Not the mermaids. And then the man said you could hear them talk. And I saw gold there. It wasn't real, I know that. So I know. You know I saw a star. It looked like Bambi. And then a long time ago, you know what's gonna happen? They won't be real. I mean the star's not real. From a long time ago, they were real, but not now, they're not real.

In response to *Make Way for Ducklings* (McCloskey, 1941), Eduardo moved the story forward in time and speculated what it would be like if it took place today:

> If he didn't have a police car, he could go on the police helicopter. And then he could bring down a paper that says, "Come quick, there's family of ducks." And it fell down and then with a rock moving down it fell on a rock so they hurt it and then they send a note. And then they made another paper, a sign that they'll get there soon.

In response to *Miss Rumphius* (Cooney, 1982), he hypothesized a creation myth that could explain how Miss Rumphius was born and grew old:

> We were in a brown egg. My mom made me, but she didn't make me because she was in the brown egg. Everybody was in the brown egg. And then they turned . . . and I saw this movie, and we turned the brown egg and everything was fine. We were all yellow. And that she was turning into a baby, and then they turn into them. Yes, I saw a movie of it. And they said they used to come home, and the baby turn into a boy. Yes. What when I'm talking it goes right in there. Know what? Um. Here her hair is not white. So if she, if her hair's not white, her hair's going to turn white. And she was old now, huh? Know what? Know what? Um. That's not fair. She was at there. No. I try. She was there. Why did she turn into an old lady? [Why do you think?] The God sent her to turn into an old lady sometime.

Eduardo's hypotheses, like Anne's questions and Juan's family associations, often lead him to develop his own explanations for things. He had an interesting speech tag leading into this; he often said, "Know what?" and then hypothesized and developed an explanation. I think he meant, "Do you want to know what I'm thinking?" It's obvious that what he wanted was simply somebody to listen to him. And at that point he was most actively engaged with the text and using language.

Compared with his behavior in kindergarten, the first time I read in first grade, Eduardo talked a lot about the story, but his responses were restrained. The book was *Alexander and the Terrible, Horrible, No Good Very Bad Day* (Viorst, 1972), and he did not tell the extended stories he had told before. His responses were more like those of other students. Several times he simply noted a part that interested him, but he still questioned and hypothesized throughout. He also started to read it to me, like both Juan and Anne. It seems significant that out of 38 students in this study in first grade, only 4 volunteered to read and 2 of those were the only 2 Latino students.

Eduardo was less restrained while I read *Umbrella* (Yashima, 1958) and renewed his free spirit. Throughout the reading, he talked about a magic umbrella:

> On the front, she's saying, "This must be a magic umbrella. She thinks it's magic . . . .
> It fly wherever she wanted. I know where dragonflies are. In the park. She didn't want to leave the umbrella. She thought it was magic.

Here again, Eduardo used the text as a starting point to tell his own stories; this was when he was truly engaged in reading. He seemed to be brimming with other stories that were triggered by the one in the book and that were much more compelling to him because they were his own. Then he volunteered to read to me again: "Want me to read this story to you? I know how. Let's try." While he read, he continued to ask questions and develop hypotheses and then explanations for what was happening. He told me, "I knew that because I heard you." His understanding of the story was deepened. He laughed at the end and said, "How'd I do?"

Eduardo's response pattern and that of the others suggest that teachers should rethink the traditional way of teaching reading through stories—with the teacher introducing it and the students reading aloud or silently to themselves. When I read aloud to these students and they were allowed to respond freely—and go as far afield as Eduardo liked to—they were ready to build on that engagement and pleasure in the story and to use it as a basis to read on their own. They had already heard the story and analyzed it; now they had a chance to experience it and enjoy it, instead of the other way around—read the story, answer efferent questions, and write or do an art activity. Let's think about reversing this order and ask an open, aesthetic question first, letting the efferent emerge from the aesthetic, which is the natural way these students responded.

In second grade the first time, Eduardo made fewer comments than in kindergarten or first grade, but he was more focused on the story itself. He pointed at many things in the text with his finger.

Something different occurred in Eduardo's response to the first book I read in second grade, *Caps for Sale* (Slobodkina, 1947). He asked many questions about words: "Where's sale, for sale? Where does it say cents?" He did this throughout the reading. He continued his hypothesizing, extending the story, and making up his own version:

> The caps can't talk. He thinks the caps are going to get mad at him, when the caps can't do nothing to him . . . . My favorite page was when . . . this one because they look like they're flying. And the monkeys . . . oh, I know. I know why they did it because when he would do something then they would copy him.

Here he goes from what appears to be a tangent about personified caps that can get mad and fly, to a succinct and plausible explanation of the peddler's actions. It is Eduardo's way. He listens, catches a piece of the story and puts his own spin on it, and then comes to a reasonable explanation or goes beyond that to a generalization—what a teacher wants students to do when they read. Again, order was important; he needed to play around with the story first before he nailed it, like cats playing with a mouse or a bird before they kill it. He needed time and the freedom to do that.

After he basically explained that the monkeys had the hats because they copied the peddler, he rewrote the story, focusing on the problem the peddler had selling caps in the first place. He "fixed" the peddler's problem:

> He should have done it with a, like a car, then he could show everybody and go other places. Like that, so he could make it better. Try to go other places, not just around the town. Because um . . . then people might see him and they might buy them. [That's a good idea.] yeah, but he didn't try that. He thought that going around the town he would make it, huh? Make money.

He appeared very satisfied with himself at this point, and he should have been. He had fun with this story. He listened to it, asked about words he wanted to read, pictured flying caps that got mad, developed plausible explanations for characters' actions, and then hypothesized a whole new ending for the story that would resolve the main character's problem of selling caps. Next, he said the words that should warm the cockles of any primary teacher's heart: "I want to read the story to you." He did, asking for a word or a word meaning in a very relaxed, natural way. He read haltingly, one word at a time, but his mood was upbeat, positive. He asked for many words, he stopped when he wanted to clarify meaning or to talk about something of interest to him, but he read the entire book to me.

Finally, Eduardo saw some information about the author–illustrator, Esphyr Slobodkina; the blurb on the back cover said the book had won an award. Eduardo told me about another book he was reading at home with his mom and offered to bring it to show me. This was an extremely satisfying reading episode with Eduardo.

In response to *The Nicest Gift* (Politi, 1973), Eduardo stopped me at the same point in the story as Juan had, the part where I read the word in Spanish; ". . . *caballito* means little horse." Whereas Juan had corrected my pronunciation, Eduardo simply said, "I know that," and "I know Spanish, too." He read a little, asked more questions, told me it was "great," and offered a simple explanation at the end: "Blanco was scared and ran far away." He did not provide the rich associations for family and culture that Juan had provided simply because he is not the same person as Juan.

It is important to remember that language and culture are two of the many things that make people different. This idea points up the highly idiosyncratic nature of the response process, and teachers should be careful not to assume that all Spanish-speaking Latino students will respond similarly to a book like *The Nicest Gift,* anymore than all girls or all boys or all oldest children in a family will respond in the same way. What is important is to listen to what each child had to say, keeping in mind the general tendencies of children at that age but not forgetting what a unique individual each one of them is.

When Eduardo was repeating second grade, he was subdued when I read *Ira Sleeps Over* (Waber, 1972). He listened attentively, asked one question, and then asked to read the book to me, which he did. He was proud of his reading.

In third grade, Eduardo talked throughout my reading of the book. He was more mature and focused that year but still imaginative and insightful. He could talk about reading. When I praised him, he told me he read to his 2-year-old brother in English.

In response to *A Chair for My Mother* (Williams, 1982), Eduardo's predominant response type again was hypothesizing. He guessed that it was a big fire and wondered how it started in the house and speculated that it might have been cooking carrots that had exploded and started the fire. This is classic Eduardo, imagining another whole scenario. Although no exploding carrots are shown in any picture, a potted snake plant is show in an orange pot on the stove, and the border around the edge of the page is a jagged white and orange shape that looks something like the shape of carrot. This is speculation on my part. What is not speculation is that it takes very little to trigger Eduardo's fertile imagination and to set him spinning another story in his mind.

In fourth grade, in response to *Song of the Swallows* (Politi, 1949), Eduardo shared what he had been learning about the California missions and what he'd heard on the news about the swallows returning to Capistrano. He still wove his own stories throughout the reading, speculating about what types of formations different types of birds made in flight, as well as that young Juan was going to be the gardener someday like old Julian and that he imagined that Father Serra would be like his imaginary friend. After reading, he told at length about his dreams of becoming a scientist or doctor and going all around the world looking for plants to help people or perhaps discovering a new species of animal because "no one's ever seen all of the world, have they?" Eduardo may not see all of the world either, but he roams through all sorts of possible worlds in his mind as he responds to literature.

A Thought from Paul

Exploring literature, developing literacy, and differentiating instruction are engaging and strategic endeavors. Authentic responses to literature do not appear as polished works; they are raw and rough, unfinished thoughts. And they can unsettle an inexperienced teacher. When a child like Eduardo describes angels and mermaids and Bambi all within a single response to *The Snowy Day,* it can leave a teacher wondering how to rein him or her in and get back on topic. In an authentic setting, the teacher utilizes instructional tools strategically to help the child learn how to finish and polish those thoughts.

Imagination is not preprogrammed. Rather than reining in an authentic, imaginative response, the skilled teacher can help the child explore his or her imagination further by asking aesthetic questions to follow up and by providing a means of self-expression. Follow-up questions can be as simple as "Can you tell me more about angels and mermaids? What were you thinking?" A response option can be something as conventional as asking the child to compare angels and mermaids in writing; a simple Venn diagramming activity can facilitate the comparison. It is when children put their raw, rough, and unfinished thoughts on paper that they begin to clarify their thinking and develop skills using writing conventions.

This coming together of imaginative responses, aesthetic questions, and options for self-expression presents a naturally differentiated instructional product that is tailored to a child's ideas and needs. The content of the instruction has multiple sources, including the work of literature, the child's imaginative responses, and the conventions that the teacher has identified for an instructional focus. The needed tools are questions and graphic organizers used to deepen and order the ideas. Once the ideas are put on paper, the conventions of spelling, punctuation, grammar, syntax, paragraph formation, and process writing are applied to the response. In this way, the child is contributing to his or her own instruction. And the differentiation is product driven, coming about naturally in a confluence of story, response, questions, conventions, organizers, and means of expression. It is a collaboration of the child and the teacher.

I can sense the reader thinking. "But doesn't the teacher lose control of instruction? How do I address mandated benchmarks? What will I tell the principal?" The teacher does *not* lose control of instruction. Instead, the teacher initiates the discussion of the literature, asks questions, suggests response options, and focuses the instruction on specific conventions according to observed strengths and needs and grade-level benchmarks. For example, let's say that the benchmarks state that the student will compare and contrast story characters and will also master use of quotation marks. When a student like Eduardo discusses angels and mermaids, the teacher can suggest framing those responses as a comparison. Further, as the student diagrams and writes about that comparison, the teacher can require that quotations be used to contrast what angels and mermaids would say. During whole-group direct instruction, the teacher can demonstrate the conventions of using quotations and can state the expectations for that day's writing. The teacher can also set up an assessment rubric that addresses the required conventions and the content contributed by the child. In this way, the teacher strategically addresses specified conventions, and the child engages his or her reading, imagination, and self-expression.

EXPLORING IDEAS

1. Compare Eduardo with both Juan and Anne in terms of background and home influences, language development, and success as a student. How could you differentiate the response products for each child when they were reading the same story?

2. What do you see as the literacy development needs of Eduardo, Anne, and Juan? How are they the same, and how are they different?

3. Practice using aesthetic questions and prompts during literature discussions. At first, plan on using one or two during a discussion, and try different questions with each discussion. If you forget them, post them on a wall chart. Encourage students to use the same kinds of questions when discussing with each other.

4. If you are teaching, consider the following ways to create home–school connections with English learners like Eduardo and Juan:

   ▲ Ask students to interview their parents about the parents' experiences with literature, and then discuss them.

   ▲ Encourage students to compare story characters to family members and friends.

   ▲ Require parents to listen to their child read from his or her literary journal once a week and to ask the child two to three questions that the child will then respond to in writing. Over time, this becomes a significant record of parent–child interactions about literature.

CHILDREN'S BOOKS

Blegvad, L., & Blegvad, E. (1985). *Anna Banana and me*. New York: Margaret K. McElderry.

Brown, M. (1957). *The three billy goats gruff*. New York: Harcourt Brace.

Brown, M. W. (1942). *The runaway bunny*. New York: Harper Junior Books.

Brown, M. W. (1947). *Goodnight moon*. New York: Harper & Row.

Buck, P. S. (1986). *The big wave*. New York: Harper Trophy.

Cooney, B. (1982). *Miss Rumphius*. New York: Viking.

Cooney, B. (1988). *Island boy*. New York: Viking.

Hutchins, P. (1968). *Rosie's walk*. New York: Macmillan.

Keats, E. J. (1963). *The snowy day*. New York: Viking.

Kunhardt, D. (1940). *Pat the bunny*. New York: Golden Books.

Lee, D. (1975). *Alligator pie*. Boston: Houghton Mifflin.

Lowry, L. (1979). *Anastasia Krupnik*. New York: Houghton Mifflin.

Martin, B. (1967). *Brown bear, brown bear, what do you see?* New York: Holt, Rinehart, Winston.

McCloskey, R. (1941). *Make way for ducklings*. New York: Viking.

Politi, L. (1949). *Song of the swallows*. New York: Scribner.

Politi, L. (1973). *The nicest gift*. New York: Scribner.

Rey, H. A. (1944). *Katy no pocket*. New York: Houghton Mifflin.

Roberts, W. D. (1991). *Scared stiff*. New York: Atheneum.

Rojankovsky, F. (1942). *The tall book of mother goose*. New York: Harper & Row.

Scieszka, J. (1992). *The stinky cheeseman and other fairly stupid tales*. New York: Viking.

Sharmat, M. W. (1986). *Nate the Great*. New York: Putnam.

Silverstein, S. (1992). *The giving tree*. New York: HarperCollins.

Slobodkina, E. (1947). *Caps for sale*. New York: Harper Junior Books.

Steig, W. (1976). *Abel's island*. New York: Farrar, Straus, & Giroux.

Viorst, J. (1972). *Alexander and the terrible, horrible, no good very bad day*. New York: Atheneum.

Waber, B. (1972). *Ira sleeps over*. New York: Houghton Mifflin.

Weiss, E. (1990). *The adventures of ratman*. New York: Random House.

Williams, V. B. (1982). *A chair for my mother*. New York: Greenwillow Books.

Wright, B. R. (1987). *A ghost in the window*. New York: Holiday House.

Yashima, T. (1958). *Umbrella*. New York: Viking.

Series

American Girl (published by Pleasant Company)

The Baby-Sitter's Club by Ann Martin (published by Scholastic)

The Boxcar Children by Gertrude Chandler Warner (published by Whitman)

Zoobooks (published by Wildlife Education)

Subject Index

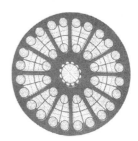

Name Index